GREEK AMERICANS

ETHNIC GROUPS IN AMERICAN LIFE SERIES

Milton M. Gordon, editor

GREEK

CHARLES C. MOSKOS, JR.

Northwestern University

AMERICANS

Struggle and Success

PRENTICE-HALL, INC., ENGLEWOOD CLIFFS, N.J. 07632

Library of Congress Cataloging in Publication Data

Moskos, Charles C (date).
  Greek Americans, struggle and success.

  (Ethnic groups in American life series)
  Bibliography: p.
  Includes index.
  1. Greek Americans.   I. Title.
E184.G7M67   973'.04'893   79-17924   28Apr '80
ISBN 0-13-365106-1
ISBN 0-13-365098-7 pbk.

10 9 8 7 6 5 4 3 2 1

Printed in the United States of America

PRENTICE-HALL INTERNATIONAL, INC., London

PRENTICE-HALL OF AUSTRALIA PTY. LIMITED, Sydney

PRENTICE-HALL OF CANADA, LTD., Toronto

PRENTICE-HALL OF INDIA PRIVATE LIMITED, New Delhi

PRENTICE-HALL OF JAPAN, INC., Tokyo

PRENTICE-HALL OF SOUTHEAST ASIA PTE. LTD., Singapore

WHITEHALL BOOKS LIMITED, Wellington, New Zealand

Grateful acknowledgement is made to the following for permission to reprint
previously published material:

The Greeks in the United States by Theodore Saloutos. Copyright © 1964 by Harvard
University Press.

New Smyrna: An Eighteenth Century Greek Odyssey by Epaminondas P. Panagopoulos.
Copyright © 1966 by University Presses of Florida.

"Growing Up Greek American" by Charles C. Moskos, Jr. in *Society*, Vol. 14, No. 2
(1977). Copyright © 1977 by Society, Transaction, Inc.

Dedicated To:

PFC Peter Shukas (1923–1944), uncle, killed in action, France;

SP4 James C. Shukas (1948–1970), cousin and godson,
killed in action, Vietnam;

Patricia Shukas (1923–1977), aunt, of Scotch, Irish and German
descent, she became the center of a Greek-American Family.

MAY THEIR MEMORY BE ETERNAL

Contents

Preface

In this book I have tried to present a perspective on the Greek experience in America by employing those insights of sociological, historical, and cultural learning of which I have been a beneficiary. At the same time, the writing of this book was a personal statement inseparable from my background as a Greek American. We Greek Americans are sometimes a contentious people, and there will be few who will not take exception to some of what is written here. This too is part of the Greek-American experience.

If this study has value, it reflects the generous investment of time and thought by dozens of people who have helped and informed me over the years. I have been especially appreciative of the friendship and intellectual support of Theodore Saloutos who is truly the dean of Greek-American studies. The manuscript in entire draft form was read by Michael N. Cutsumbis, Milton M. Gordon, Alexander Karanikas, George A. Kourvetaris, and Nicholas Tavuchis. Their comments were enormously helpful.

For tracing down elusive material on Greek Americans, I am grateful to Dimitri Parry, Andrew T. Kopan, Helen Zeese Papanikolas, John Rexine, and Alice Scourby. Along the way toward completion of this book, the number of people who have given me insights on Greek Americans is beyond recounting. But I would like to single out John P. Anton, Panos Bardis, Elias Dimitras, Leon Marinakos, Harry Mark Petrakis, Nikos Petropoulos, M. Byron Raizis, Constantina Safilios-Rothschild, and Evan C. Vlachos. Lest this list sound too ethnically bound, I must mention those non-Greek colleagues in sociology who have given me the benefit of their astute observations: Janet Abu-Lughod, Bernard Beck, Howard Becker, Leonard Broom, Remi Clignet, Andrew M. Greeley, Irving Louis Horowitz, Morris Janowitz, and Edward Shils.

For uncovering statistical data on Greek Americans and making it available to me, I express my thanks to the following individuals and the institutions they represent: Spyridon Dokianos, Consulate General of Greece; John P. Kaiteris, Hellenic American Neighborhood Action Committee of New York City; Paula R. Knepper, American Council on

Education; and Paulette Poulos, Greek Orthodox Archdiocese of North and South America.

In the fall of 1977 I was most fortunate to be invited to address a conference on Greek ethnicity in Australia to commemorate the eightieth anniversary of the Greek Orthodox community of Melbourne. George Papadopoulos, Chris Mourikis, and Petro Georgiou greatly expanded my understanding of Greek Americans by the comparisons they made with Greek Australians.

I wish to acknowledge a grant from the Research Committee of Northwestern University to underwrite the collection of materials used in this study. Mrs. Elizabeth Conner, who has always been able to meet my impossibly short deadlines, typed the manuscript in her own inimitable manner of good humor and dispatch. Of course, none of the persons who assisted me must be held responsible for any factual errors or flaws of interpretation that remain.

The first Greek to set foot on these shores was Christopher Columbus. Such at least is the belief of many Greek immigrants in America. Columbus's purported Greek lineage was to be given credence in a full–length treatise—*Christopher Columbus: A Greek Nobleman*—by Seraphim G. Canoutas, a major figure in Greek-American letters during the first half of this century.[1] Canoutas, himself an immigrant, devoted the last years of his life to prove that Columbus was a member of a distinguished Greek family that had gone to Italy from Byzantium. Whatever the ancestry of the Great Discoverer—and one is obliged to admit that Columbus's Greek background is not accepted by non–Greek historians—the belief in his Greekness does reveal two enduring qualities of Greek immigrants: their overweening pride in their Hellenic background, and their striving to assert some psychic precedence over the dominant groups in American society.

The Greek Comes to America

The Greek experience in the United States has been a blend of ethnic pride and resourceful participation in American society. In its early years it is the story of immigrants who suffered incredible hardships, many of whom, nevertheless, eventually became secure members of the middle class. It is a story of the children of the immigrants, the second generation, most of whom have enjoyed levels of education and income surpassing the American average, and some of whom have been outstandingly successful in the country of their birth. And there are the third and fourth generation who are still half-sketched figures in the unfinished canvas of Greek America. It is also the still unfolding story of the new immigrants from Greece who have been coming to America in large numbers over the past decade and a half. The Greek experience in the United States also has a darker side: immigrants whose lives drained away in poverty and loneliness after serving the demands of an expanding industrial economy, exploitation of Greek by Greek, conflicts across

[1]Seraphim G. Canoutas, *Christopher Columbus: A Greek Nobleman* (New York: St. Mark's Press, 1943). Canoutas's treatise is not the first on the subject. In 1937 Spyros Cateras of Manchester, New Hampshire, privately printed a small book entitled *Christopher Columbus Was a Greek Prince and His Real Name Was Nikolaos Ypsilantis from the Greek Island of Chios.*

generations, and misunderstandings between older and newer immigrants. Yet in its broad outlines, the sociological portrait of what are today some one million Greek Americans is one of an ethnic group that has maintained a remarkable degree of communal and family cohesion while also comfortably accommodating itself to the achievement standards of the larger society. This almost self-congratulatory "best of both worlds" adaptation may well be the distinguishing quality of Greek Americans.

BEGINNINGS AND FALSE STARTS

Leaving aside the tenuous and self-serving belief that Columbus was descended from Byzantine nobility, one may ask who was the first Greek to arrive in America. This distinction goes to Don Teodoro or Theodoros, a sailor and ship caulker serving aboard the expedition of the Spanish explorer Panfilio de Narvaez. In October, 1528, Narvaez anchored off what is now Pensacola, Florida, to secure fresh water. An agreement was reached with the Indians on the land who, however, insisted on keeping a hostage while the water was to be procured. Don Teodoro volunteered himself as the hostage and went ashore. He never returned to the ship and was presumably killed by the Indians. Though his life ended tragically, Don Teodoro is the first Greek known to have set foot on American soil.[2]

The Eighteenth Century

We are fortunate that the historian E.P. Panagopoulos has given us a full and absorbing account of the first large migration of Greeks to America—the ill-fated New Smyrna colony.[3] It involved a trans-atlantic odyssey that started with high hopes and was to end in privation and misery. The story began in 1763, when Florida passed from Spanish into

[2]The fate of Don Teodoro is related in *The Journey of Alvar Nunez Cabeza de Vaca and His Companions from Florida to the Pacific, 1528–1536*, trans F. Bandelier (New York: A.S. Barnes & Co., 1905), cited in E.P. Panagopoulos, "The Greeks in America during the Eighteenth Century" (paper presented at the Bicentennial Symposium on the Greek Experience in America, University of Chicago, 1976), p. 2. The question of who were the first Greeks in America is one that has many answers in diverse Greek-American sources. It has been asserted that Greek sailors accompanied Columbus during his various voyages. Some claim the Spanish admiral and explorer, Juan de Fuca, who in 1592 discovered the straits south of Vancouver Island that bear his name, was a Greek sea-captain, Ioannis Phocas, from the island of Cephalonia. Panagopoulos, who has made the most thorough and reputable examination of the early Greeks in America, holds that these and similar claims are plausible, but that there is no solid historical evidence to sustain them.
[3]E.P. Panagopoulos, *New Smyrna: An Eighteenth Century Greek Odyssey* (Gainesville: University Presses of Florida, 1966). The account of the New Smyrna Greeks given in the text is essentially a paraphrase of Panagopoulos.

British hands. Several influential people in Great Britain became intrigued with the idea of establishing plantations in the newly acquired territory by bringing in Greek settlers. Among these was Andrew Turnbull, a Scottish doctor, who was married to Maria Gracia Rubini, the daughter of a Greek merchant in London. Maria Rubini had been born in Smyrna, Asia Minor. Turnbull secured a royal grant of twenty thousand acres (eventually to grow into a land area of over one hundred thousand acres) about 75 miles south of St. Augustine, Florida. He named this land New Smyrna to honor the birthplace of his wife.

Funded by a generous subsidy from the Board of Trade in London, Turnbull was able to sail in April, 1767, into the Mediterranean to recruit his colonists. These were to be indentured laborers, the terms of whose contract specified that after completion of their service—between five and eight years—they would acquire a certain amount of land in their own right. Turnbull first stopped at the island of Minorca to arrange an assembly point for his settlers. There he found willing volunteers for his venture, Italians from nearby Leghorn, as well as Minorcans. By the following year, Turnbull had been able to recruit a total of 1,403 people for his Florida colony, about four to five hundred of whom were Greeks, principally from Mani on the southernmost tip of the Greek mainland. He then left for Florida with eight ships carrying the colonists. On June 26, 1768, the first ship arrived at St. Augustine. The others caught up soon afterwards. From St. Augustine the colonists continued southward to the site of New Smyrna. A contemporary report stated this to be the "largest importation of white inhabitants that was ever brought into America at a time."[4]

The conditions the settlers encountered were appalling. Over half of the colonists died within two years of their arrival in New Smyrna. Not only was food scarce, but also the colonists were put to brutally heavy labor in clearing the wilderness under the supervision of former noncoms of the British army. Flogging was common. On August 19, 1768, the colony exploded in anger. A riot started, overseers were attacked, and a ship was seized and readied to set sail for Havana and freedom. Quickly a British frigate was dispatched and prevented the colonists' escape. A detachment of soldiers was landed, which was able to suppress the rebellion.

Three of the leaders of the rebellion—two Italians and a Greek from Corsica, Elia Medici—were sentenced to death. The Court, however, in what seems to have been an obvious attempt to create divisiveness among the colonists, promised the Greek his life on condition that he personally execute the two Italians. A Dutch surveyor who eyewitnessed the event gives us the following description:

[4]*Ibid.*, p. 54.

On this occasion I saw one of the most moving scenes I ever experienced; long and obstinate was the struggle of this man's mind, who repeatedly called out, that he chose to die rather than to be executioner of his friends in distress: this not a little perplexed Mr. Woolridge, the sheriff, till at last the entreaties of the victims themselves, put an end to the conflict in his breast, by encouraging him to act. Now we beheld a man thus compelled to mount the ladder, take leave of his friends in the most moving manner, kissing them the moment before he committed them to an ignominious death.[5]

After the suppression of the rebellion, the colony sullenly resumed working operations. Things were going badly for the landowners. When colonists applied for discharges after serving their work time, they were turned down and a few thrown into confinement. Finally, in the late spring of 1777, the several hundred surviving colonists simply picked up and moved to St. Augustine. Because of their repeated petitions seeking freedom, the conditions of the colonists had become an open scandal within British circles. The British courts formally freed the colonists from their indenture on July 17, 1777. By that time New Smyrna had already been completely abandoned.

The Greek remnant of New Smyrna—probably no more than about one hundred—found a new life in St. Augustine. A census in 1783 reports that most of the Greeks in St. Augustine were prospering, some had established themselves as merchants, and a few even owned slaves. John Giannopoulos left a deep imprint in the educational history of Saint Augustine by establishing a school in his house; now restored, it stands as the oldest school building in the United States. But the first Greeks in the New World were to disappear without a trace by the middle of the nineteenth century. Although some left Florida for other places, the majority were absorbed into the general population. During the nine years of New Smyrna's existence, Greek intermarriage with fellow Minorcan and Italian colonists had already become the rule. Without their own Greek Orthodox priest, the Greek settlers took refuge in the Roman Catholic Church, a practice that continued in St. Augustine. With Catholic forbearance a small Greek chapel was established in St. Augustine in November, 1777, where Greeks could pray to God in their own way. Almost two hundred years later this building was designated a shrine by the Greek Orthodox Archdiocese of America to commemorate the trials of the first Greeks who came to this country.

Other "firsts" in early Greek-American history can be noted.[6] Records show that a Greek, Michael Ury (Youris), became a naturalized

---

[5]*Ibid.*, p. 62.

[6]There is a report, which is impossible to verify, that a Cretan, one Konopios, started a Greek coffeehouse in New England in 1652. Melvin Hecker and Heike Fenton, eds., *The Greeks in America 1528–1977* (Dobbs Ferry, N.Y.: Oceana Publications, Inc., 1978), p. 1.

citizen by act of the General Assembly of Maryland in 1725.[7] This makes Ury the first Greek positively known to reside permanently in what is today the United States. The first Greek-American scholar was John Paradise.[8] Persuaded to come to this country by Benjamin Franklin and Thomas Jefferson whom he met in Europe, Paradise in 1787 married into the Ludwell family, one of Virginia's most distinguished. (The Ludwell-Paradise home was the first to be restored in Williamsburg, Virginia). Coming to America by the back way, so to speak, of the Bering Strait was Eustrate Delarof, a native of the Peloponnesus in Greece.[9] From 1783 until 1791 Delarof was in charge of all Russian trading operations in the Aleutians and Alaska and is considered by some reckoning to have been the first de facto governor of Alaska.

The first marriage between two Greek Americans we know of occurred in 1799 in New Orleans, when Andrea Dimitry, a native of the Greek island of Hydra, married Marianne Celeste Dracos, the daughter of Michael Dracos, a well-to-do merchant who had come to New Orleans from Athens around 1766. With indisputable Greek lineage from her father's side (her mother was of mixed French Acadian and American Indian ancestry), Marianne Celeste, who was born in Louisiana on March 1, 1777, may qualify as the Greek "Virginia Dare." The children and grandchildren of Andrea and Marianne Dimitry were leading professionals and business figures in the antebellum South. One of their sons, Alexander, became the first superintendent of education in the state of Louisiana and was assistant postmaster-general of the Confederacy.

The Nineteenth Century

Passing out of the mists of Greek-American antiquity we come to a remarkable episode of Greek-American relations. The Greek War of Independence (1821–1827) against the Ottoman Turks had gained the sympathy of many American and European philhellenes. One major impetus for philhellenism in the United States was that our own founding fathers had consciously looked to the culture of classical Greece as a model for their own endeavors. Thus, when the Greeks began their own war of independence only a generation after that of the Americans, it seemed only fitting that the Hellenic cause would garner support in leading circles in this country. Throughout the United States groups were set up to raise funds and supplies for the beleaguered Greeks. A few individuals—notably, Lieutenant General George Jarvis, Colonel

---

[7]George J. Leber, *The History of the Order of Ahepa* (Washington, D.C.: Order of Ahepa, 1972), p. 7.

[8]*Ibid.*, pp. 7–8.

[9]Thomas Burgess, *Greeks in America* (Boston: Sherman, French & Co., 1913), p. 192.

Jonathan P. Miller, and Dr. Samuel Gridley Howe—went so far as actually to fight with the Greek insurgents.

One of the fascinating results of this outpouring of American philhellenism was that a remarkable group of about forty orphans was brought to this country during or shortly after the war.[10] Some were brought over by individual patrons, while others came through the efforts of the American Board of Commissioners for Foreign Missions (Congregationalist). The Foreign Missions Board sponsored the education of Greek boys in America with the intent of eventually returning them home, where they would contribute to the uplift of their native country (and presumably spread the Calvinist gospel). Several of these orphans did, indeed, return to Greece. Alexander Paspatis, an Amherst graduate, spent his last years in Athens where he acquired an international reputation as a Byzantine scholar. Christodoulous Evangelides, after graduating from Columbia College, returned to his native Syra, where he established an American type of school. Evangelides is said to have been the inspiration for William Cullen Bryant's poem "The Greek Boy."[11]

Our interest, however, is with those who stayed in America, many of whom became quite prominent in their adopted country. Among those whose later careers can be documented are: John Zachos, an educational pioneer among blacks after the Civil War and early proponent of equal education for women, who served as the curator of Cooper's Union in New York; Evangelos Sophocles, who became professor of Greek at Harvard University; Constantinos and Pantias Rallis, brothers who established a worldwide commercial firm; and Luca Miltiades Miller, U.S. Representative from Wisconsin (1891–1893), the first Greek-American Congressman. Several of the orphans were to make names for themselves in the U.S. Navy: Photius Fiske, who became a Navy chaplain and left his estate to the abolitionist cause; George Marshall, who wrote the first manual on gunnery to be used in the American fleet; and Captain George Colvocoresses, who commanded the *Saratoga* in the Civil War (his son, Rear Admiral George P. Colvocoresses, fought in the Spanish-American War and was commandant of midshipmen at the U.S. Naval Academy). Another Greek orphan, Michael Anagnos, came to the

[10]The first and still most informative account of the orphans brought to America during or shortly after the Greek War of Independence is Burgess, *Greeks in America*, pp. 192–207. A useful systemized list of the origins, education, and adult careers of the Greek orphans is George A. Kourvetaris, "Greek-American Professionals: 1820's–1970's," *Balkan Studies*, 18, no. 2 (1977), 318–23. The two most prominent of the nineteenth-century Greek Americans have been the subject of extended study: see Franklin Sanborn, *Michael Anagnos 1837–1906* (Boston: Wright and Potter, 1907); and Eva Catafygiotou Topping, "John Zachos: American Educator," *Greek Orthodox Theological Review*, 21, no. 4 (winter, 1976), 351–66.

[11]Burgess, *Greeks in America*, p. 194.

United States in 1867 at the bequest of the philhellene Dr. Samuel Gridley Howe. Eventually, he married Howe's daughter and succeeded his father-in-law as head of the Perkins Institution for the Blind in Boston, a position he held for thirty years. Under Anagnos's administration, the Perkins Institution became the leading school for the blind in the world.

At about the time the Greek war orphans were making their mark, another group of Greeks appeared on the American scene. Starting in the 1850s a small number of Greek merchants began to set up their import-export business in such port cities as New York, Boston, San Francisco, Savannah, Galveston, and New Orleans. It was in New Orleans that the first Greek Orthodox church in America was established in 1864.[12] The founders were mainly Greek cotton merchants—Nicholas Benakis being the prime mover—but the church also served non-Greek communicants of the Orthodox faith, as well as Greek sailors in port. The parish minutes were kept in English—reflecting the pan-Orthodox nature of the congregation in the early years—until 1906, when Greek prevailed. Maintaining its existence into the present, Holy Trinity in New Orleans can rightfully claim to be the oldest Greek church in the Western Hemisphere. Almost three decades would pass before another Greek Orthodox church would be organized anywhere else in America.

Another trickle of Greeks to come to this country in the nineteenth century consisted of sailors from ships arriving in American ports. Most of these Greek sailors began to work on ships in the Great Lakes and on steamboats plying the Mississippi River and its tributaries. A few became oyster fishermen in the Gulf states. The number of such Greeks— probably several hundred—working and residing in the United States was sufficient enough to merit the attention of a *New York Times* story in 1873.[13] In whatever employment they found in America, Greek sailors were praised for "their abstinence from drinking and their hard work."[14]

Neither the educated Greek Americans of the orphans' generation, nor the Greek merchants, nor the Greek sailors were, of course, typical of the waves of Greek immigrants who were to come to these shores in a

[12]The best account of the founding of the New Orleans church is Alexander Doumouras, "Greek Orthodox Communities in America Before World War I," *St. Vladimir's Seminary Quarterly*, 11, no. 4 (1967), 177–79. Doumouras also reports fragmentary evidence of the founding of a Greek church, Sts. Constantine and Helen, in Galveston, Texas, in 1862. Little is known of the Galveston church except that it served a small pan-Orthodox community of Serbs, Russians, and Syrians as well as Greeks and that it later passed into the hands of the Serbs who had split from the Greeks. On the Galveston church see also *Orthodox America 1794–1976* (Syosset, N.Y.: Orthodox Church in America, 1975), pp. 37–38.

[13]"The Greeks in America," *New York Times*, August 4, 1873, reprinted in Hecker and Fenton, *The Greeks in America*, pp. 61–64.

[14]*Ibid*., p. 63.

later age. Nineteenth-century Greek arrivals did not establish deeply rooted Greek-American institutions. This was to be the accomplishment of the poor and uneducated, but energetic and resourceful, immigrants who came to this country later, from the villages of rural Greece. It is the saga of these immigrants that was to mold the Greek experience in America.

THE ERA OF MASS MIGRATION

The world of the Greek peasant at the turn of the century was desperately poor. Simply having enough to eat was a constant concern though actual starvation was rare. Whatever the glories of its classical monuments and the beauty of its seas and mountains, Greece was a harsh land from which to wrest a living. But the Greeks of the countryside knew they were poor. They made invidious comparisons with the small bourgeoisie and the petty government functionaries of their homeland. The notion of moving to better places—anticipated in the Greek maritime tradition and entrepreneurialism in the cities of the old Ottoman Empire—was already part of the common worldview. As the refrain of the folk song went:

> Mother, I want to go to foreign lands.
> To foreign lands I must go.[15]

It was a world in which the Greek Orthodox Church was an embodiment of historical, cultural, and social as well as religious experience. The holy days of the liturgical calendar dominated the year-long cycle—the climax being the Passion of the Holy Week. It was a society of parental authority, puritanical strictness, and sexual segregation. Fathers and brothers were committed to come up with a suitable dowry—the *prika*—if their daughters and sisters were to marry. Not to do all that was possible to insure the marriage of female relatives would be a violation of one's *philotimo*—a concept hard to translate, but connoting values of self-esteem, dignity, and obligation.[16]

[15]Helen Zeese Papanikolas, *Toil and Rage in a New Land: The Greek Immigrants in Utah*, 2nd ed. (Salt Lake City: Utah Historical Society, 1974), p. 107.
[16]Discussion of *philotimo* and its centrality in the Greek national character is found in Dorothy Lee, *Freedom and Culture* (New York: Spectrum Books, 1959), pp. 141–49; and John G. Peristiany, "Honour and Shame in a Cypriot Highland Village," *Honour and Shame*, ed., Peristiany (London: University of Chicago Press, 1966), pp. 171–90. In June, 1978, President Jimmy Carter called a meeting of Greek-American leaders at the White House to explain why he reneged on a campaign promise to retain the U.S. arms embargo against Turkey (passed by Congress in the wake of the 1974 Turkish invasion of Cyprus). One of the American-born Greeks in attendance, Christos Spirou, Democratic leader of the New Hampshire legislature, characterized the Administration's bid for support as "offending Greek philotimo." When reporters asked what the word meant, a chorus of voices shouted back, "Love of honor." *Washington Post*, June 23, 1978, p. A14.

It was a time in which the nationalism engendered by the Greek War of Independence still burned strong. The pantheon of Independence heroes was more vivid and empathetic than the distant immortals of classical Hellas. At the time of its independence, in 1830, Greece consisted of the Peloponnesus, the peninsula forming the southern part of Greece, the adjacent mainland regions of Roumeli and Attica, and certain nearby islands. The still "unredeemed" Greek lands waiting to be liberated only exacerbated the Greeks' hypernationalism. The Ionian Islands were ceded to Greece by Great Britain in 1864. In time (principally through wars with Turkey and Bulgaria) Greece expanded to include Thessaly (1881), Crete (de facto in 1898), Macedonia and Southern Epirus (1913), the Aegean Islands (1914), and Western Thrace (1919).

Despite the territorial expansion of modern Greece, the maximum goal—the "Great Idea"—of a reconstituted Byzantine Empire was to be irrevocably shattered in 1922, when Turkish forces inflicted a catastrophic defeat on the Greek Army in Asia Minor. The 1922 disaster was a watershed event for modern Greece: a three-millennia Hellenism was eradicated from Anatolia, over 1,300,000 refugees had to be absorbed by the mainland population, and Greece was destined to remain a minor nation, a perpetual pawn of the major powers. Even today, the "Great Idea" still evokes memories of opportunities lost.

After World War II the Dodecanese Islands were acquired from Italy. Hopes to incorporate Northern Epirus (in southern Albania) are periodically raised, but the claim has not been pushed seriously in recent decades. The issue of Cyprus *enosis* (union) with Greece resulted in a compromise of sorts with the establishment of an independent Cyprus republic in 1960. But following the Turkish invasion of the island in 1974, the ultimate status of Cyprus has remained unsettled. Throughout the twentieth century, the Greek-American community has played an important role in Greek irredentism.

The Greek immigrant around the turn of the century was coming out of a homeland where internal politics had become highly personalistic and often turbulent. Seeking to usher Greece into the modern era, a group of reformist military officers in 1909 summoned a Cretan liberal, Eleutherios Venizelos (1864–1936), to head the government. Soon Venizelos was to be locked in a bitter struggle with the newly crowned King Constantine I (1868–1923). The schism between the royalist adherents of Constantine and the more republican supporters of Venizelos was to dominate Greek political life for a generation. It was a political schism that was to be carried over with a vengeance into the Greek community of America.

It cannot be overstated that the overriding motive for Greek migration to the United States was economic gain. The intent of the overwhelming majority of immigrants was to return to Greece with sufficient capital to enjoy a comfortable life in their home villages. At the least, they expected to insure the proper marriages of their daughters and sisters by building up dowries with their American earnings. The only major exception to the immigrant goal of returning home were the Greeks who came from what is today Turkey. Correctly foreseeing that the aborning Turkish republic would reverse the relative tolerance that the older Ottoman order had displayed toward its non-Muslim minorities, these Greeks saw their move to America as a permanent one. (One important impetus was the 1908 promulgation that Greeks must serve in the Turkish army.) Why is it that many Ottoman Greeks chose as their destination the faraway and strange America over the nearby and familiar "free Greece"? Again the answer is simple—money.

Thus whether from "free" or "enslaved" Greece, the move to America was to become a virtual exodus. A Greek writing in 1909 observed:

> "So and so from such and such village sent home so many dollars within a year," is heard in a certain village, and the report, flashed from village to village and growing from mouth to mouth, causes the farmer to desert his plow, the shepherd to sell his sheep, the artisan to throw away his tools . . . and all set aside the passage money to that they can take the first possible ship for America and gather up the dollars in the streets before they are all gone.[17]

In the early decades of the twentieth century, whole villages were stripped of their young and middle-aged males. When sons went, driven by the hope of escaping a limited existence, there was the tearing away from distraught mothers and grim fathers. When husbands went it was with the promise that they would soon return after making their fortunes. Many husbands did not return to the old country; some sent for their wives, others never did bring their families over to America. Because so few young men remained in the villages, moreover, dowries became exorbitant, in order to attract the eligible males still residing at home. By the time the men who had emigrated to America were themselves ready to marry, they sought girls younger than the ones they had left behind in their own generation. It was a cruel piece of historical irony that precisely because so many men went to America to insure their sisters' marriages, many young women in Greece had to face the probability of remaining single or marrying old men.

The great roll of the Greek mass migration to America is headed by Christos Tsakonas, who was born in 1848 in a village near Sparta.[18]

[17]Seraphim G. Canoutas cited in Henry Pratt Fairchild, *Greek Immigration to the United States* (New Haven: Yale University Press, 1911), p. 224.

[18]Christos Tsakonas is described as the precursor of the Greek immigrant in Theodore Saloutos, *The Greeks in the United States* (Cambridge: Harvard University Press, 1964), p. 24. Andrew T. Kopan identifies Tsakonas as settling in Chicago. See Kopan, "Education and Greek Immigrants in Chicago, 1892-1973: A Study in Ethnic Survival" (unpublished doctoral thesis, University of Chicago, 1974), p. 113.

Tsakonas was a prototypical immigrant in many ways. After completing a few years in the village school, he set out to improve his financial circumstances, first in the Greek port of Piraeus, then in Alexandria, Egypt. Making little headway in his ambitions, Tsakonas decided to leave for America in 1873—an unprecedented step for a man of peasant background—thereby earning the sobriquet the "Columbus of Sparta." Tsakonas found America to his liking. He returned briefly to Greece and, in 1875, left for America again. This time he was accompanied by five compatriots from Sparta. This party of Spartans—the precursor of the succeeding waves of Greek immigrants who came to America— settled in Chicago where they became fruit peddlers.

During the 1880s about two thousand Greeks came to America, mostly from Sparta. During the 1890s over fifteen thousand Greeks coming from a wider regional base left for the United States. The departures of the nineties were precipitated by the collapse in the European market for raisins, Greece's principal export, and the greater impoverishment which resulted in the countryside. But the flood of Greek immigrants occurred in the first two decades of the twentieth century. Indeed, from 1900 to 1915, close to one in every four Greek males between the ages of fifteen and forty-five departed for America!

The outlines of this mass migration are shown in Table 1-1. In the decade 1901–1910 some 167,000 Greeks came to these shores, and from 1911 through 1920, despite the interruption of World War I, over 180,000 Greeks migrated to America. These figures refer only to Greeks born in Greece proper and, therefore, do not include immigrants of Greek heritage who came from Turkey, the Balkan countries, Egypt, or

TABLE 1-1.

GREEK IMMIGRATION TO THE UNITED STATES BY DECADES

Decade	Number*
1881–1890	2,308
1891–1900	15,979
1900–1910	167,519
1911–1920	184,201
1921–1930	51,084
1931–1940	9,119
1941–1950	8,973
1951–1960	47,608
1961–1970	85,969
1971–1980**	102,000

*Refers only to those born in Greece proper. Persons of Greek ethnic stock coming from outside Greece not included.

**Immigration figures for 1977–1980 estimated at 9,000 annually.

Source: Immigration and Naturalization Service, *1976 Annual Report* (U.S. Government Printing Office), pp. 87–88.

Cyprus. We do not have accurate statistics as to how many Greeks came from outside Greece, but one hundred thousand is an informed estimate.[19] Thus, well over four hundred thousand Greeks—the vast majority males—arrived in the United States between 1900 and 1920.

Once the first group of immigrants had settled in America, they wrote to their home villages to encourage other male relatives to follow. A typical letter from an older brother in the United States to a younger one still in the old country went as follows.[20]

December 28, 1908

Dear Costa,

The time we have been so long expecting has at last arrived. Our business has reached the point where we need another helper, and we want you to come over and help us. I enclose a complete ticket from Tripolis [a town in the Peloponnesus] to Chicago, all paid for. All you have to do is show it to the men as you go along. Have dear mother give you a written paper showing that you have her permission to come, as you are not yet sixteen. We will pay you the same wages as we would pay any other clerk. Take the greatest care of yourself, dear Costa, and come quickly. Kiss our beloved mother and sisters for me. I kiss you on the two eyes.

Those without relatives in America to bring them over were often recruited by labor agents scouring the Greek hinterland. Sportily dressed and wearing a gold watch, the agent promised passage money and a job in America working in a factory, packing house, mine, or on a railroad gang. Repayment for the ticket would come from garnishments on one's wages in America. The agent was usually a Greek himself who had come from America and his retelling of the "gold in the streets" legend found willing ears. Too many of these agents were unscrupulous individuals who fleeced the unwary peasant of his few acres by demanding collateral. Too often the promised jobs did not exist. Even when the work was there, the living conditions were shocking. More than one shepherd boy, accustomed to sleeping under the stars, would find himself in America, sharing quarters with six others in a room with no windows.

However he acquired his passage money, the immigrant's trauma began even before he left for America. Wrenched from his familiar surroundings, he was assembled into groups at the point of embarkation—usually the ports of Pireaus or Patras. Brusquely when not rudely treated by port authorities and steamship personnel, the immigrant was consigned to the nether regions of his ship. The crossing in unbelievably cramped quarters could take as little as three weeks or as

[19]Theodore Saloutos, "Causes and Patterns of Greek Emigration to the United States," *Perspectives in American History*, 7 (1973), p. 390.
[20]Fairchild, *Greek Immigration*, p. 96.

long as several months, depending upon the number and length of stays in other Mediterranean ports. But discomfort and humiliation were nothing as compared to the one absolute fear gripping all immigrants: that a cough or an eye infection might cause one to fail the physical examination required for entry into America. In the early years the physical examinations were conducted in the Castle Garden buildings— the *kastengardi* of Greek immigrant lore—on Ellis Island. Starting around 1910, however, preliminary examinations were increasingly held at the ports of embarkation.

Once through the processing of Ellis Island and admission to the United States, the newly arrived immigrant would head by train toward his destination: the relatives who had preceded him, or the job promised him by the labor agent. If he had no firm destination, he would seek out a place where some of his fellow villagers might be found. The flood of Greek immigrants who arrived in America before 1920 can be traced along three major routes:

1. Greeks going to the Western states to work on railroad gangs and in mines;
2. Greeks going to New England mill towns to work in the textile and shoe factories;
3. Greeks who went to the large Northern cities, principally New York and Chicago, and worked in factories, or found employment as busboys, dishwashers, bootblacks, and peddlers.

Each of these groups shared many things in common, but also differed from one another.

The West

As early as 1907 the Greek Consul General in New York estimated that there were between thirty and forty thousand Greek laborers in the American West.[21] These Greek workers found employment in the mines and smelters of the Rocky Mountain region—especially Colorado and Utah—and on the railroad gangs throughout the West. In some locales the Greeks constituted the largest ethnic group among such workers. Greek railroad laborers were especially concentrated in California, where in 1910 there were more Greeks proportionate to the total state population than anywhere else in America.

Men would be hired through labor agents representing the big companies.[22] Often they would have to pay a bribe to a "padrone," a fellow Greek who would act as intermediary between the recently ar-

---

[21]Stephanos Zotos, *Hellenic Presence in America* (Wheaton, Ill.: Pilgrimage, 1976), p. 92.

[22]The discussion on early Greek immigrants in the Rocky Mountain states is adapted from Papanikolas, *Toil and Rage*.

rived worker and his employer. The most powerful and notorious of the padrones was Leonidas G. Skliris, the "Czar of the Greeks." Skliris's power was based not only on the money he extorted from his compatriots, but, more important, on the fact that he could supply men to the managers at lower than prevailing rates and, when labor troubles broke out, he could provide strikebreakers as well. For these services, Skliris was given the authority to deduct his charges directly from the workers' wages. Though occurring in a decidedly American context, Skliris's position resembled nothing so much as that of an Ottoman despot.

It was as strikebreakers that the first sizeable group of Greeks arrived in the West. A 1903 strike of Italian coal miners in eastern Utah was broken by Greeks quickly brought in from the East. (The striking Italians had been brought into the area several years earlier as strikebreakers themselves.) Though most Greeks were not to be stirred by the workers' movement gaining strength in the West in the years before World War I, they did, nevertheless, take a leading role in some major strikes. But it was more a sense of violation of their dignity—the Greek's *philotimo*—than class consciousness that caused them to strike. Greeks in the West, especially those from Crete, were quick to strike when they found others were making more money for the same work, when they were cheated on the mine's weighing scales, or if they could seize an opportunity to escape from the control of the padrones.

In 1912 copper miners in Bingham Canyon, Utah, went out on strike. The main issue for the Cretan Greeks among the strikers was to force the company to get rid of Skliris. This was finally accomplished, but not before blood was shed and the Cretans had taken up armed positions in the surrounding mountains, a tactic they adopted in other strikes. Meanwhile, Skliris had brought in mainland Greeks to take over from the striking Cretans. The use of Greek against Greek in labor strife was to poison intra-Greek relations in the West for a generation to come. In 1922 Greek coal miners were involved in a major strike that took place in Carbon county, Utah (the same area where Greeks nineteen years earlier had first entered the West as strikebreakers). The Greeks' immediate cause for participation in this nationwide coal strike was their being shortweighed on the coal scales. Animosity between Cretan and mainland Greeks, however, prevented a united front.

A truly heroic Greek labor leader—Louis Tikas, a Cretan—appeared in the 1913–1914 coal strike at Ludlow, Colorado. Tikas was killed on April 20, 1914, when he was caught in a crossfire between strikers and national guardsmen, while attempting to escort women and children to safety under a flag of truce. Upon hearing of Tikas's death, hundreds of Greek workers left their jobs and walked across the mountains of southern Colorado and northern New Mexico to take part in his funeral. On a monument erected by the United Mine Workers in memory of those who died at Ludlow, Tikas's name is the first of many.[23]

If conditions in the mines were harsh, the situation for those working in the railroad gangs was not much better. A Greek passing through the American West in 1911 writes in his diary:

> A Greek traveling by rail over these immense western states cannot but feel grief and sorrow and be plunged into sorrowful thoughts, when he sees at nearly every mile of railway little groups of his own people with pick and shovel in their hands. All these have left their beloved fatherland, their families, their fellowcountrymen, and their lands, and come here to build and repair railroads in the hope of acquiring a few thousand francs—instead of which they acquire rheumatism, tuberculosis, venereal diseases, and those other ills, while others are deprived of feet, hands, eyes, and some their lives! This is unhappily the bitter truth.[24]

With good reason the Greek workers feared they would die young or be permanently maimed in America. Doctors were accused of amputating limbs too quickly, and injured men often asked to be first taken to folkhealers among their own kind. Still, thousands must have died from work injuries. In isolated Western towns it was common to have a "Death Wedding" funeral—a Greek custom for the unmarried dead. The young man would be dressed as a bridegroom in his casket: a wedding crown on his head, a gold band on his finger, and a white flower in his lapel. Without Greek women, there was not even the solace of the funeral wailing of the *mirologhia*—the "words of fate," an extemporaneous account of the departed's life and unfulfilled promise.

Life in the mining towns and railroad camps was, perhaps inevitably, coarse. Gambling was endemic and prostitutes were the only available women. Male comaraderie based on shared nationality and present circumstance could suddenly change into hostility if one's honor was slighted. Men fought over transgressions to that honor; political disputes between royalist supporters of King Constantine and republican adherents of Venizelos were always an ever present cause for intra-Greek bitterness in America as well as in Greece; lifelong feuds could spring from marriage arrangements that went awry after the woman reached America.

[23]Grim testimony to the number of Greeks who labored in the mines is found in the death toll of major mining disasters. On October 22, 1913, 263 men were killed in the "No. 2" mine at Dawson, New Mexico, of whom about a hundred had identifiable Greek names. Another explosion in Dawson on February 8, 1923, killed 120 miners of whom about twenty were Greek. F. Stanley, *The Dawson Tragedies* (privately printed, 1964), pp. 8–16. An explosion on March 8, 1924, in the Castle Gate mine near Price, Utah, caused the deaths of 172 men including 50 Greek miners. Papanikolas, *Toil and Rage*, p. 177.

[24]Seraphim G. Canoutas cited in Burgess, *Greeks in America*, pp. 43–44.

A perceptive account of the early Greek-American West has been given us by an unusual Greek woman. Maria S. Economidou, the spirited wife of an Athenian publisher and well educated in her own right, took upon herself to report on the conditions of the Greeks in America in 1914.[25] Usually understanding of what she saw, Mrs. Economidou was, nevertheless, disgusted with the enthusiasm the Greek men in one mining town showered on a "Madame Sophia," a somewhat tarnished Greek performer who toured the mining camps. "She danced and sang," Mrs. Economidou wrote, "with the grace of an elephant and the voice of a wolf." But, as one of the miners explained, "If we did not have even this diversion from time to time, we would become animals completely."[26]

As in other parts of the country, the Greeks in the West were to confront a virulent nativistic reaction. But it was in the West, where their relative numbers made them more visible, that the Greeks faced the most serious incidents. In McGill, Nevada, three Greeks were killed in an antiforeign melee in June, 1908. In Utah conflict with Mormons seemed to compound the general prejudice against foreigners in the air. A sampling of the characterizations of Greeks printed in Utah newspapers in the years just before and after World War I include "the scum of Europe," "a vicious element unfit for citizenship," and "ignorant, depraved and brutal foreigners."[27] In 1917 a Greek accused of killing the brother of the boxer Jack Dempsey was almost lynched in Salt Lake City. In 1923 in Price, Utah, local citizens took matters in their own hands by breaking up Greek stores and ordering the "American girls" who worked in them to return to their homes. When the Ku Klux Klan was active in the Utah of the early 1920s, Greeks were singled out as a special target. The Greeks always believed their robed enemies were Mormons jealous of the newly successful Greek businesses.

The most publicized anti-Greek assault took place in 1909 in the city of South Omaha, Nebraska.[28] On the outskirts of the city was a shantytown of several thousand Greek laborers, a number swollen by unemployed railroad workers waiting out the winter. Anti-Greek feeling in South Omaha was already intense owing to the carousing and gambling of the Greeks and, possibly, because many of them were viewed as strikebreakers. The precipitating incident occurred on February 19 when a Greek, John Masourides was stopped by a policeman, while he

[25]Maria S. Economidou, *The Greeks of America as I Saw Them* [*E Hellines tis Amerikis opos tou Eida*] (New York: D.C. Divry, 1916).

[26]Cited in Papanikolas, *Toil and Rage*, p. 138.

[27]*Ibid.*, p. 112.

[28]The account of the 1909 anti-Greek riot in South Omaha, Nebraska, is based on Saloutos, *Greeks in the United States*, pp. 66–70; Zotos, *Hellenic Presence*, pp. 96–99; Papanikolas, *Toil and Rage*, p. 112; and my own conversations with elderly Greek men who had personally witnessed some of the events in their early days in America.

was with a prostitute. An argument ensued and Masourides killed the officer. The Greeks claimed the policeman was drunk and enraged in seeing a Greek publicly walking with a "white" prostitute, and that Masourides killed in self-defense. In any event, the townspeople were ready to be whipped into a frenzy ("One drop of American blood is worth all the Greek blood in the world!") at a mass meeting presided over by local officials. A mob rampaged through the Greek quarter burning most of it to the ground, destroying some thirty-six Greek businesses, and driving all the Greeks from the city. The South Omaha riot was given wide coverage in the Greek press in America and in Greece. The Greek government lost no time in protesting the acquiescence of the local authorities to the brutality of the mob. The Greek government lodged a formal demand that the victims be compensated with $135,000. In 1918 the U.S. Congress did indemnify the Greeks but only to the amount of $40,000.

Although Greeks were often targets of native American hostility and although they came to the West as manual laborers, many began to move into the middle class early on. Even before World War I, but especially in the 1920s, many Greeks began to leave the mines and railroads to become store owners. They established restaurants, bars, candy stores or confectioneries, hotels, and other businesses at a rapid rate. Some Greeks became quite well to do by investing shrewdly in real estate. Another group of Greeks in the West became sheepmen, ironically the very occupation they had left Greece to avoid. The sheepmen attained a modicum of prosperity in the 1920s, although most of them were to lose their holdings in the Depression. The appearance of a Greek-American middle class after World War I, however, should not obscure the many Greeks in the West—and elsewhere—who remained blue-collar workers for all of their lives. But the main development was clearly toward the emergence of a Greek-American bourgeoisie. In time, as women arrived from the old country, a normal family life was made possible, which further accentuated middle-class aspirations. This pattern was to be recapitulated among Greek Americans throughout the country.

New England

A second major destination of Greek immigrants was New England, to work in textile and shoe factories. In the first decades of this century sizeable Greek colonies could be found in Manchester and Nashua in New Hampshire, Bridgeport, New Britain and Norwich in Connecticut, and Chicopee, Haverhill, Lynn, Peabody, New Bedford, and Springfield in Massachusetts. Early on there was a major Greek concentration in Boston centering around Kneeland and Washington streets. The settlements of Greek workers in New England had counterparts in the factory towns of Ohio, Pennsylvania, and upstate New York. But for Greeks the foremost mill town was Lowell, Massachusetts, a community that has a special significance in the history of Greek Americans. In 1906 the first Greek Orthodox church in America with a Byzantine motif, Holy Trinity, was erected in Lowell. By 1910 Lowell, with a total population of about one hundred thousand, had at least twenty thousand Greeks. Even as late as 1920, Lowell had the third largest Greek population in America, trailing only New York and Chicago.

The reception accorded the new Greek arrivals by the larger community was generally hostile. An observer of early Greek immigrants noted that the "average American citizen" of Lowell regarded Greeks as "a quarrelsome, treacherous, filthy, low-living lot."[29] But it was with fellow immigrant workers that the Greeks ran into the most difficulty. The Greeks were the third major immigrant group to come to the mill towns, following French Canadians and the Irish. Each migration in turn underbid the wages of the earlier workers. Moreover, the Greeks also had the reputation of being less inclined to drink than the Irish or French Canadians and therefore more reliable workers. A contemporary account describes the situation the Greeks encountered:

> From the very beginning these two dominant races [the Irish and French Canadians] attacked and ill-used the new Greek laborers and hounded them from good lodgings. Their attacks grew as the Greek colony grew. At night when the mills poured out their operatives, the poor, scared Greeks would gather twenty or so together, take the middle of the street, scatter to their lodgings and dare not stir out till morning.[30]

In the later decades of the 1930s and 1940s, a generation of Greek Americans who grew up in the mill towns would remember childhood experiences of taunts and fights with the children of other immigrant nationalities.

Another account is given in an interview in 1966 with a retired non-Greek foreman of one of the mills. He reminisced about the first Greek workers over a half century earlier.

> Every time we'd hire one, he would tell us of brothers or cousins or other relatives who were planning on coming to this country. We noticed that there were more and more Greeks every year, and I never believed what some of them told me that they were going back to the old country again. They stuck pretty much to themselves. If you happened to go down near the shanties in the evening, especially on weekends, you'd hear loud talking, arguments, or weird singing. They drank Greek whiskey and Turkish

[29]Fairchild, *Greek Immigration*, p. 144.
[30]Burgess, *Greeks in America*, p. 141.

coffee. At work they were friendly with the others, but they always talked Greek. Sometimes we laughed at them and at the way they were living. But they were good workers.[31]

The living conditions of the early Greek immigrants in the mill towns were, to say the least, frugal. Extreme parsimony was the operating principle, the object being to save as much money as possible to send back to Greece. Modern hygiene and a balanced diet were not commonly practiced. Tuberculosis was a frequent scourge and has always been a special dread in the Greek-American community. Usually a half-dozen or so men would rent a cheap apartment and share expenses collectively. Often one among their number might be designated as cook and housekeeper and be excused from working in the mills. The permanent menu, too typical, of one such household was:[32]

Monday: rice and wieners
Tuesday: potatoes and wieners
Wednesday: eggs and wieners
Thursday: lentils and wieners
Friday: greens and wieners
Saturday: beans in cottonseed oil
Sunday: meat, soup, and beer

"Greektowns" appeared in all parts of the United States wherever a sufficient number of Greek immigrants had located. Lowell, Massachusetts, had one of the first and most extensive of such Greektowns. In 1913 a Greek business district centered on Market Street included:

2 drug stores
2 newspapers
3 ticket agencies
2 photographers
1 importing house
several dry goods stores
tailor shops
shoemakers

[31]Quoted in James W. Kiriazis, "A Study of Change in Two Rhodian Immigrant Communities" (unpublished doctoral thesis, University of Pittsburgh, 1967), p. 75. But a superintendent of a leather factory in Nashua, New Hampshire, could describe the early Greek workers in less favorable terms: "They had no sense of honor; you can't rely upon them; they lie and do it cunningly." Peter Roberts, The New Immigration (New York: Macmillan Co., 1912), p. 99.
[32]Theodore Saloutos, They Remember America (Berkeley: University of California Press, 1966), p. 18.

4 restaurants
some 30 groceries
a wholesale meat dealer
6 bakeries
25 or 30 coffee houses
1 model saloon
about 10 confectioneries and fruit stores
a number of barbers
and a number of shoe shine parlors.[33]

Although nearly all of these shopkeepers were of peasant origin and had been in America only a few years, the nascent entrepreneurialism of the Greek immigrant was already evident. In fact, it was common for a Greek businessman first to start a business limited to Greek clientele and then to expand his horizons—and if need be to change locations—to the larger buying public.

Many of the Greek immigrants in New England, however, were to remain in the mills for at least a decade or two if not for their entire working lives. Yet, even those Greeks who stayed in the factories played only a marginal role in labor union activity. An observer in 1911 describes the Greek mill workers in the following terms:

> Socialism finds no followers among the people of this race in the United States, though it is beginning to get a slight foothold in Greece. Greeks are apparently not inclined to join trade unions, partly because there are comparatively few of them who are laborers in unionized trades, partly because they prefer their own organizations, and partly because they are not wanted by the unions.[34]

Two years later another commentator similarly concluded, "In Lowell and elsewhere the Greeks . . . care naught for labor unions nor the I.W.W."[35]

Greek mill workers had practically no working-class identity. Several factors accounted for this. The majority of the Greek workers in the early years saw themselves as temporary sojourners in the United States. Strikes, layoffs, and even union dues could only detract from the immediate goal of accumulating as much money as possible. Linguistic and cultural isolation also played a part. Greek immigrants could organize themselves, but only in self-contained and ethnically homogeneous groups. They were more concerned with common national identification than with working class solidarity. Also, enough of the Greeks did set up

[33]Burgess, *Greeks in America*, pp. 146–47.
[34]Fairchild, *Greek Immigration*, pp. 209–10.
[35]Burgess, *Greeks in America*, p. 154.

small businesses early on to serve as role models and local leaders for their countrymen who stayed in the factories. In time, nearly all the Greek immigrants, whether behind the looms in the mills or the counters of their stores, sought to enjoy the material comforts and emulate the middle-class standards of their adopted country. In this regard the Greek workers in New England were very much like their compatriots in all parts of the United States.

The Big Cities

The third major destination of the Greek immigrants was the big cities of the Middle Atlantic and Great Lakes states. By the eve of World War I there were at least several thousand Greeks in each of such cities as Philadelphia, Pittsburgh, Buffalo, Cleveland, Toledo, Detroit, Gary, and Milwaukee. But Chicago and New York became the preeminent Greek-American cities, a position which has solidified over the decades. A conservative estimate of the Greek population in 1913 placed the number at about twenty thousand in each,[36] which augmented to at least fifty thousand by the early 1920s. With some hyperbole Chicago's Greeks would claim that theirs was the third largest Greek city— surpassed only by Athens and Thessalonica—in the world.

The Chicago Greek community was the most geographically concentrated of any in America. An early Greektown in the 1890s formed at Clark and Kinzie streets just north of the city's Loop. But, beginning around the turn of the century, Greek immigrants settled on the near West side at the "Delta," a triangular area bordered by Halsted and Harrison streets and Blue Island Avenue. This "Halsted Street Greektown" became the largest in the country. With about twenty thousand inhabitants between the two world wars, Chicago's Greektown developed into an ethnic enclave with its own churches, schools, businesses, coffee-houses, restaurants, newspapers, doctors, lawyers, and voluntary associations. It remained a viable community for over half a century and served as the focal point of Greek life in metropolitan Chicago until displaced in the early 1960s by the erection of a new campus of the University of Illinois.

Chicago's Greektown was adjacent to Hull House, Jane Addams' famed settlement project, whose activities played an important and beneficial role for many early Greek immigrants. The special attention Jane Addams gave to Greek immigrants and her espousal of Greek culture did much to buttress the ethnic pride of the sorely tried Greek immigrants of Chicago. The Hull House Theater opened its doors in 1899 with a production of the classical Greek tragedy "The Return of Odys-

[36]Fairchild, *Greek Immigration*, pp. 125, 148.

seus" with a cast made up of Greek immigrants from Chicago. After seeing one performance Loredo Taft, the renowned sculptor, wrote:

> The thought which came over and over again into every mind was: These are the real sons of Hellas chanting the songs of their ancestors, enacting the life of thousands of years ago. There is a background for you! How noble it made these fruit merchants for the nonce; what a distinction it gave them![37]

Many Chicago Greeks, like their compatriots in other big cities, found work in meatpacking plants, steel mills, and factories. But many others took the entrepreneurial route. It was in this capacity that the Greek immigrant was to make his most distinguishing mark on American society. Greek immigrants, newly arrived and often still boys, would start out as bootblacks, busboys, or peddlers of fruit, candy, and flowers. Somehow setting aside a portion of their meager profits, their mercantile future seemed almost predestined. Thus, Henry Pratt Fairchild, an otherwise caustic observer of the early Greek-American community, could, nevertheless, write:

> The average Greek immigrant does not bring enough money with him to establish himself in a fixed business. But he can buy a push cart, or even a small tray hung over his shoulder, on which he can place a small stock of candy or fruit, and, stationing himself on a street corner, begin doing business. Give a Greek a start in business and he will do the rest. However small his earnings he manages to save a part of them, and in the course of time he has amassed enough to enter on the second state of progression. He gets control of a small sidewalk space and puts up a little stand where he can keep a larger stock of goods and have a permanent location. From now on his advancement is rapid. Very soon he is able to rent a small store, with or without sidewalk space in front, and it is only a matter of time and ability until he is operating a finely appointed store on one of the best streets of the city, or perhaps own a chain of stores which ensures him the bulk of the trade of the place.[38]

[37]Cited in Kopan, "Education and Greek Immigrants," pp. 148–49. The contrast between the real-life Greek immigrants at the turn of the century and the idealized Hellenes of classical antiquity was always good for comment by native American observers. "We never picture the heroes of Greek epics, undersized, like these moderns; round headed, looking into the world out of small, black, piercing eyes, their complexion sallow and their hair straight and black." Edward A. Steiner, *On the Trail of the Immigrant* (New York: Fleming H. Revell Co., 1906), p. 283.

[38]Fairchild, *Greek Immigration*, p. 167. The entrepreneurship of the early Greek immigrants was noted by just about all contemporary observers. Two representative accounts follow. "Full of this pride and confidence in themselves, they are nevertheless ready to blacken our boots for ten cents, and they do it remarkably well, displacing negroes and Italians, until later, they open stores and sell American candies to an undiscriminating public, hungry for cheap sweets. No labour is too hard for them, although they prefer to stand behind the counter." From Steiner, *On the Trail of the Immigrant*, p. 285. "The push cart trade of New York city is in the hands of Greeks, and it is affirmed that the shoe shining parlors in Chicago are in the hand of a Greek company, which reaps a harvest by gathering in the nickels and dimes. In these ancient peoples there is what may be called a parasitic streak, which enables them to live by catering to the minor wants of Americans." From Roberts, *Tne New Immigration*, p. 60.

The Greek reluctance to work for wages was remarked upon almost from the very start. A *Chicago Tribune* story in 1897 stated the "Greek will not work at hard manual labor like digging sewers, carrying the hod . . . He is either an artisan or a merchant, generally the latter."[39] Further recognition of the pecuniary acumen of the early Greek immigrant is found in a 1909 article on Chicago's Greektown in the *American Journal of Sociology*:

> During the short time he has been in Chicago the Greek has established his reputation as a shrewd businessman. On Halsted Street they are already saying, "It takes a Greek to beat a Jew."[40]

Thus it was in the role of small businessmen that Greek Americans were to find their archetype.

Greek businesses in Chicago, as in other cities, tended to concentrate in certain areas: confectioneries or sweet shops, food service, retail and wholesale produce, floral shops, hatters, dry cleaners and pressers, and shoeshine parlors. In Chicago the Greek monopoly on sweet shops was virtually total. By 1908 there were already 237 Greek-owned confectioneries in the city. It is claimed that the sundae was first invented in a Greek-owned ice cream parlor in Chicago![41] The Greek proclivity in the food service business was evident early. In 1913 there were several hundred Greek-owned lunchrooms and restaurants in Chicago.[42] In addition to the bulk of the Greek business community that catered to the general public, of course, there were the stores in Greektown that serviced the needs of an almost exclusively Greek clientele.

The Greek population of New York City was about the same number as that of Chicago. The earliest Greek neighborhood was centered around Madison Street between Catherine and Pearl Streets in Manhattan's Lower East Side, but this area never developed into a definable enclave. Other smaller Greek neighborhoods were scattered throughout Manhattan and in the other boroughs. After World War I the main body of Greek immigrants settled along Eighth Avenue, between 14th and 45th Streets. Even though New York never produced a concentrated Greektown in the manner of Chicago, it could always lay claim to being the most important in the national Greek-American community. New York became the home of the first Greek-American

---

[39]Cited in Kopan, "Education and Greek Immigrants," p. 123.

[40]Grace Abbott, "A Study of the Greeks in Chicago," *American Journal of Sociology*, 15, no. 3 (November, 1909), p. 386.

[41]The dominance of Greeks in confectioneries is described in Fairchild, *Greek Immigration*, pp. 127–28 and Burgess, *Greeks in America*, pp. 34–36. The claim that Greeks in America invented the ice-cream sundae goes back some years. See Louis Adamic, "Greek Immigration to the United States," *Commonweal* Magazine, 33 (January 31, 1941), pp. 366–68, reprinted in Hecker and Fenton, *The Greeks in America*, pp. 88–92.

[42]Burgess, *Greeks in America*, p. 37.

daily newspapers with national circulation and became the headquarters of the Greek Orthodox Church in America.

The Greek entrepreneurial spirit noted in Chicago was equally evident in New York City. The kinds of businesses toward which New York Greeks gravitated, moreover, reflected the common Greek-American business pattern. A 1909 survey of Greek-owned businesses in Manhattan reported: 151 bootblack parlors, 113 florists, 107 lunchrooms and restaurants, 70 confectioneries, 62 retail fruit stores, and 11 wholesale produce dealers.[43] A few wealthy Greeks were in the travel and import business. Except for cigarette manufacturing, only a small number of New York Greeks worked in factories. Many who did not have their own businesses or who did not work for other Greeks became peddlers and pushcart vendors. One New York occupation that did not have a major counterpart among Greeks elsewhere in the United States was the fur industry. And Greeks employed by furriers— especially in the years between the two world wars—constituted one of the few Greek workers' groups to be attracted to communist labor organizations. But the clearly significant trend in New York, Chicago, and other cities was for the Greek immigrant to start off in menial tasks and then move on to a small but self-owned business.

A uniquely Greek mainstay in the early immigrant economy was the shoeshine or bootblack business.[44] Throughout the North there were literally scores or even hundreds of shoeshine parlors in each of the big cities. For the boy who had no better choices, there was always work to be found in a shoeshine parlor run by a fellow Greek. From our present perspective it is hard to realize how lucrative a shoeshine parlor could be in the early decades of this century. It was a time when walking was more common and shoes became dirtier than today; it was a time when the full high shoe was in fashion and standards of shoe presentation more particular than at present. With the cheap labor of young boys, the owners of bootblack establishments could do quite well indeed. Some of the more enterprising owners managed to set up chains of shoeshine parlors.

The bootblack business also led to some of the most unsavory exploitation of Greek by fellow Greek. Owners of shoe shine parlors developed a padrone system which was little more than indentured labor. Passage money was sent to boys in Greece to come and work as bootblacks in America. Once under the control of the padrone, the bootblack might not be paid anything for a year, after which he might

[43]Fairchild, *Greek Immigration*, p. 150.

[44]The description given on bootblacks in early Greek America is based on Saloutos, *Greeks in the United States*, pp. 48–56; Fairchild, *Greek Immigration*, pp. 171–84; and the reminiscences of old Greeks who worked as boys in the shoeshine parlors.

earn a salary of twenty dollars a year! (This compared to about ten to fifteen dollars a week for a mill worker in New England.) The working conditions were wretched. The shops opened up at about 6:00 A.M. and closed at 9:00 P.M. on weekdays, and later on weekends. There were no days off. After the doors were closed at night, the boys had to clean the shop and prepare things for the following day.

Unbeknownst to many of the bootblacks, all they had to do in order to escape their situation was simply to walk away from the shoe shine parlor. The padrone tried his best to keep his charges ignorant of this option or at least to overstate the bleakness of alternative employment. He would censor their mail lest complaints crossing the ocean cut into his future supply of bootblacks. After Greek-American newspapers raised their voices against the "flesh peddlers," some improvement did occur.[45] Yet the fact remained that most of the boys considered their privations worthwhile if they were the only way to get to America. In time, partly as a result of increasing familiarity with American opportunities, partly due to the decline of the shoe shine business, most of the bootblacks found employment in other fields. But for many years bootblacks and Greeks were synonymous in our large urban centers.

The South and Tarpon Springs

Only a small number of Greek immigrants headed toward the South. Of all the Greeks who came to America before 1920 fewer than one in fifteen settled in the states of the old Confederacy. A region with little industrial employment or commercial opportunity and one in which antiforeign sentiment was most pronounced, the South played a minor role in the early Greek experience in America. Those Greeks who did live in the South, however, prospered; almost all ran their own small businesses—restaurants and lunchrooms, confectioneries, fruit stores, and shoe shine parlors. A Greek or two could be found in almost any Southern city, but their numbers were most visible in places such as Birmingham, Alabama, Greensboro, North Carolina, and Savannah and Atlanta in Georgia.

There is a small community in the South, however, which does occupy a singular position in Greek America—Tarpon Springs, Florida, on the coast of the Gulf of Mexico.[46] Founded in the 1880s as a spa and

[45]Saloutos, *Greeks in the United States*, p. 54.

[46]Accounts of the Greek colony in Tarpon Springs, Florida, are found in: Helen Halley, "A Historical Functional Approach to the Study of the Greek Community in Tarpon Springs" (unpublished doctoral thesis, Columbia University, 1952); George T. Frantzis, *Strangers at Ithaca* (St. Petersburg, Fla.: Great Outdoors Publishing Co., 1962); and Edwin C. Buxbaum, "The Greek-American Group of Tarpon Springs, Florida" (unpublished doctoral thesis, University of Pennsylvania, 1967).

winter haven for wealthy Northerners, Tarpon Springs underwent a dramatic transformation at the turn of the century. In 1905 under the entrepreneurship of John Cocoris and his brothers, five hundred Greek spongers from the Aegean and Dodecanese Islands were brought to Tarpon Springs. From that time until the end of World War II, Tarpon Springs was the sponge center of America. Greeks dominated the industry through all of its stages—diving, hooking, cleaning, sorting, stringing, clipping, packing, and buying. During Prohibition times the Greek boat owners were also known to augment their incomes by smuggling liquor into the United States from Cuba. With the thriving sponge industry as its basis, Tarpon Springs became more than a "Greektown" enclave; it became a Greek town in fact. From 1905 into World War II, Tarpon Springs had a majority Greek population, a situation without parallel in any other town in the United States. In 1940 there were 1,000 men engaged in the sponge industry who, with their families, constituted about 2,500 Greek Americans in the town's total population of 3,402.

Although the Greeks of Tarpon Springs were concentrated in an area known as "fishtown," bordered by Pinellas and Tarpon Avenues and Dodecanese Boulevard, they were in political control of the town for most of the years between the two world wars. Some attribute the departure of the earlier established families of Tarpon Springs to the Greek ascendancy. As early as 1907 the spongers established their own Greek Orthodox church, St. Nicholas, named after the patron saint of seafarers, and much of their communal life centered around the liturgical calendar. The high point of the year still is the feast of the Epiphany on Janury 6, when local boys dive to retrieve a cross cast into the waters by a Greek prelate.

After World War II the sponge industry of Tarpon Springs went into a precipitous decline. The spongers were unable to withstand the double catastrophe of the introduction of syntheic sponges on the market and the "red tide" which decimated the sponge beds of the Gulf of Mexico. Today the sponge industry is only a remnant of its former self and has become part of a tourist scene accentuating the local Greek ambiance. By the late 1970s the town had a population of around thirteen thousand of whom about a third were of Greek descent. Although the non-Greek population was growing at a rapid rate, some fresh Greek infusion was also apparent. Greek-American retirees from the North— several score a year—were increasingly finding Tarpon Springs an attractive place to spend their remaining years. Small numbers of young men from the Greek islands were also coming over. Though nominally entering the United States to work in the town's small sponge and shrimp fleet, most of the newcomers, it seemed, were likely to become busboys and waiters in the local Greek restaurants.

It was the arrival of Greek women in significant numbers that anchored the Greek community in this country. It was on these women that the main burden and credit of the Greek-American family came to rest. Before the turn of the century only a trickle of Greek women entered the United States, each of whom must have been a pioneer in her own right. Between 1900 and 1910 less than one in twenty Greek immigrants were women, and only one in five between 1910 and 1920. According to the U.S. census the ratio of males to females among Greek-born Americans was a remarkably high 2.8 to one even in 1930, and a still disproportionate 1.6 to one as late as 1960.[47]

The preferred way for a Greek woman to come to America was to be accompanied: with her husband or in the company of brothers or cousins. But since marriages were frequently arranged across the ocean, many "picture brides"—who came from the same or nearby village of their prospective grooms—had to travel to America on their own. Whether betrothed or not, the trip to America could not be but a wrenching experience for single women. As Helen Zeese Papanikolas writes:

> Such women suffered not only from the fear of coming alone to a country whose language they did not know, but from violating the rigid code of their people. In the Mediterranean countries where a poor man's only possessions were his self-respect and his daughters' virginity, women were chaperoned with paranoid obsession. Women traveling alone to America were tragically burdened with the anxiety that they would be suspected forever of having questionable morals.[48]

By and large Greek immigrant women—married and unmarried—did not work outside the household. If a man's wife, daughters, or even sisters had to seek gainful employment, it was considered a poor reflection on his ability to provide. Indeed, many immigrant men never married precisely because they knew they could not support a family without reliance on a wife's income. There were, however, some exceptions to the general pattern. For a woman to work in the family store was acceptable, although even this was not a rule. In the West in the early years, moreover, many married women ran boarding houses for Greek laborers. But it was in New England that the likelihood of women working was highest. A large proportion, some say a majority, of the

---

[47]Evan C. Vlachos, "Historical Trends in Greek Migration to the United States" (paper presented at the Bicentennial Symposium on the Greek Experience in America, University of Chicago, 1976), p. 67.

[48]Papanikolas, *Toil and Rage*, p. 142.

Greek immigrant women in the mill towns were operatives in the textile and shoe factories. But even there most women did not continue working once they were married or after their husbands had secured a modicum of economic stability. The clearly dominant standard—and one that was usually adhered to—among early Greek immigrants was for women not to work. A Hull House study of Chicago's Greektown in 1909 reports that out of 246 women investigated only five were found to be employed.[49]

In a culture where men were supposed to be concerned mainly with the rigors of earning a living, the mother often became the emotional center of the family, If the husband was a responsible man the wife usually stayed at home. Though formally submissive to her husband, the wife was frequently dominant in the practical affairs of running the household and disciplining the children. Not only tradition but practical sense enforced this division of labor; it took so much energy just to cook, clean, shop and bring up the children. A wife was to be treasured more for her abilities as a *kali nikokira*—good housekeeper— than for any marketable skills outside the home.

The Greek immigrant woman typically learned little English— though perhaps more than she let on—especially in the urban Greek enclaves. She led a full, if circumscribed, social life which revolved around her family, a circle of Greek friends, and church activities. The Greek immigrant wife of the early era could expect realistically a long period of widowhood, inasmuch as she was often a decade or two younger than her husband. She fervently prayed that her grown children would marry "Greek" and that, once widowed, she might move in with them. Whatever the immigrant woman's personal circumstances, it was only with her arrival that the groundwork for a permanent Greek-American community could be laid.

The migration experience was a profound culture shock—for women and men alike—for which it took many Greek immigrants years to adjust. Some never did. The traditional peasant life of the mass of the immigrants was mean and should not be romanticized. But at least it was a thoroughly familiar way of life to these people. To move into an urban setting, not to know the English language, to be targets of hostility by most people, including other immigrant groups was, of course, a painful transition. Little wonder that the dominant mood among the immigrant Greeks of the early decades was an upswell of nostalgia for the old country.

Yet, for all the difficulties encountered by the pioneer Greeks in America before World War I, the basic fact remained that almost all of

[49]Abbott, "Greeks in Chicago," p. 388.

them were able to make more money here than they would have at home. Slowly, with resistance, but inevitably, the Greek immigrants became persuaded that their future was to be found in this country.

CHAPTER TWO

Early Greek immigrants in America, regardless of employment or location, were almost exclusively male. Prior to World War I about 90 percent of all of them were males. Some of the immigrants married American women, but many others never married at all. Still others had wives but left them in Greece. Even among those men who did eventually bring brides over from the old country, marriage would not often occur before their middle years. The Greek-American community in its early years was thus mainly a bachelor's community.

The bachelor existence of the large majority of the Greek immigrants gave rise to a uniquely Greek-American institution—the *kafenion* or coffeehouse. Almost from the time of the first arrivals, an enterprising Greek would rent a space in a cheap location, install a few tables and chairs, purchase a dozen decks of playing cards, and serve sweets and thickly brewed coffee in the manner of the old country. A few basil plants might be planted in rusty tin cans. The decor would include lithographs of classical or revolutionary scenes—"The Vengeance of Achilles" or "Lord Byron Taking the Oath of Allegiance."

Greek America Forms

Though sometimes frowned upon by established Greeks who saw the coffeehouse as a place for idlers and gamblers, it was the *kafenion* where Greek men could find surcease from this strange land. Theodore Saloutos gives us a good description.

> The coffeehouse was a community social center to which the men retired after working hours and on Saturdays and Sundays. Here they sipped cups of thick, black Turkish coffee . . . played cards, or engaged in animated political discussion. Here congregated gesticulating Greeks of all kinds: railroad workers, factory hands, shopkeepers, professional men, the unemployed, labor agitators, amateur philosophers, community gossips, cardsharks, and amused spectators. The air of the average coffee house was choked with clouds of smoke rising from cigarettes, pipes, and cigars. Through the haze one could see the dim figures of card players or hear the stentorian voices of would-be statesmen discussing every subject under the sun.[1]

The coffeehouse, especially in the larger cities, could also be the scene of more planned entertainment. A *bouzouki* or mandolin player, a

[1] Theodore Saloutos, *The Greeks in the United States* (Cambridge: Harvard University Press, 1964), p. 79.

belly dancer, or a strong-man act—the inevitable "Hercules"—would occasionally appear and earn a living from a tray passed through the coffeehouse audience. Much more common were the performances of the *karaghiozi*. Coming out of a Turkish tradition, the *karaghiozi*—shadow silhouette shows performed on a white sheet—were a popular form of entertainment throughout rural Greece in the nineteenth century.[2] Although there were innumerable variations, the basic plot was one in which the seemingly stupid but actually sly Greek, Karaghiozis, would always get the better of the officious and superordinate Turk.[3] As one-man shows the *karaghiozi* were readily adaptable to performers who traveled from Greektown to Greektown throughout the United States in the early decades of this century. The *karaghiozi* were to disappear in America by about the end of the 1930s, but not before they had become an indelible part of the Greek immigrant experience. In Greece itself the live *karaghiozi* lingered on into the 1960s, but now appear only on television.

RETURNEES AND THE END OF MASS MIGRATION

The mass of the Greek immigrants—railroad and mine workers in the West, textile and shoe factory workers in New England, peddlers and bootblacks in the large Northern cities, nascent entrepreneurs everywhere—somehow managed to save money from their meager earnings. Funds in large amounts were sent back to Greece; remittances from Greeks in America totaled over $650 million in the years between 1910 and 1930. Many immigrants, moreover, accomplished exactly what they had set out to do—to make money and return to Greece. Estimates are that about forty percent of all Greeks admitted to the United States before 1930 went back to their homeland: some after only a short stint in America, others after five or ten years here.[4] Some 45,000 returned to volunteer in the Greek army during the Balkan Wars of 1912–13, a most remarkable testimony to the Hellenic patriotism of Greek immigrants in America.[5] We do not know how many of these early returnees eventually decided to come back to America and stay for good. For sure, many Greeks counted as "repatriated" were simply returning to the old country to bring relatives or newly acquired wives back to America. Certainly the number of such two-time immigrants in the early decades of this

[2]Linda S. Myrsiades, "The Karghiozis Performance in Nineteenth-Century Greece," *Byzantine and Modern Greek Studies*, 2 (1976), 83–98.
[3]L. Danforth, "Humour and Status Reversal in Greek Shadow Theater," *Byzantine and Modern Greek Studies*, 2 (1876), 99–112.
[4]Theodore Saloutos, *They Remember America* (Berkeley: University of California Press, 1956), p. 29.
[5]Theodore Saloutos, "Causes and Patterns of Greek Emigration to the United States," *Perspectives in American History*, 7 (1973), p. 407.

century was considerable. In fact, almost any tracing of a Greek-American family tree will uncover ancestors who crossed and recrossed the Atlantic several times before finally deciding to settle in America or remain for good in Greece.

It was with the utmost reluctance that the Greek immigrant gave up the idea of returning home. A 1930 survey of twenty-four nationality groups showed that Greeks ranked last in aquisition of American citizenship—holding length of residence constant.[6] Yet, contrary to their initial intentions, those immigrants whose economic fortunes turned out best were the most likely to put down roots in America. Those who earned only a livelihood or little more, on the other hand, were the ones most likely to return permanently to Greece. Even among the less economically successful of the immigrants who did stay in America, a disproportionate share never did marry. In fact another wave of returnees started in the 1950s—and continues into the present—which consists of elderly bachelors retiring to Greece on their social security benefits.[7] In brief, those immigrants who prospered in America, or at least had steady employment, were the most likely to establish families here. It was this element that became the bedrock of the Greek-American community.

The transformation of the Greek immigrant colony in America into a Greek-American community was presaged by the passage of restrictive immigration starting in 1917. It was not until 1921, however, that Congress first passed immigration legislation based on nationality quotas. The move toward restrictive immigration culminated in the Reed–Johnson Act of 1924, in which the number of entering immigrants was determined by a formula based on nationality distribution of the 1890 census. The clear intent and accomplishment was to exclude immigrants coming from southern and eastern Europe. The Greek quota was set at only 100 immigrants per year! This number contrasted with 28,000 Greeks who came to this country in 1921, the last year of relatively open immigration. In 1929 the annual Greek quota was raised to 307, where it remained for most of the next three decades. Nonquota immigrants, however, were allowed—principally through the mechanism of reuniting immediate family members—and Greek entry into the United States averaged about 2,000 yearly between 1924 and 1930.

The immigration legislation of 1921 and 1924 closed what had been a virtually open-door policy for Greeks and other European immigrants. The halt in mass migration had two profound consequences for

[6]Frances J. Brown and Joseph S. Roucek, *One America* (Englewood Cliffs, N.J.: Prentice-Hall, 1945), p. 657.

[7]In the mid-1970s, there were an estimated 19,000 Greek Americans residing in Greece receiving social security pensions. *New York Times*, Nov. 26, 1976, p. 31.

Greek America—one immediate and the other long-term. First, there was a frantic scramble to acquire American citizenship. The immigrant realized that only a naturalized citizen could hope to bring over family members, or even he himself if he sought to return to America after visiting Greece. Where in 1920 only one in six Greek male immigrants had acquired American citizenship, by 1930 half of these immigrants had become naturalized Americans.[8] Second, without the transfusion of new arrivals from Greece, American-born Greeks would eventually replace the immigrants as the core Greek-American population. Proponents of maintaining traditional Greek culture in the adopted country would dominate for a generation, but the arithmetic of the American ascendancy was inevitable. In 1920 only one in four Greek Americans was born in this country, but by 1940 American-born Greeks were in the majority.[9] Thus legislative restrictions on immigration set into motion both individual and demographic forces that molded the Greek-American community.

The formation of the Greek-American community was also affected by the regional origins of the immigrants. The first small group of Greek immigrants in the 1880s came from Laconia, a province located in the Peloponnesus. By the 1890s most came from Arcadia, another province in the Peloponnesus. In time, Greek immigrants would be drawn from all parts of "free" Greece as well as the unredeemed lands. The expulsion of the Greeks from Asia Minor by Turkey in 1922 resulted in a number of these refugees coming to America just before the closing of the immigration gates. But the Peloponnesus, the southernmost region of mainland Greece, has always remained the main place of origin of Greek Americans. By way of comparison, about one in seven persons in contemporary Greece lives in the Peloponnesus, whereas at least four out of seven Greeks who ever came to this country were Peloponnesians.

DISORDER AND EARLY PROGRESS

The Greek Church

The basic organizational unit of the Greek immigrants was the *kinotis* or "community." When a sufficient number of Greeks had settled in one place, a community would be formed which broadly included all the Greeks in the area. In practice, however, the *kinotis* consisted of those who took part in the community's general assemblies—increasingly lim-

---

[8] Saloutos, *Greeks in the United States*, p. 239.

[9] Evan C. Vlachos, "Historical Trends in Greek Migration to the United States" (paper presented at the Bicentennial Symposium on the Greek Experience in America, University of Chicago, 1976), p. 35.

ited to dues payers—which elected their own board of directors or *symvoulion*. The main purpose of the *kinotis* was to raise enough funds to found and maintain a local Greek Orthodox church. The first step in this was to acquire a charter of incorporation from the state, and then to find a priest. A priest could be obtained through a request sent to either the Church of Greece or the Patriarchate of Constantinople (Istanbul in Turkey). Often enough, however, a Greek Orthodox priest could be found from among the immigrants themselves.

Among the earliest church communities were New York's Holy Trinity established in 1892 by the Society of Athena, Chicago's Annunication founded in 1893 by the Society of Lycurgus, and Boston's Holy Trinity founded in 1903 by the Society of Plato. The *kinotis* in a typically Greek way symbolized the immigrant's dual pride in their classical heritage and commitment—perhaps even more in America than in the old country—to their Byzantine Church. In 1916 there were about sixty Greek churches in the United States, and about 140 by 1923.

The significant point of the appearance of Greek Orthodox churches in America was that they originated from the actions of the immigrants themselves and were not instituted by the ecclesiastical authorities in Athens or Constantinople (Istanbul in Turkey). Unlike the situation in the old country, moreover, priests in America were hired directly by the *kinotis* rather than assigned by bishops. The governance of the church community in the early years was something like that of Congregationalism, with decisive power in the hands of the locally elected *symvoulion*. The priest was usually regarded as an employee who must minister the sacraments and attend to the spiritual needs of his congregants, but not make too many demands of them. Each church community "was governed by a board of trustees, many of whose members were small independent businessmen, marked by that commanding proprietary air so often found in the self-made man."[10]

Democratic control of the parishes by the laity did not by any means imply that a state of harmony existed within the churches. Quite the contrary; personality clashes and disputes over administrative matters and the qualifications of the priest were commonplace. Frequent schisms were disaffecting many congregants. Clerical commercialism and parish raiding also marred the early Church scene. It was becoming apparent that a more systematic organization was required and one which would be consistent with canonical principles, that is, authority deriving from a recognized Eastern Orthodox episcopacy in the old world. Early efforts toward affiliation with other Eastern Orthodox bodies in the United States—principally Russians—did not succeed. Pan-Orthodoxy with its dilution of the essential Hellenism of their

---

[10]Saloutos, *Greeks in the United States*, p. 129.

Church was not a congenial choice for the Greek immigrants. The Church for them was as much a vehicle for the transmission of Greek national values as it was a religious vessel.

The early Greek Orthodox churches in America, although independent for all practical purposes, were under the spiritual aegis of the Patriarchate of Constantinople. In 1908, however, the Patriarchate formally placed the Greek churches in America under the authority of the Church of Greece led by the Metropolitan of Athens. At this point a brief explanation of the jurisdictional structure of Eastern Orthodoxy is required. There are four ancient patriarchates of which the Ecumenical Patriarch of Constantinople ranks first in honor. There are also autocephalous ("self-headed") or independent national Churches, such as the Church of Greece and the Church of Russia. Thus, although the Constantinople Patriarchate and the Church of Greece are identical in theology, liturgy, and Hellenic culture, the two bodies have for historical reasons become jurisdictionally independent of each other. The 1908 decision of the Patriarchate to place the American churches under the authority of Greece was in large part dictated by the threat of Turkish reprisals against the Patriarchate for the anti-Turk agitation of Greek immigrants in the United States. There was also the Patriarchate's apprehension that it would be unable to counteract efforts by Russian Orthodox bishops in America to bring the Greek-American churches under their control.

Placing the Greek Orthodox churches in this country under the authority of the Church in Greece did not bring order to the Greek-American community. Quite the contrary. The Holy Synod in Athens—the ruling body of the Church of Greece—became embroiled in a game of musical chairs, as the royalist supporters of King Constantine and the liberal backers of Venizelos alternated in power. The consequences of the royalist–Venizelist struggle in America led to a situation which has been aptly termed "the civil war within the Church."[11] In 1918, the Metropolitan of Athens, Meletios Metaxakis, came to America to organize the Church in this country. Metaxakis returned to Greece promising to establish a bonafide American Archdiocese. However, Metaxakis, a Venizelist, was deposed in 1920 as head of the Church in Greece and replaced by a royalist. Metaxakis came back to the United States, claiming to be rightful head of the Church of Greece; and, as such, he assumed the administration of the Greek churches in this country. In turn, the Church of Greece sent its own bishop to America to rally royalist congregants to its fold.

In 1921 Metropolitan Metaxakis convened the first clergy-laity conference of the Greek communities in the United States. This laid the

[11]*Ibid*., pp. 281–309.

groundwork for the formal incorporation, under statutes of the state of New York of the Greek Archdiocese of North and South America. Shortly after founding the Archdiocese, Metaxakis—in a dramatic turn of events—was elevated to the position of Patriarch of Constantinople. Once enthroned as Patriarch, Metaxakis transferred the Archdiocese in America to dependency on Constantinople and appointed a trusted supporter, Archbishop Alexander, as its head. Throughout his archbishopric—from 1922 to 1930—Alexander was bitterly opposed by royalists along with those Greeks in America who preferred Athens over Constantinople as the seat of their Orthodoxy. Alexander faced several rival claimants to his leadership of the Greek churches in America. The most formidable opponent was Archbishop Vasilios, an ardent royalist, who waged a relentless campaign to bring the Greek-American communities under his sway. Court battles ensued, excommunications were exchanged, and there was "hysterical violence even within the sanctuary of the Holy Altar. Police were stationed at strategic positions within some of the churches to prevent actual bloodshed."[12]

There were some 200 Greek Orthodox churches in the United States in 1930, about two-thirds of which were under the jurisdiction of the Archdiocese under Archbishop Alexander with most of the remainder following Archbishop Vasilios. Although the royalist-Venizelist schism cut across class and regional lines, there were some discernible patterns. The more traditional and working-class Greeks—especially in New England—were the most likely to be found in the royalist camp and with Archbishop Vasilios, whereas the more assimilationist and middle-class elements—especially in the Middle West—were the most likely to be supporters of Venizelos and Archbishop Alexander. Although the contending ecclesiastics certainly displayed little talent for accommodation, they were in actuality reflecting the more basic proclivity of the mass of the Greek immigrants to continue the royalist-Venizelist struggle in this country.

By the close of the 1920s the Greek Orthodox churches in the United States were in a state of acute disarray and demoralization. The time for reconciliation was overdue. In 1930 the Constantinople Patriarchate with the concurrence of the Church of Greece dispatched the respected Metropolitan Damaskinos of Corinth on a peacekeeping mission to America. After much acrimony and negotiation it was agreed that all the feuding bishops in America would accept reassignments in Greece. Further, upon Damaskinos's recommendation, Athenagoras, the Metropolitan of Corfu, was selected to head the Archdiocese in America. Athenagoras's long tenure as Archbishop here—actually eigh-

---

[12]Peter T. Kourides, *The Evolution of the Greek Orthodox Church in America and Its Present Problems* (New York: Cosmos Printing Co., 1959), p. 8.

teen years, 1931–1948—proved to be of major significance in the development of the Greek-American community.[13]

Athenagoras's first task—in which he well succeeded—was to defuse the royalist-Venizelist collision in this country. Through personal trips to each of the Greek Orthodox parishes and by patience and tact, he calmed and then dissipated the royalist-Venizelist conflict. To be sure Athenagoras's efforts were aided by a changing political situation in Greece which was moving beyond the events of the World War I period, and by the increasing number of American-born Greeks for whom the old country fights of their predecessors were irrelevant if not incomprehensible. Yet, while external factors facilitated the Archbishop's achievements, it was his own time-consuming pastoral visits that finally laid to rest the generation-long political feud which had divided the Greeks in America.

Athenagoras's second and more controversial goal was to centralize the administration of the Greek churches in the Archdiocese. He was ultimately successful in this endeavor, but not before setting off another round of intercommunal fighting. Starting in the 1930s, the Archdiocese began to implement policies to regularize its revenues and to enforce uniform bylaws in all parishes. Bishops previously in control of their own dioceses became auxiliaries of the one ruling archbishop. Athenagoras sought to increase the prerogatives and prestige of the clergy, which necessarily meant a diminution of the influence of the laity in parish affairs. Thus it was made mandatory that priests be appointed by the Archbishop and not directly by the parish. To say the least, many congregants took exception to vesting so much executive power in the Archdiocese. At the same time, Athenagoras's efforts to professionalize the clergy met with resistance from those priests who feared the new order would jeopardize their positions.

The opposition to Athenagoras's centralization policies coalesced around the priest Christopher Kontogeorge of Lowell, Massachusetts. Having been unfrocked by the Patriarchate at Athenagoras's behest, Kontogeorge was ordained a bishop in an irregular ceremony and declared himself head of his own independent "Archdiocese of America and Canada, Inc."[14] The Kontogeorge forces catered to dissident groups of various stripes and posed a continuous challenge to Athenagoras's authority for over fifteen years. Court battles and litigation again ensued. In a moment of despair Athenagoras would write of his opponents: "They opened drains and sewers and, with their hands, scattered

---

[13]An indispensable history of Greek Orthodoxy in the United States is George Papaioannou, *From Mars Hill to Manhattan: The Greek Orthodox in America under Athenagoras I* (Minneapolis: Light and Life Publishing Co., 1976).
[14]*Ibid.*, p. 105.

everything that was filthy."[15] The cause of the decentralists faltered after Kontogeorge's death in 1950 and collapsed entirely by the mid-1950s. Although never receiving widespread support, the Kontogeorge movement did appeal to arch-traditionalist elements—for example, supporters of the old Julian calendar—and thereby acted as a brake on Americanization trends within the Archdiocese itself.

The Press and Voluntary Associations

The internecine events occurring within the Greek Orthodox Church were mirrored on the secular side. The Greek language press in America was quick to take positions—and, some would say, exacerbate matters— in the conflicts between royalists and Venizelists and between contending church factions. The mortality rate of Greek newspapers was exceedingly high, but two—the *Atlantis* and *National Herald* [*Ethnikos Kyrix*]— were destined to play a powerful role in the immigrant community for many decades. The two newspapers were the only Greek-American dailies to last more than a few years and both operated from New York City.

The *Atlantis* was published first in 1894 as a weekly and then as a daily starting in 1904. Its publisher, Solon J. Vlastos, was a fervent admirer of King Constantine and defended the monarch's policy of Greek neutrality in World War I. Ardently royalist during its early years, the *Atlantis* continued to take conservative positions on political matters in Greece and backed the Republican Party in this country. The *National Herald* made its appearance in 1915 in support of Venizelos and Greece's entry into the war on the side of the Allies. Under the editorship of Demetrios Callimachos, it consistently identified with liberalism in Greece and later the New Deal in America. For over a half century the two rivals competed with each other. At their peak circulations in the 1920s, they each had daily press runs of around thirty thousand. By the end of the 1930s, though still wielding major influence, their circulations had dropped to about thirteen thousand each. Although both newspapers maintained national readerships, their constituencies hardly overlapped. To read either the *Atlantis* or the *National Herald* was to choose sides on the issues dividing the Greek-American community.

Those who read the established dailies or weeklies could take comfort in the reinforcement of their already held political attitudes and in the fact that these newspapers informed them of the larger events throughout the Hellenic world. Indeed, during the World War I period the *Atlantis* in America enjoyed a circulation exceeding that of any daily newspaper in all of Greece![16] There were also the more marginal Greek

---

[15]*Ibid.*, p. 103.

[16]Victor S. Papacosma, "The Greek Press in America," *Journal of the Hellenic Diaspora*, 5, no. 4 (winter, 1979), p. 49.

newspapers of the early era that must be seen less as ventures in journalism than as parochial voices in a communal dialogue. Such newspapers were heavily laden with effusive accounts of baptisms and weddings and laudatory coverage of the social affairs of Greek-American associations. There was also a journalistic genre of an extremely personalistic nature. Saloutos describes some of the more unseemly types.

> Men presuming to be editors wrote vituperative articles against a particular individual, showed these handwritten pieces to rivals of the attacked man, received from them the cost of the newsprint or the salary of the typesetter, and then printed the articles as "newspapers" ... And there were newspapers which on one day would heap praises on Mr. X, calling him a merchant, a man of eminence, a friend of the people, and a patriot, and on the next would denounce him as a nonentity, a traitor, an illiterate, and a bootblack.[17]

The high fecundity rate of Greek newspapers in the early years was more than matched by a plethora of Greek fraternal societies. There were over one hundred such societies in this country by 1907.[18] It seemed that wherever a score or so of Greek immigrants would come together, a voluntary association would spring forth—complete with lengthy constitution, colorful banners, and adornments for the officers' uniforms. The large majority of these associations were *topika somateia*, societies whose members came from the same region or village in the old country. Besides offering social opportunities among familiar compatriots, the regional associations would often collect money for projects benefiting the home village. Dissidence and personality conflict, however, were a chronic trait of the Greek fraternal societies, and their demise was about as frequent as their appearance. Moreover, unlike the *kinotis* that sought to establish the institutions of a permanent Greek community in America, the early *topika somateia* were groups of transitory Greeks preparing for the—hopefully not too distant—day when they would return to their true home in Greece.

The idea of a national association that would embrace all Greek immigrants was initially voiced by Michael Anagnos, the director of the Perkins Institute for the Blind and America's most renowned early Greek immigrant. In 1904 Anagnos did obtain a charter for a National Union of Greeks in the United States, but the association died with him in 1906. Shortly thereafter and in part inspired by his efforts, the first truly national Greek organization in America was established in 1907— The Pan-Hellenic Union.[19] By 1912, probably with some exaggeration, the Pan-Hellenic Union claimed a nationwide membership in 150

[17]Saloutos, *Greeks in the United States*, p. 89.
[18]*Ibid.*, p. 75.
[19]Thomas Burgess, *Greeks in America* (Boston: Sherman, French & Co., 1913), pp. 63–67.

branches throughout the United States. The appeal of the Pan-Hellenic Union was helped by its simple ceremonies, small dues, and promise of welfare benefits. Increasingly, however, the organization harked to old country patriotism. With the open support of the Greek Embassy, the Pan-Hellenic Union unabashedly promoted the Greek cause in whatever way it could. When the Balkan wars of 1912–13 broke out, the Pan-Hellenic Union served as a recruiting office for the Greek government in this country. These activities brought the organization under severe attack—from Greek Americans as well as American sources—for what was regarded as patent disloyalty to America. Suffering as well from financial mismanagement, internal squabbles, and political confusion in Greece, the Pan-Hellenic Union withered away by the time America entered World War I.

The pattern of fragility and localism of Greek-American associations was broken in 1922. In that year, a group of Greek businessmen in Atlanta, Georgia, founded the American Hellenic Educational Progressive Association—usually referred to by its acronymn as the Ahepa.[20] A fraternal association with Masonic influences, the Ahepa was to become the leading Greek-American lodge. The official headquarters in 1924 was moved to Washington, D.C.—symbolically important because of its location in the nation's capital rather than in a city with a large Greek population. By 1928 the Ahepa had over 17,000 members and 192 chapters in all parts of the United States. By 1930 the "Ahepa family" had expanded to include a women's auxilliary, the Daughters of Penelope, and counterpart organizations for boys, the Sons of Pericles, and girls, the Maids of Athena.

The growth of the Ahepa is to be understood in large part as an answer to the prevailing feeling against foreigners in postwar America. One of the objectives of the Ahepa was "to advance and promote pure and undefiled Americanism among the Greeks of the United States."[21] English was the official language of the organization and membership was not limited to persons of Greek descent or Greek Orthodox religion, although in practice virtually all of the membership was of Greek ethnic stock. Prominent non-Greek Americans would be initiated into the Ahepa, but with the implicit understanding that their obligations did not extend beyond lending their names to add to the lodge's public luster. The trend toward Americanization was captured more revealingly in the names of some of the organization's leading members. An inspection of the 1924 roster of the Ahepa convention shows, in addition to the usual

[20]Much of the material dealing with the Ahepa is drawn from George J. Leber, *The History of the Order of Ahepa* (Washington, D.C.: Order of Ahepa, 1972).
[21]*Ibid*., p. 150.

polysyllabic Greek names, Anglicized ones such as Miller, Nixon, Walker, Adams, Campbell, and Kirby.[22]

Even though its official face was one of assimilationism, the Ahepa, nevertheless, was from its inception deeply committed to Greek identity, albeit in an American context. There was much more to the purpose of the order than outflanking American nativism. It represented the social aspirations of a growing Greek middle class, which could not be met by traditional, if not obscurantist, Greek associations. Most important, the Ahepa acknowledged the wrenching reality that most Greeks were in this country to stay. An Ahepa president in 1925 could finally state the unthinkable:

> Today ninety per cent at least of our compatriots have definitely decided to remain in America permanently. They are fast becoming American citizens; are acquiring American culture; are establishing their homes and businesses here; and are rearing their children to be real Americans. This is the country where they will die—the country where their children will live.[23]

The Ahepa also believed that only American fraternal forms would enable its membership to escape the morass of intercommunal fighting which had become synonymous with Greeks in this country. By having an American referent, the lodge would transcend the battles of royalists and Venizelists. By being secular, the Ahepa would stay removed from the partisanship of opposing church groups. In avoiding these entanglements the Ahepa was in large measure successful. But Ahepa's own internal politics could generate a factionalism of its own. Almost from the start competing groups coalesced around the personalities of V.I. Chebithes and Harris J. Booras, two men who labored prodigiously for the organization, each in his own way. The two Ahepa contending parties they led would outlive them both and continue to animate the lodge into the present day.

Despite the acrimonious maneuvering as to who would lead the organization, the Ahepa was always in the forefront in pressing the good name of the Greek American. No opportunity toward this end seemed to be passed by. The Ahepa was involved in many activities during the 1920s and 1930s. Classes on naturalization procedures were held by the local chapters. A statue was erected to commemorate George Dilboy, a Greek immigrant posthumously awarded the Congressional Medal of Honor for valor in the battle of Belleau Woods of World War I. Banquets were held in which U.S. Senators and state governors gave ad-

---

[22]*Ibid.*, p. 177.
[23]*Ibid.*, p. 178.

dresses extolling the Greek contribution to civilization in general and to America in particular. Yale University was criticized in 1931 for abolishing the Greek or Latin language requirement for the baccalaureate. Jim Londos, the world's wrestling champion, was regularly honored. Franklin Delano Roosevelt was initiated into the lodge while governor of New York. An Ahepa sword was given to each graduate of Greek descent from the service academies at West Point or Annapolis. Dialogue considered derogatory of Greeks was removed from the movies *The Yellow Ticket* (1932) and *Bureau of Missing Persons* (1934). The first National Olympiad of Ahepa was held in 1939. Placing third in the 100-yard dash was a boy named Spiro T. Agnew.

The Ahepa was not without its strong critics in the Greek community. Even among those who recognized the permanency of the Greek settlement here, there were many who viewed the Ahepa as an instrument of unwarranted de-Hellenization. Because it adopted English as its official language, the Ahepa came under severe attack from much of the Greek language press, notably the *National Herald*. Moreover, even though Ahepans as individuals and through their lodge have been major benefactors of the Greek Orthodox Church, there has always been an element of strain between these two bodies. In contrast to the relationship of the Knights of Columbus with the Roman Catholic Church, the Ahepa has not become a lay arm of Greek Orthodoxy.

Those who wished to preserve Greek life as much as possible in this country formed in 1923 their own organization—the Greek American Progressive Association, or Gapa—only a year after the founding of the Ahepa. The Gapa employed Greek as its official language and openly supported the Greek Orthodox Church. Its membership was restricted to ethnic Greeks and Greek Orthodox communicants. It was more than coincidental that the Gapa's organizational name began with "Greek American . . . ," whereas the Ahepa's began with "American Hellenic . . ." The contrast between the two organizations was clear even in their social affairs. Gapa affairs consisted entirely of Greek folk dances, whereas at Ahepa dances there was a predominance of "American" waltzes and fox trots. Also, when the Ahepa did emphasize Greek culture it was likely to be in terms of classical Hellas, while the Gapa espoused the traditions of living Greece. Yet despite the Gapa's antiassimilationist philosophy, the organization always considered its first loyalty to be to America. In this fundamental political sense, the Gapa and Ahepa were alike.

The Gapa claimed more than fifty chapters by 1928, principally in the more traditional and working-class communities of New England and the Middle Atlantic states. But it was never able to rival the Ahepa in membership rolls, financial resources, administrative efficiency, and national visibility. The Gapa leadership was sincerely dedicated to its cause,

but it was fighting a rearguard action against the tide of Americanization. In later years the organization would become increasingly
moribund. Unlike the Ahepa, the Gapa found it difficult to make the
transition from an immigrant to an American-born membership.
Nevertheless, some of the Gapa philosophy did carry through. As early
as the 1930s, the Ahepa had retreated from the ultra-assimilationist
policies of its founding and took many actions to show it was neither
anti-Greek nor anti-Church. In the post-World War II period, the
Ahepa would become a major factor in the preservation of Greek ethnic
identity in America.

Crime and Gambling

The Greek quest for respectability in America was in part indicative of
sensitivity to charges that the immigrant enclaves were breeding grounds
for crime. A 1908 campaign in Chicago against "Greek dives"—ice-
cream parlors (!)—purportedly used for purposes of prostitution,
brought much unfavorable publicity to the Greek community.[24] In 1932
the Wickersham committee, a panel appointed by President Hoover to
investigate criminality in America, included in its report some statements
that were construed as reflecting badly on Greek Americans. The Ahepa
immediately reacted by assembling documentation on the sparse
number of Greek immigrants in American penal institutions.[25] Certainly
the early Greek community was worried about the incidence of crime,
more than it allowed itself to say in public or admit to non-Greeks. But
much of the crime could be regarded as "innocent" resulting from not
knowing whom to pay graft, for example. Peddlers could not avoid
breaking local regulations if they were to make a living. Health code
violations in Greek-owned lunchrooms could be invoked capriciously by
inspectors.

In the everyday life of the Greek community, however, crime was a
marginal phenomenon, one which Greeks more quickly attributed to the
amerikanoi. This was to become even more the case once women arrived
and normal family life could be established. Hardly any of the Greek
immigrants had either the training in, or understanding of, or appetite
for, criminal methods. In time, as the possibilities of American enterprise became clearer, a few—a very few—Greeks found their way to
more sophisticated crime and became highly placed in the Mafia. But in
the main, crime—certainly violent crime—was a source of shame. It was
never at the center of Greek immigrant life.

There was, however, one illegal activity which was recurrent among

---

[24]Theodore N. Constant, "The Greek and the Law in the U.S." *Athene*, 4 (December,
1944), p. 48.
[25]Leber, *Order of Ahepa*, pp. 282–87.

the Greek immigrants—gambling. For many a coffeehouse owner, the margin of survival rested on the tips he garnered from the gamblers who frequented his premises. The Greek propensity to wager on games of chance was in part a carryover of habits from the old country, where gambling was common and legal, and in part an outcome of the virtually all-male makeup of the early Greek settlements in America. A researcher who conducted a survey of Greek Americans concluded: "Almost every answer to my questionnaire mentioned gambling as the chief evil among the Greeks in America."[26]

It is no surprise that one of the most famous of all Greek Americans made his reputation at the gaming tables and race tracks. Nick "the Greek" Dandolos was born in Crete and came to this country at eighteen, in 1902. After trying his hand in the fig business, Nick began his gambling career in the coffeehouses of Chicago's Greektown. His willingness to risk extravagant sums became legendary. In a memorable game in 1926 between Nick the Greek and Arnold Rothstein there was $797 thousand on the table, the biggest pot in the history of stud poker.[27] Nick the Greek's reputation in betting circles was enhanced by his unusual behavior. He not only was unconnected with the rackets, but also he disdained ostentatious living and often made allusions to classical Greek philosophy. A millionaire for much of his life, Nick's luck turned sour in his later years. When Nick the Greek died in Las Vegas in 1966, he was broke.

Greeks in Business

More than a few Greek immigrants had already become proprietors and entrepreneurs before World War I. But it was the general rise in American affluence in the 1920s that carried a large number of them into ownership of their own small businesses. In big cities and small towns throughout the United States, Greek immigrants were joining the middle class more and more. Bootblacks moved into their own shoe-repair, hat blocking, and dry cleaning establishments. Fruit peddlers and flower vendors became owners of groceries and florist shops. Confectioners opened up their own stores to such an extent that sweet shops became virtually a Greek monopoly in this country. Pool halls were another venture with a heavy Greek concentration. Still other Greeks went into business for themselves in a variety of retail, wholesale, and manufacturing enterprises. Many Greeks became wealthy in real estate and stock market speculation. The affinity between Greeks and food service be-

---

[26]J.P. Xenides, *The Greeks in America* (New York: George H. Doran Co., 1922), p. 89.
[27]Cy Rice, *Nick the Greek* (New York: Funk and Wagnalls, 1969), p. 141.

came an American social phenomenon about which more will be said later. For the time being, however, it suffices to note that the Greek entry into American capitalism was most notable in the restaurant business.

A new area of business in which some enterprising Greeks flourished was movie theaters. One of these was Alexander Pantages, who came to this country as a boy in 1893.[28] He first sought to strike it rich in the Klondike gold rush but lost his grubstake in a card game. He did make a fortune, however, by becoming a purveyor of commercial entertainment for the miners. Upon his return to Seattle, Pantages set up a one-man movie theater operation. Unschooled but shrewdly ruthless, he parlayed his movie theater holdings to the point where in the late 1920s he owned a chain of about eighty theaters. Pantages claimed to be the first to combine movies with vaudeville. His indubitably Greek name became a permanent fixture on many West Coast "Pantages Theaters."

The three Skouras brothers[29] brought even greater prominence to the Greek name in the entertainment industry. Charles, the eldest, came to this country in 1908 at the age of nineteen. He settled in St. Louis, where he worked as a waiter and bartender. In the typical Greek immigrant manner, Charles soon sent for his younger brothers, Spyros and George. All three brothers worked in menial tasks during their first years in America. Spyros, however, also went to night school, where he studied English and learned elementary business methods. By 1914 the brothers were ready to step into the business world on their own and begin a Horatio Alger climb to the pinnacles of monetary success. They bought a nickelodeon which they converted into a movie theater and renamed the "Olympia." By 1926 the Skouras brothers controlled thirty-seven theaters in St. Louis. It was in a Skouras St. Louis theater that the first precision dancing team—the Missouri Rockets—appeared as a stage presentation, the lineal ancestor of the Music Hall Rockettes in New York's Radio City.[30] During the 1930s the brothers had a chain of over four hundred theaters and were major figures in the motion picture industry in Hollywood itself. In 1942 Spyros Skouras became president of Twentieth Century-Fox. He and his brothers were movie magnates of the very first rank in this country. Though operating at the top

---

[28]This capsule biography of Alexander Pantages is adapted from Saloutos, *Greeks in the United States*, pp. 273–78.

[29]On the Skouras brothers, see *Ibid.*, pp. 278–80. George Anastaplo, a second-generation Greek American who teaches at the University of Chicago and Rosary College, tells the following story about his father. Anastaplo's father, when he was a young immigrant confectioner in St. Louis, was approached by the Skouras brothers to join them in their new movie venture. He declined and admonished the Skouras brothers to "stay in candy."

[30]*New York Times*, April 2, 1978, p. D15.

levels of finance, the Skouras brothers always remained active in the Greek-American community and were major benefactors of the Greek Orthodox Church and Greek charities.

The Skouras brothers and Pantages were, of course, the rare exception and not the rule of the Greek immigrant experience. They did demonstrate, however, that it was possible for immigrants to become millionaires even if they came to this country without money, without the English language, and without much formal education. Larger than ordinary life to be sure, the Skourases and Pantages typified the hopes of lesser Greek entrepreneurs that they too could grasp a part of the American Dream.

FROM THE THIRTIES TO THE FIFTIES

The Greek advance into the American middle class was abruptly set back by the Depression. The thirties were grim years for most Americans and Greek Americans were not an exception. Working-class Greeks suffered a significant drop in earning power, even among those fortunate to have a job. Marginal Greek-owned businesses went under in dismaying numbers. Individuals who had made paper fortunes on Wall Street or who had invested in real estate saw their stocks become valueless or their holdings taken over by creditors. Import houses and travel agencies dealing with Greece—the initial mainstay of the Greek-American bourgeoisie—suffered especially and were never to regain their influence in the Greek-American economy. Greek-American voluntary associations declined in membership and the Greek language press saw its circulation and advertisements shrink. Even the Greek Orthodox Church was sorely pressed to find the funds to maintain itself. For the only time in history, the outflow of Greeks back to the old country exceeded the numbers coming over to America during most of the 1930s.

By and large, however, the middle-class aspirations of Greek Americans were shaken but not destroyed by the Depression. Many small businessmen persevered by the simple means of working excrutiatingly long hours. The immigrant entrepreneurial spirit also received a respite following the repeal of Prohibition in 1933, when many Greeks gravitated to the bar and package liquor business. Mitigating to some extent the trauma of the Depression years was the additional fact that most of the Greek immigrants were at the peak of their physical vigor. Many would look back upon this period of their lives as the time when they enjoyed good health and found satisfaction in raising their young families.

A certain amount of resiliency and maturation was evident as well in the Greek-American community collectively. Old country regionalism and politics were giving way to a more composite Greek-American culture. The royalist-Venizelist feud was dying out, along with much intercommunal rancor. To be sure, when the quasi-fascist General Metaxas became dictator in Athens in 1936, his supporters and opponents in this country reacted accordingly. But the acrimony and numbers of the contending partisans never came close to the virulence of the earlier political feuds that had split Greek America.

It was apparent in the 1930s that Greek-American energies were increasingly drawn from and focused upon the American scene. Somehow the Greek-American community found the wherewithal to establish an extensive network of Greek-language afternoon and Saturday schools. In the late 1930s there were 450 such schools with 25,000 students.[31] The Greek Orthodox Archdiocese was winning its battle to bring the local churches under its central direction. One immediate outgrowth of the Depression was the Archdiocese's centralization and the reinvigoration of the women's church organization, the Philoptochos, or "Friends of the Poor." The Philoptochos undertook many charitable activities and continues today to be a major outlet for women's volunteer work within the Greek Orthodox community. The permanency of the Greek community in this country was reinforced by the founding of a Greek Orthodox seminary, Holy Cross, in Pomfret, Connecticut, in 1937 (which was relocated in Brookline, Massachusetts, ten years later). This laid the base for American-educated Greeks to enter the clergy in significant numbers. It also showed that the church was no longer a Greek immigrant church but a true Greek-American church.

From a political standpoint the Depression moved the large majority of the Greek community into the Democratic party. Whereas the Greek commercial community was strongly Republican in the 1920s, small businessmen came to identify closely with New Deal recovery measures as much as working-class Greeks. Even today the Greek business community largely supports the Democratic party. Certainly there was a recognizable Republican element among Greeks even during the Depression, but Franklin Delano Roosevelt was probably supported by over three-quarters of the Greek-American electorate. The liberal *National Herald* was an early and consistent supporter of Roosevelt and even the conservative *Atlantis* moderated its stand toward the President to conform more closely to the New Deal sentiments of its Greek-American readership.

Unlike some other immigrant groups, the Greeks in America never produced a major socialist constituency even during the Depression.

[31]Papaioannou, *From Mars Hill to Manhattan*, p. 149.

There was a vocal radical press in the Greek language, but it was always at the margin of the Greek-American community.[32] A monthly Greek publication of the Socialist Labor party, *Organization (Organosis)*, appeared during World War I and survived for about a decade. In 1918 the first in a succession of Greek communist newspapers, the *Voice of the Worker (Phone tou Ergatou)*, commenced regular publication. It changed its name in 1923 to *Forward (Embros)* and declared itself the official organ of the "Greek section of the American Communist Party." *Forward* was superseded by *Freedom (Eleftheria)* in 1938 during the Popular Front era. Then, in 1941, the *Greek-American Tribune (Vima)* replaced *Freedom* as the voice of the Greek-American left. The *Tribune* had a readership of several thousand, was well edited, and included occasional English pieces. The *Tribune* continued publication until after World War II, when it was suppressed under provisions of the Smith Act. True to its ideology, the Greek leftist press composed articles in the demotic speech of spoken Greek and avoided the more formal and stilted Greek conventionally adopted by Greek newspapers both in America and Greece.

Although the left was never to exert a major influence on the Greek-American community, it did and continues to display certain enduring strengths. The Greek-American left initially consisted of immigrant workers in communist leaning unions and a sprinkling of Marxist intellectuals. The International Workers Order had an active Greek branch from the 1920s until after World War II when it was banned under the anti-communist legislation of the Smith Act. A Greek Seamans Union of indeterminate Marxist lineage and membership size has existed for over forty years. By far the most significant left-wing Greek group was local 70 of the Fur Workers Union. Most of the four thousand or so Greeks working in the fur industry of New York City were members of Local 70. During the thirties and forties, the communist hold on the furriers—then affiliated with the CIO—seemed unbreakable. In the years just before and during World War II, the Greek furriers of Local 70 could be counted upon to give some mass to Greek-American leftist demonstrations. But in the McCarthyite atmosphere of the early 1940s, the Fur Workers Union was vulnerable and an anti-communist drive in the CIO threatened to destroy it. Grappling for survival, party strategists sought sanctuary in the AFL and the furriers became a division of the Amalgamated Meat Cutters Union in 1955. This step along with sectarian infighting effectively compromised the militancy of the furriers.[33]

The lack of broadly based support for leftist causes among Greek immigrants is at first glance surprising. After all, the immigrants almost to a man started off in menial labor. In the years before World War I, as

---

[32]The summary of the Greek-American leftist press is adapted from Papacosma, "The Greek Press," pp. 54–55.

[33]Irving Howe, *World of Our Fathers* (New York: Harcourt Brace Jovanovich, 1976), pp. 340–41.

the Greek countryside began to empty a large portion of its male youth into the work gangs and mills of the United States, a Greek-American proletariat appeared which preceded that of Greece proper.[34] On closer inspection, however, the failure of the left becomes perhaps a little clearer. The split between Venizelists and anti-Venizelists over the issue of the monarchy deflected enormous political energies into a conflict basically unrelated to class formations in Greek society. It was even more so a complete irrelevancy to the immigrants' position in American society. Also, most of the Greeks who initially came to this country saw themselves as temporary workers here; class-based activities in America could only detract from the goal of returning home. Greek participation in strikes in the American West was sparked more by feelings of discriminatory treatment as Greeks than by notions of an encompassing working-class identity. In the mill towns as well, Greek immigrants were linked much more to those who shared their tongue and heritage than to abstract "fellow workers" in the new world.

Even after Greeks began to root themselves a little in America, socialist organizing seemed not to answer the immediate wants of their existence. Life in America was hard, work exhausting, and the imperatives of daily need overwhelming. Organization, especially that which looked outward toward the American milieu, was always difficult for the Greek immigrants. The *kafenion*, the workers' most common grouping, drew minds away from America and back toward nostalgic memories of the old country. Moreover, in the twenties and thirties, it seemed foolish to align oneself with "unpatriotic" causes at the very time Greeks were questing for American acceptance. There was the family in which the concerns of children, brothers, sisters, and other relatives were more pressing than those of something called "labor." And there was the final overriding factor that a large number of Greek immigrants had moved out of the working class into small businesses of their own; for such petty bourgeoisie, socialism was anathema.

The Italian invasion of Greece in the fall of 1940 brought Greece into World War II. The initial successes of the Greek army in throwing back the Italian invaders had an exhilarating effect on the Greek-American community. The heroism of the Greeks was given laudatory coverage in the American media and Greek Americans basked in unaccustomed glory. In a matter of days following the Italian invasion, a Greek War Relief Association (GWRA) was formed.[35] Archbishop

---

[34]Detailed accounts of the emergent working class and nascent socialist activity in Greece itself at the time of the mass migration to the United States are found in the studies of George B. Leon. See his *The Greek Socialist Movement and the First World War*, East European Monograph Series (New York: Columbia University Press, 1976); and "The Greek Labor Movement and the Bourgeois State, 1910–1920," *Journal of the Hellenic Diaspora*, 4, no. 4 (winter, 1978), 5–28.

[35]The organization and activities of the Greek War Relief Association are covered in Saloutos, *Greeks in the United States*, pp. 345–53; and Papaioannou, *From Mars Hill to Manhattan*, pp. 134–39.

Athengoras was designated honorary chairman and Spyros Skouras elected the first national chairman. Greek church communities and associations all gave support, but it was the Ahepa which provided most of the volunteer labor at the local level. In the five-month interval between the Italian attack and the subsequent German occupation of Greece, over $5 million in money and supplies was raised. Though Greece became an occupied country, many Greek Americans believed that Hitler's rescue of the Italian army in Greece postponed his invasion of Russia, and thereby set in motion the final defeat of Nazi Germany. During the fascist occupation of Greece, the GWRA devised a program by which seven hundred thousand tons of food, clothing, and medicines were shipped to Greece on neutral Swedish vessels. It is estimated that a third of the Greek population were saved from death because of the efforts of the GWRA. The relief work of the GWRA during and after the war was a sincere reflection of the love Greek Americans retained for the mother country.

Once America itself entered World War II on December 7, 1941, Greek-American support for the war effort was wholehearted. After Pearl Harbor, Greece and the United States were united in the struggle against the Axis powers. Greek and American interests came together as they never had before. In 1942 Archbishop Athenagoras issued an encyclical directing Greek Orthodox priests to make supplications to God during the liturgy for the President of the United States and the American armed forces.[36] The Ahepa, in cooperation with the Treasury Department, launched a drive which eventually sold a half billion dollars worth of U.S. war bonds. The first bond in the drive was purchased by Sam Rayburn, Speaker of the House, from Steve Vasilakos, a peanut vendor who worked the White House sidewalk. Another Ahepan, Michael Loris, was named champion U.S. war bond salesman in 1943, a year in which he sold 24,142 individual bonds.[37] One need not read too much into it, but it is worth remembering that the Andrews sisters—Laverne, Maxine, and Patty—whose "support-our-boys" tunes made them the most popular singing group of the war years were second-generation Greek Americans. Certainly World War II was a watershed in Greek America: the war effort became a matter that combined Greek ethnic pride with American patriotism.

In Greece itself during World War II a resistance was mounted whose main body was a coalition of leftist groups in which communists increasingly took the lead. The valor of the Greek resistance under the occupation was so exceptional that it evoked great admiration from Greek Americans of all political stripes. But even before the Germans

[36]*Ibid.*, p. 180.
[37]Leber, *Order of Ahepa*, p. 345.

were defeated, Greek political differences were being felt in the Greek-American community. The communist-led resistance in Greece and the British-supported government in exile were both girding for control of a liberated Greece. Closely following upon the heels of the German evacuation in late 1944, the British-supported royalist government returned to Athens. A vicious civil war broke out between the government and the communists that lasted until 1949. In this country, a group of Greek-American liberals and leftists formed in 1945 the Greek American Council as a means to lobby against, first, the American acquiescence to the British actions in Greece and, later, American aid to the Greek government. But it was abundantly clear that the large majority of the Greek-American population and all major Greek-American organizations were committed to a pro-Western government in Greece. One of the historic consequences of the Greek civil war was that, under the mantle of the 1947 Truman Doctrine, the United States replaced Great Britain as the Western patron of Greece. American military aid and advisers were crucial in the final defeat of the communist forces. The Truman Doctrine initiated a military alliance between Washington and Athens which was to lead over the next generation to increasing American influence in Greek political and economic life.[38]

The foreign policy initiatives that brought Greece into the American sphere were also to make President Harry Truman popular within the Greek-American community. (There is no evidence, however, that Truman ever canvassed any Greek Americans before he implemented the policies which so directly affected Greece.) Archbishop Athenagoras hailed Truman as "a man sent from God."[39] When the Truman Doctrine was promulgated, the Archbishop was so gratified that he ordered a special thanksgiving service in which a traditional hymn invoking the blessings of God for Orthodox kings was revised to name President Truman and his family.[40] When in 1948 Athenagoras was elevated to the Ecumenical Patriarchate, some say with the help of the American government, he was flown to Constantinople on the President's personal airplane. Truman was also the only President to be initiated into the Ahepa at a White House ceremony. In 1963 the Ahepa erected a Truman memorial statue in Athens. Truman's own personality and small business background always seemed to resonate with the immigrant Greek Americans who could understand the plain talk of the man from Missouri. If Franklin Roosevelt was venerated by most Greek Americans, Harry Truman was much more an object of genuine affection.

[38]A balanced view of American influence in Greece is found in Theodore A. Couloumbis, John A. Petropulos, and Harry J. Psomiades, *Foreign Interference in Greek Politics* (New York: Pella, 1976), pp. 113–53.

[39]Saloutos, *Greeks in the United States*, p. 368.

[40]Papaioannou, *From Mars Hill to Manhattan*, p. 181.

The postwar period was one in which the bulk of Greek Americans became solidly entrenched in the middle class. In point of fact, it was the prosperity generated by World War II which brought about a major social ascent exceeding even that of the 1920s. The Greek-American occupational structure in its main body of immigrants was dominated by small businessmen. Among the American born, the large majority were in white-collar occupations and the professions. By the end of the 1950s it almost seemed abnormal for Greek Americans to work for wages. Although overall economic improvement was felt by many Greek Americans, there were important exceptions. A minority, principally old bachelors, were still trapped in poverty. In the factory towns of the North there was still an immigrant proletarian segment, but it was shrinking in both absolute numbers and relative weight. The general picture was indisputable. Greek Americans had comfortably arrived in American society.

The fifties were also a time of general serenity within the Greek-American community. To be sure the social base of the most traditional immigrant associations was approaching dissolution, but those incorporating the American born—such as the Ahepa—were displaying sufficient appeal to insure their longterm viability. The Greek Orthodox Church enjoyed a period of unaccustomed equanimity. Archbishop Michael succeeded Athenagoras as head of the Greek Archdiocese in 1949. Under Michael's stewardship, the Church took the first steps to accommodate second- and third-generation Greek Americans. The Greek Orthodox Youth of America, an organization in which English was the official language, was established in 1950 and grew rapidly over the next few years. At the time of Michael's death in 1958, there were about 250 Greek Orthodox churches in this country, all of which were in the fold of the Archdiocese. Michael also pressed for acknowledgment of Eastern Orthodoxy as a major religious group, along with Protestantism, Catholicism, and Judaism. Toward this end, twenty-six state legislatures passed resolutions recognizing Orthodoxy as a major faith.[41] A symbolic threshold was crossed in January, 1957, when Archbishop Michael became the first Orthodox hierarch to take part in the Presidential inaugural ceremony. On a more mundane level, the Defense Department finally authorized an Eastern Orthodox "dog tag" in 1955. No longer would Greek-American servicemen resign themselves to the nebulous "Other" category or force fit themselves into misleading Catholic or Protestant designations.

The postwar period was also one in which Greek immigrants again began to arrive in this country. Greek-American associations, notably the Ahepa, along with other Eastern and Southern European nationality

[41]*Ibid.*, p. 190.

groups exerted pressure on Congress to liberalize immigration laws. The Greek quota had been set at 307 annually since 1929, but under special refugee legislation in 1948 it was made possible to borrow from the future. By 1952 the Greek quota was mortgaged to the year 2014! Hopes for less restrictive immigration policies were set back by the passage of the McCarren–Walter Act of 1952, over President Truman's veto. The nationality quota system was maintained and the Greek quota raised by only one person—to 308 per year. Legislation passed in 1953 and 1954, however, permitted non-quota Greeks to enter either as displaced persons or through preferences given to close relatives. Under these acts, some 17,000 non-quota Greeks came to this country in the middle 1950s. All told, about 70,000 Greeks—either by borrowing on future quotas, by qualifying for displaced persons status, or by utilizing provisions enabling citizens to bring over relatives—came to America between the end of World War II and 1965.

Another group, numbering several thousand at least, were Greek students who received their advanced education in the United States and eventually acquired permanent residency or American citizenship. This development led to the appearance of an immigrant professional class in the 1950s and early 1960s—physicians, academics, engineers, and others—which added a new dimension to the Greek-American community.[42]

Although there were fewer postwar arrivals than there were during the era of mass migration, they still had a retarding effect on the assimilation of the Greek-American community. The fresh wave of immigrants replenished Hellenism in America. Greek Orthodox membership grew, the circulation of the Greek-language press revived, travel to and from Greece expanded, and Greek food and other items were increasingly marketed. Although the new arrivals meant the Greek-American community would not be completely cut off from the wellsprings of Greek culture, it did not imply that the processes of Americanization were being reversed. The American-born ascendancy was undeniable. There were no longer any Greektowns in which young children were brought up to speak Greek as their first language. Throughout the United States, the Greek community was moving from one made up of Greeks with American citizenship to one consisting of Americans of Greek descent.

A thoughtful observer in 1960 would have predicted a lingering sort of Greek ethnic consciousness within an overarching American social identity. The power of the immigrant past was fading. This seemingly natural progression of events, however, was not to happen, at least not at its expected speed. Instead, Greek America entered a period of

[42]George A. Kourvetaris, "Greek-American Professionals: 1820s–1970s," *Balkan Studies*, 18, no. 2 (1977), pp. 285–323.

growth and turbulence. This development was partly a result of the new ethnic pride in the descendants of the immigrants which was to become part of the American mood in the sixties and seventies; but it was especially due to the reopening of the immigration doors to large numbers of Greeks.

THE NEW GREEKS

The Immigration Act of 1965 finally abolished the basis of selecting immigrants according to country of, origin. An annual ceiling of 170,000 immigrants from the eastern hemisphere and 120,000 from the western hemisphere was established, with no more than 20,000 from any one country. From 1966 to 1971, during the first flush of the new legislation, about 15,000 Greeks came to this country annually. Since the mid-1970s the figure has stabilized at around 9,000 Greek immigrants per year. That Greeks account for such a disproportionate share of the total eastern hemisphere allotment is due almost entirely to that feature of the 1965 Act giving preferential advantage to persons who have close relatives in the United States. Since 1966 over four out of five Greek immigrants have entered under the preferences enjoyed by relatives.[43] Thus, for example, a Greek with American citizenship would send for a brother, who would then bring over his wife, who would in turn send for her brothers and sisters, and the chain would continue until a whole clan had arrived in America. It may not have been its intent, but the new immigration legislation in fact has given special advantage to nationalities with strong kinship ties such as the Greeks.

The new arrivals were more likely to be better educated and more urbane than their predecessors. Indeed, enough Greek professionals have migrated to America in recent years to cause concern of a "brain drain" from Greece.[44] Most newcomers, however, have come from a rural background, although they might claim otherwise. But the most signifant difference between the older and newer immigrants was in their sex ratio and familial status. The demographic composition of the recent arrivals since 1966, unlike the original immigrants who were mainly single men, was much more balanced, with almost as many women as men coming over. Moreover, many of the new Greeks were arriving in this country as married couples with small children. Most of the women with blue-collar husbands have themselves entered the labor

[43]Vlachos, "Historical Trends in Greek Migration," p. 22.
[44]George A. Kourvetaris, "Brain Drain and International Migration of Scientists," *The Greek Review of Social Research*, nos. 15–16 (Jan.–June, 1973), pp. 2–13. In 1974 Krikos, an association of Greek-American scientists, engineers, educators, and other professionals, was formed to reverse the brain drain by devoting expertise to the development of Greece.

force, principally in light factory work. This differs sharply from the stay-at-home Greek women of the earlier immigration. The large proportion of employed mothers among the new arrivals has led to a growing acceptance of day-care centers. But resistance to the idea of leaving one's children with strangers dies hard. Some families with working mothers bring over grandparents from the old country to watch over the children; a few will even send their young children back to Greece where they will be cared for by relatives.

The old pattern of exclusively male arrivals from Greece, however, continues in one enduring form—the illegal immigrant. In point of fact, more Greek seamen have abandoned their ships in American ports than any other nationality. From 1957 through 1974, over thirty thousand Greek nationals jumped from their ships and disappeared somewhere in this country (in distant second place were the thirteen thousand Chinese who illegally left their crafts during the same period).[45] The life of illegal immigrants is difficult to research but we know they can work only on the margins of the economy—as dishwashers, assistant cooks, garage attendants, and movers.[46] Often they work for established Greek Americans in manipulative if not extortionate relations. Even if illegal immigrants do somehow manage to acquire a decent job, their status is fraught with uncertainty and apprehension. One Greek ship jumper put it as follows:

"Each of us has two nightmares. One is that he will die here in America. The other is that he will be caught by the immigration authorities and sent home to die in Greece."[47]

Many of the recent Greek immigrants followed in the path of their predecessors and went into the food service business. Greek cuisine restaurants increased dramatically with the advent of the new migration. In 1966, for example, there was only one Greek cuisine restaurant in the entire city of Chicago. By 1978, there were over twenty full-menu Greek cuisine restaurants in the city and hundreds of establishments featuring a selection of short-order Greek foods. Almost all of the new Greek-food restaurants were owned by recent arrivals. In New York City and New England, in a curious ethnic turnabout, new Greek immigrants began to operate pizza parlors. Throughout America a large number of the newcomers from Greece had become owners of bars, small restaurants, and

[45]Theodore Saloutos, "The Greeks in America: The New and the Old" (paper presented at the Bicentennial Symposium on the Greek Experience in America, University of Chicago, 1976), p. 18.

[46]Hanac staff, *The Needs of the Growing Greek-American Community in the City of New York* (New York: Hellenic American Neighborhood Action Committee, 1973), pp. 38–39.

[47]*Hellenic Times*, Sept. 23, 1976, p. 6.

coffeeshops, more than replacing the decline of older Greek tavern keepers and restaurateurs. Besides being involved in the traditional food and drink business, the new Greeks were also becoming proprietors of tailor shops, shoe repair shops, dry cleaners, grocery and produce stores, and, in New York especially, taxi cabs.

As in the past, many of the new Greeks were finding first employment as push cart vendors of frankfurters, ice cream, and sandwiches. Even hot chestnuts, which had not been seen on American streets in well over a generation, were making a comeback in New York City. A glance at the classified section of the Greek-language press revealed an array of advertisements offering push carts, hot-dog wagons, and restaurant trucks. In a rerun of the tribulations of the first immigrants, the new Greek push cart vendors and peddlers ran into frequent trouble with the health departments and licensing agencies of city governments.

Most of the new Greek immigrants, of course, were not proprietors or even peddlers, but worked for someone else. Some went into factories, but more were moving into construction, painting, and maintenance work. A large number also became waiters, grillmen or chefs in Greek-owned restaurants. Those employed by fellow Greeks were sometimes cajoled into working "off the books."[48] Employers would convince the new immigrants that in this way they could make good money because they would not have to pay taxes or union dues. Under such conditions, workers were not eligible for health insurance, paid sick leave, or unemployment benefits. If they were laid off or a family member became seriously ill, the situation could only be described as desperate.

The new Greeks were located in all parts of the United States, but especially in communities where relatives had previously settled; mainly in the cities of the North and West Coast. New York City and Chicago, however, have attracted by far the largest number of recent arrivals. Both cities witnessed the reappearance of Greektowns, swelling neighborhoods where the newcomers from Greece overlaid earlier concentrations of Greek Americans. The Astoria section of Queens with sixty to seventy thousand Greeks became the largest Hellenic settlement outside of Greece or Cyprus. Sizeable numbers of Greeks were also to be found in Washington Heights in Manhattan and Bay Ridge in Brooklyn. In Chicago, the new Greektown centered at Western and Lawrence avenues and had a population of between 20,000 and 30,000 Greeks. (The old Chicago Greektown on Halsted Street, though now devoid of Greek residents, has acquired a second life with its Greek restaurants, nightclubs, and retail stores). The metropolitan dailies of New York and Chicago found the new Greektown always good for colorful if

---

[48]Hanac staff, *Needs of the Growing Greek-American Community*, p. 42.

stereotypic copy. Described as law abiding and hard working, the new Greek immigrants seemed to be recapitulating the success story of their predecessors.

In the main, the picture of adjustment of the recent arrivals to their new land was probably accurate. But beneath the surface, especially in the New York community, one could hear disturbing things—deplorable housing, exploitation of new immigrants, family fights, adolescent misbehavior, and mental health problems. Encouraged by a group of Greek-American activists including many prominent members of the Ahepa, a Hellenic American Neighborhood Action Committee (HANAC) was founded in 1972 and began a network of services for the Greek-American population of New York. Substantial public funding was obtained and by 1978 HANAC had a staff of sixty paid members working in over a dozen offices throughout the city. HANAC established programs for youth, the aged, job placement, and family counseling. It has sponsored symposia on Greek-American social needs, initiated English language instruction for Greek adults, and worked for Greek-English bilingual education in the public schools. HANAC defined its mission as serving all Greek Americans in New York City, but its major thrust was geared toward the problems of the recent arrivals from Greece. The Hellenic Foundation of Chicago, though operating on a much smaller scale, was engaged in parallel activity in the nation's second largest Greek community.

The new Greektowns—Astoria, in Queens, Western and Lawrence in Chicago—were very visible to the casual observer. A stroller in these Greek neighborhoods of the late 1970s would have seen full-menu restaurants serving only Greek cuisine, produce stands, fish stores, bakeries and sweet shops, stores retailing Greek newspapers, books, musical recordings and souvenir items, offices of Greek-language newspapers, radio, and television programs, social clubs (that could also serve as the home for amateur Greek-American soccer teams), travel agencies, and funeral parlors. There would be more Greek grocery stores than one could readily count, each with their selections of Greek cheeses, six kinds of olives, cuts of lamb unfamiliar to American butchers, Greek bread, olive oil, and jars of sweets made from orange or watermelon rinds. These stores were patronized not only by neighborhood Greeks, but also by large numbers coming from the suburbs for weekend shopping. Cars in the neighborhood have the telltale *kompoloi* (Greek worry beads) dangling from inside rear-view mirrors. Offices abounded in which Greek-American professionals practiced medicine, dentistry, or law for their predominantly Greek clientele. The public elementary schools of the neighborhood would operate on a bilingual Greek-English curriculum. The parish churches would find it necessary to offer the Sunday liturgy in shifts to accommodate overflow flocks.

The number of Greek nightclubs catering to both Greek and "American" trade has mushroomed in recent years in both New York and Chicago. The new cabarets have eclipsed belly dancing acts—which were, after all, a Turkish rather than a Greek art—and are instead places where the foremost singers and musicians of Greece can be heard. Contemporary Greek popular music dominates but the traditional folk music of the villages can also be heard and, if one is fortunate, the *rebetika* as well.[49] The *rebetika*, which emerged out of the bars, brothels, and drug dens of Greek port cities and spread abroad with the diaspora of Greek laborers in foreign countries, has been likened in theme and origin to American jazz and blues.

The preferred housing pattern in Greektown—today as in times past—is to buy a two or three bedroom flat, then move into the ground floor and rent the upper stories to tenants who are also Greek. It is a source of wonderment how a Greek working in a menial job somehow manages to make the down payment on a building after only a few years in this country. The new Greektowns are not as thoroughly Greek as those that appeared around World War I. Non-Greek residents are interspersed throughout the neighborhood. Chain supermarkets and fast food operations along with other "American" stores juxtapose purely Greek shops. Yet on most summer nights the old time ambiance seems to come back. In the early evening Greek men stand on street corners talking loudly and gesticulating. Women visit with each other on the front steps of their houses or in nearby parks. Children shouting in Greek and English play street and alley games. Later at night the married men will return to their families, while the single men retreat to their "social clubs"—the modern day equivalent of the venerable *kafenion*—or neighborhood nightclubs. The merchants and homeowners of Greektown are constantly vigilant lest their neighborhood acquire a bad reputation and attract unsavory types. Efforts to prevent gambling are persistent but Sisyphean. Greek youth gangs of a rudimentary sort have surfaced in both the New York and Chicago Greektowns, apparently in reaction to the incursions of Puerto Rican youths. Still it is no accident that Chicago's Greektown was singled out in 1975 as the city neighborhood where property values were increasing most rapidly.[50]

The long-term viability of the new Greektowns directly depends upon the arrival of new immigrants. If new Greeks ceased to come in, the neighborhoods would soon change. Many of the newcomers move out of Greektown once they are financially able, usually to higher in-

[49]Nicholas Gage, "Greek Cabarets Changing," *New York Times*, May 7, 1976, pp. C1, C9. An interpretation of the rebetika is offered by A.A. Fatouros, "Night Without Moon," *Journal of the Hellenic Diaspora*, 3, no. 4 (December, 1976), pp. 17–18.
[50]Chicago Daily News, Oct. 18, 1975, p. 14.

come neighborhoods in the city or to the suburbs. Most of the children of the immigrants will move out when grown and on their own. A core of middle-class people does remain in Greektown simply because of old neighborhood ties and conveniences, but most of those who stay are those with no language skills and with limited economic opportunities. It does appear, however, that the infusion of new immigrants will be sufficient to maintain the Greektown of New York and Chicago into the foreseeable future.

The newcomers did not always meld easily into the existing Greek-American community. On the whole, they were more cosmopolitan than their predecessors and some may have tended to view the Greeks already established in America as boorish and uncultivated. They could demean the humble origins of the earlier immigrants by referring to them as bootblacks or *piatades*—dishwashers. The recent arrivals were perhaps too quick to contrast their good Greek with the deteriorated Greek—which in any event was less polished to begin with—spoken by most of the oldtimers. The new Greeks saw a Greek Orthodox Church and a Greek-American community in which Hellenism had been diluted to an extent unrealized by the older immigrants. On their part, the older generation of immigrants was put off by what seemed to be an anti-American if not socialist tendency among some of the new Greeks. The old Greeks often described the new arrivals as being adverse to toiling long hours and unwilling to appreciate the privation which had led Greek Americans into the middle class. There was also some concern that the new Greeks were too calculating, too grasping, and would ruin the good name the Greeks in America had worked so hard to attain. The old Greeks might say of the new that they expected too much for nothing, "they found the table all set."[51]

It was perhaps inevitable and understandable that there would be some strain between the new immigrants from Greece and the earlier arrivals. It would be a gross exaggeration, however, to assume that the newcomers and the oldtimers fell into two antagonist groups. In many cases extended families were reunited with extreme cordiality. To be able again to converse comfortably in one's native tongue with members of a younger generation was a boon many older Greeks thought they had forsaken forever. There was also the common recognition that, without the infusion of the new Greeks, Hellenism in this country would never have maintained itself. If on occasion the new and the old Greeks found themselves at odds, both groups, nevertheless, found that what they shared in common overrode what separated them.

[51]Saloutos, *Greeks in the United States*, pp. 380–81.

Relations between American-born Greeks and the new immigrants are much more problematic. Excepting relatives, most of the second and third generations come into contact with new Greeks only at church services and Greek-American social affairs. The social distance between the American-born and the new Greeks finds expression in diverse ways. There is the bemoaning of the apparent unwillingness of the new arrivals to contribute either time or money to Greek Orthodox parishes or Greek-American voluntary associations. (That both time and money may be in short supply for many of the new immigrants is rarely acknowledged.) The new Greek, on the other hand, is dismayed by the lack of Hellenic consciousness among American-born Greeks as typified by their alleged indifference to the Turkish invasion of Cyprus. (It is rarely acknowledged that the considerable domestic pressure brought to change American foreign policy toward Cyprus and Turkey was spearheaded by American-born Greeks.)

The term "D.P." (from Displaced Person) has become part of the Greek-American lexicon and is used as a generic expression by the second and third generations to describe negatively recent arrivals from Greece. One of the surprising differences between the two groups is that American-born Greek women often describe the new male immigrant as too forward and taking too much for granted in his contacts with the opposite sex. In a gathering in which several young Greek-American women were present, the term D.P. was being used rather frequently. I asked the women to define a D.P. "Well, you know, a D.P. is a D.P." Still not satisfied, I asked for further explication. "Just go to a Greek dance, then you'll know what a D.P. is." With this Delphic answer, the conversation turned to other matters.

The negative stereotype many American-born Greeks have of the new Greek immigrants can be understood as a form of filial respect for their parents and grandparents. The recent arrivals from Greece, that is, are held to a standard—self-sacrifice, moral rectitude, feeling for family, commitment to Greek-American institutions—that is ascribed to an idealized older generation. Whether in fact the new Greeks are all that different from the older immigrants is a question that cannot be answered with precision. Certainly Greece today is not the same as it was before World War II; neither is modern urban America with its street crime and social disorder the same America of the early immigrants.

Although there are real differences between the old and the new Greek immigrants, there are many more important similarities between the two groups. It is not fair to say that the vast majority of the recent arrivals are not just as hard working as the early immigrants. Indeed, the economic advancement of the newcomers may be even more impressive than that of their predecessors. If some of the new Greeks may espouse a politically more liberal line than the oldtimers, this should not obscure their continuing basic conservatism on family and personal matters. If the new immigrants do not participate in the Greek-American community to the purported degree of the older immigrants, this is largely due to the fact that it is a community which they did not shape and whose control has increasingly entered the hands of the American-born generations.

When all is said and done, both the old and the new Greeks share in common a strong motivation to succeed in American society while retaining an abiding pride in their Hellenic origins. It also seems that many of the "old" new immigrants—those who have been in this country for five or so years—take the same critical attitude toward the "new" New Greeks as do the old immigrants, a kind of process whereby earlier immigrants look upon newcomers as less morally upright than themselves. Our newly arriving cousins from Greece are indeed very much like our immigrant parents and grandparents.

A commonly told tale in Greek-American circles relates the adventures of a Greek immigrant in the days of the untamed West. A covered wagon train on which the Greek is traveling is suddenly attacked by Apaches. After each assault, the survivors retrench and fight back, but to no avail. Finally, only the Greek is left. Just as he is about to be scalped by Geronimo himself, the Greek falls to his knees, crosses himself, and pleas—in Greek—"Mother of God, save me!" Geronimo casts his knife to the ground, pulls the Greek up, embraces him, and exclaims—in Greek—"What, you a Greek too!"

The ubiquity of the Greek is a popular topic in Greek-American parlor conversation. Every Greek American has his or her favorite "Geronimo story" of a personal encounter with another Greek in the most unlikely place or situation. This perception of the omnipresence of Greeks in America, however, can lead to gross exaggeration as to the actual umber of Greek Americans. The uestion of the total Greek-American opulation is a continuing one and not be answered with precision. come up with relevant figures inves matters of definition as well as measurement. Is descent from Greek stock the determining variable? How does one count those of mixed Greek and non-Greek ancestry? Is it more an issue of affiliation with Greek-American communal institutions? Or is it the social-psychological sense of being ethnically Greek in American society that matters? How does one categorize permanent residents with Greek citizenship, those on student visas, or illegal aliens? These are all questions that generate controversy. We also know little of the birth rate of Greek Americans. One can note, impressionistically, that the Greek-American family has never been a large one. Among earlier as well as more recent immigrant families, three or four children tend to be the outer limits. The American-born generations are barely reproducing themselves, if that.

The broadest definition of Greek Americans is to include all descended from Greek stock—immigrants from Greece or elsewhere, and those born in America of fully Greek or mixed ancestry. To define them based on their participation or at least affiliation with organized Greek-American institutions would lead to much lower estimates. And to use self-identity as the criterion for defining them would probably result in a

The Greek-American Community

figure somewhere in between. This is all to say that although the actual numbers of Greek Americans are undetermined, we can, nevertheless, begin to draw conclusions based on available data and by keeping in mind the terms of the discussion.

THE GREEK-AMERICAN POPULATION

The U.S. census adopts a lineage definition of ethnicity. The 1970 census reports 177,275 Greek-born Americans (first generation) and 257,296 native-born Americans of fully Greek or mixed parentage (second generation), or a total of some 434,000 persons of "Greek stock" in this country. These numbers have been challenged as undercounting Greek Americans, especially the new arrivals in New York City and other major metropolitan areas.[1] The census, moreover, does not enumerate ethnic background beyond the second generation. Nevertheless, the census figures serve as a benchmark for informed estimates of the total Greek-American population.

A more complete and current picture of the Greek-American population can be offered by making some demographic assumptions on the ratio of births to deaths since 1970, the rate of immigration from and return to Greece in the seventies, the probable number of the third and fourth generations of Greek Americans, and the many thousand Greek immigrants probably underreported in the census. On the basis of these calculations and guesses, a maximal estimate of the total Greek-American population by 1980 would be:

first generation	350,000
second generation	450,000
third generation	350,000
fourth generation	100,000
total	1,250,000

This total figure is based on a broad definition: all persons descended from Greek stock, including those in the later generations with at least one Greek grandparent. This is far below the two, three, or even four million sometimes claimed by Greek-American spokespersons. When we use more qualified—but more socially significant—definitions of who is a Greek American, the figures are lower. National survey items that allow for ethnic or religious background measures show between seven and eight hundred thousand who consider themselves either

---

[1]Hanac staff, *The Needs of the Growing Greek-American Community in the City of New York* (New York: Hellenic American Neighborhood Action Committee, 1973), pp. 13–20.

Greek Orthodox or Greek American.[2] Although offspring of mixed marriages are less likely to identify as Greeks than others, this is not necessarily the case. The manner and degree to which ethnic identity transmits across the generations through mixed marriages is one of the most tantalizing yet least understood mechanisms of ethnic imprinting. In any event, the outer limits of the self-identified Greek-American population most likely falls short of a million persons.

The Greek-American population can also be described in terms of its regional distribution. The historical narrative of the Greek arrival in this country is reflected in the census trend data given in Table 3-1. In 1910, in addition to sizeable numbers in New England, the Middle Atlantic, and the Middle West, we find the largest Greek settlements in the trans-Mississippi states, areas in which Greeks labored on the railroads

TABLE 3-1

REGIONAL DISTRIBUTION OF GREEK-AMERICAN POPULATION BY SELECTED
CENSUS YEARS (in percent)

Region	1910	1930	1950	1970
New England	17.0	14.5	13.3	13.5
Middle Atlantic	17.7	32.4	35.7	36.1
Middle West	20.1	30.4	27.8	25.3
South	5.6	6.1	7.4	9.3
Plains and Mountain	23.7	6.8	5.2	4.1
Pacific	15.9	9.8	10.6	11.7
Total	100.0	100.0	100.0	100.0
(census total)	(98,771)	(175,302)	(169,083)	(434,571)

Source: *Thirteenth Census of the United States: 1970*, Abstract of the Census, Tables 14 and 15; *Fifteenth Census of the United States: 1930*, Population, Vol. II, General Report, Statistics by Subjects, Tables 6 and 7; *U.S. Census of Population: 1950*, Vol. IV, Special Reports, Part 3, Nativity and Parentage, Tables 12 and 13; *U.S. Census of Population: 1970*, Vol. I, Characteristics of the Population, United States Summary, Section 1, Tables 144 and 145.

[2]The American Council on Education (ACE) national survey of college freshmen in 1972 included a self-identifying ethnic measure. Among all respondents, .035 percent identified themselves as "Greek." The ACE Greek-ethnic data were made available by a special computer run commmissioned by the writer. We can conjecture that college freshmen understate the Greek-American population by the underrepresentation of new immigrants, but overstate the Greek ethnic population in that American-born Greeks are twice as likely to matriculate in college than the American average. Thus, in balance, we can surmise that the proportion of Greek Americans who are freshmen probably comes close to the proportion of Greek Americans in the total U.S. population.

A 1975 Gallup poll of American religious preferences found .031 percent who identified as Greek Orthodox. This information was obtained through Tom Reinken of the Gallup organization on August 4, 1976. If the ACE and Gallup figures are extrapolated to a total U.S. population of 222 million (the census projection for 1980) and rounded off, there are approximately 800,000 self-identified ethnic Greeks in this country, and 700,000 who identify themselves as Greek Orthodox.

and in the mines and smelters. By 1930, however, the Greeks in the West diminished in number, and the largest concentrations were almost entirely in the states of the Northeast and the Great Lakes region, a pattern which has continued into the present. A breakdown by states in the 1970 census shows the largest number of Greeks to be in New York—about one in four of all Greek Americans—followed by Illinois, California, Massachusetts, New Jersey, Pennsylvania, Ohio, and Michigan. It is revealing that in 1910, four Western states—California, Utah, Washington, and Nebraska—were among the eight states that had the largest numbers of Greeks, while in 1970 California remained the only Western state in that category.

To look at the total number of Greeks by state or region, however, does not give an indication of the proportion of Greek Americans in these areas. It helps also to know something about the relative numbers of Greek Americans. This can be done by computing the 1970 census figures of the Greek-American population over the total state population. New Hampshire has the highest ratio of Greek Americans of any state in the union, closely followed by Massachusetts. Other states with disproportionately high ratios of Greek Americans are, in descending order, New York, Illinois, Connecticut, New Jersey, Maryland, and Michigan. Conversely, Texas—which ranks thirteenth among the states in aggregate Greek population—has the lowest proportionate number of Greeks. Other states with low Greek-American ratios are Alabama, Kentucky, Mississippi, and Tennessee. Thus, though there has been some outward movement in recent years toward the Sun Belt, the main body of Greek America continues to be found in the states of the Northeast and the Great Lakes.

Greek America is overwhelmingly urban. The 1970 census shows 94 percent of all Greek Americans residing in urban areas (compared to 73 percent of the total American population). Well over half of all Greek Americans live in or near one of the nine American cities: New York (250,000–300,000); Chicago (125,000–150,000); Boston and nearby mill towns (over 125,000); Detroit (40,000); Los Angeles (30,000); Philadelphia (25,000); Cleveland (20,000); and Pittsburgh (20,000). The figures in parentheses are cautious estimates based on information from knowledgeable sources, projections from the census, and Archdiocesean data. All these estimates are lower than those usually claimed by local Greek community leaders.

The pervasive trend toward suburbanization of the middle class in America is one that also characterizes the Greek-American population, especially for the American-born generations. For example, in 1960 in the Chicago area, 98 percent of all Greek Orthodox Church members lived in the city proper; in 1978, half of them were in the city's suburbs. Even more dramatic change could be observed in Philadelphia, Cleveland, and Detroit (though the remnant of Detroit's Greektown on Monroe Street remains as a prosperous Greek commercial and entertainment area). Some of the Greek-American movement out of the cities can be attributed to rising affluence and the pull of suburban life styles, but there is also the push of racial change in the inner city. An almost endemic fear among urban Greek Americans is with the encroachment of the *mavroi*—the blacks. Unlike some ethnic groups who have developed a strong sense of territoriality in our older Northern cities, Greek Americans seem to be among the first to leave at the earliest signs of black advances in still distant neighborhoods. Were it not for the new arrivals from Greece who still locate in the older neighborhoods, the Greek-American flight from the center cities would be almost complete.

Today we encounter three rather distinctive groupings in the Greek-American population: an older immigrant cohort usually demarcated as those who came to this country before World War II or in the years immediately following; a recent wave of immigrants who have arrived in this country since the reopening of the immigration doors in 1966; and the main body of the Greek-American community which consists of the children and grandchildren of the immigrants. Each of these groups, while sharing something of a common Hellenic heritage, relates to and participates in the Greek-American community in a different fashion.

GREEK-AMERICAN INSTITUTIONS

Greek America can be likened to an archipelago, a scattering of communities—some larger, some smaller, some more Greek, some more American—across the continental expanse. It was natural that with the passing of the older generation and the move to suburbia, immigrant institutions would be profoundly changed. Yet among most second- and third-generation Greek Americans there is a reluctance to abandon all features of the parochial life of the immigrants. The overriding impression is that wherever Greek Americans come together there is a commitment to something more than just going through ethnic motions. This is how we are to understand the structure of Greek-American institutions.

The Greek Orthodox Church

The central Greek-American institution is the Greek Orthodox Church. During the Ottoman era the Church constituted the primary force for the preservation of Hellenism among the subjugated Greeks. Thus, Greek Orthodoxy and Greek nationalism became inextricably linked. For the immigrant in America, the church community became the arena in which one worshipped, attained social recognition, and made friends—and sometimes enemies. Its major function was not so much religious as social—to confer a sense of bondship within the perplexity of American society. For the American born, even as the immigrant past fades, the church community becomes the prime definer of Greek ethnicity in this country.[3] Any rearrangement of Greek-American life that would not have the Church at its core would likely be little more than a reminiscence of immigrant forebears, a dim awareness of an ancestral Hellenic homeland. It is mainly through the Church that new generations continue to be aware of sharing a destiny somehow connected with other people called Greek Americans.

Though Greek Orthodoxy and Greek ethnicity are intertwined, they do not completely overlap. In Greece, despite ongoing harassment, Jehovah's Witnesses have made gains. In this country, as well, some numbers of Greek Jehovah's Witnesses are to be found. Among the early Greek immigrants, particularly in the smaller towns and cities where no Greek Orthodox church was available, there was a drift toward established American Protestant churches; Episcopalianism had a special attraction because it possessed both doctrinal affinity with Eastern Orthodoxy and high social acceptability. There are also a few Greek Jews in America, coming out of the post-Holocaust remnant of the large Sephardic communities in Thessalonica and Yannina, but they rarely take part in Greek-American activities, even of a completely secular nature. Despite these exceptions, it would be reasonable to estimate that about four out of five persons who regard themselves as ethnically Greek in this country are Greek Orthodox—whether actively or only nominally.[4]

The embodiment of the Greek Orthodox Church in this country is

---

[3]The relationship between Greek ethnic identity and Greek Orthodoxy among American-born generations has been examined in Alice Scourby, "Third Generation Greek Americans: A Study of Religious Attitudes" (unpublished doctoral thesis, New School for Social Research, 1967); Chrysie Mamalakis Costantakos, "The American-Greek Subculture: Processes of Continuity" (unpublished doctoral thesis, Columbia University, 1971); and George A. Kourvetaris, *First and Second Generation Greeks in Chicago* (Athens: National Center of Social Research, 1971). See also Theodore Saloutos, "The Greek Orthodox Church in the United States and Assimilation," *International Migration Review* 7, no. 4 (winter, 1973), 395–407.

[4]The estimate that about four out of five ethnic Greeks in this country are at least nominally Greek Orthodox is supported by surveys of Greek Americans in Brooklyn and Cincinnati that found between 70 and 80 percent of all respondents identified as Greek Orthodox. For Brooklyn, see Costantakos, "The American-Greek Subculture," p. 165; for Cincinnati, see Nicholas P. Petropoulos, "Social Mobility, Status Inconsistency, Ethnic Marginality, and the Attitudes of Greek-Americans Toward Jews and Blacks" (unpublished doctoral thesis, University of Kentucky, 1973), p. 105. Indirect corroboration of these findings can be found in the Canadian census which, unlike that of the United States, tabulates religious preference. According to the 1951 census, 70 percent of Canadians of Greek descent reported themselves as Greek Orthodox. See George D. Vlassis, *The Greeks in Canada* (Ottawa: privately printed, 1953), p. 96.

the Archdiocese of North and South America.[5] No other institution in Greek America approaches the Archdiocese in membership, commitment, national visibility, and grass-roots organization. Since 1959, Archbishop Iakovos has been primate of the Archdiocese. In 1970, the Ecumenical Patriarch in Istanbul conferred on the Archbishop the rank of Patriarchal Exarch Plenipotentiary, signifying the large degree of autonomy the Archdiocese possesses in internal matters.

Archdiocesan administration is centralized in the New York headquarters and to a large degree in the person of the Archbishop. The archdiocese owns not only its immediate property but also controls the assets of the parishes under its jurisdiction. In addition to some 440 churches in the United States, the Archbishop oversees a panoply of Archdiocesan activities, such as an orphanage, a home for the aged, a summer camp in Greece for Greek-American youth, programs of religious instruction, and Greek Orthodox parochial schools. The Archdiocese newspaper, the *Orthodox Observer*, has a circulation of over one hundred thousand, by far the largest of any periodical in the Greek-American community.

The keystone of the Archdiocesan institutional structure is the undergraduate Hellenic College and the Holy Cross graduate school of theology located in Brookline, Massachusetts. Although priests are still brought over from Greece because of a perennial shortage of Greek Orthodox clergy in this country, the majority of new priests for some time have been American-born graduates of the Holy Cross seminary. Women now also matriculate at the Brookline campus with the usual intent to pursue careers in church related work. The 1977 inauguration of the first lay president of Hellenic College/Holy Cross, Thomas C. Lelon, an American-born educator, signified the coming of age of Greek Orthodox higher education in the United States.

The Archdiocese is organized into eight districts that cover the United States (other districts encompass Canada and Latin America). Each district is headed by an auxilliary bishop, the holder of a title of an ancient ecclesiastical see, who operates with only limited organizational authority. In the late 1970s there was a beginning recognition that the Archdiocese had grown too large to be administered adequately from New York. This has led to steps toward establishment of a "synodical" system, thereby decentralizing the Archdiocese. The restructuring of the Archdiocese entails the creation of true regional dioceses in which bishops—with a title referring to an American city—would have in-

---

[5]For all practical purposes, the Archdiocese is coterminous with Greek Orthodoxy in the United States. There are, however, a few breakaway churches, a handful of storefront churches of dubious canonicity catering to some of the new immigrants, and some archtraditionalists who follow the old Julian Calendar now thirteen days behind the modern calendar.

creased authority to handle church matters, such as assignment of priests, and in which the synod of diocesan bishops would have a voice in the selection of the Archbishop.

Completing the picture of Church governance in the United States are the Archdiocesan Council and the clergy-laity congresses. The Archdiocesan Council, a standing group made up of the Archbishop and appointed laypersons, approves and implements decisions made at the clergy-laity congresses held every two years. It is at the clergy-laity congresses, attended by priests and parish-elected lay delegates, where major decisions, if not initiated, are at least ratified by a representative body. Though sometimes criticized for being too orchestrated, the clergy-laity congresses can alternately be viewed as a workable blend of Byzantine ethnarchy and the American convention system.

The individual parish community reflects an adaptation of a centralized institution to local circumstances. Archdiocesan appointed clergy share practical authority with the broad lay control exercised by the board of trustees, who are elected at large from the members of the parish. A certain amount of conflict between the priest and factions in the parish is almost expected. Such factions usually coalesce around wealthy lay leaders upon whom the parish depends for financial support. The I-fire-dishwashers-every-week-and-I-can-do-the-same-for-priests attitude is less apparent today than in times past, but still occurs often enough to bring a priest to grief. In theory, a priest can be assigned to a community for life, but the rule in practice is for a transfer to come every few years, especially early on in a priest's career. But a measure of stability is found in most communities because of the uniform regulations of the Archdiocese and the continuity found in longtime members of the local church board.

Greek Orthodoxy allows an aspirant priest to marry only before ordination; even a widowed priest is forbidden to remarry. Bishops are elevated solely from the celibate clergy—about one in eight of all Greek Orthodox priests in this country. This means, in effect, that while priests born or educated in America predominate in the married clergy, nearly all bishops are Greek born. It is very possible that selecting qualified bishops in the near future will involve reaching into the married clergy. The priest's wife—the *presbytera*—is almost as likely as her husband to be an object of approval or approbation from the parish membership. Her role is a particularly delicate one, as she must take a leading part in church activities while not appearing overbearing. Divorce among the clergy, while not common, is enough of a problem to account for a number of priests who leave the cloth.

Greek Americans can be described as a church-going though not overly pious people. The central religious experience is the liturgy, a high church service appealing to all senses with its colorful icons, ornate priestly vestments, incense, singing of the liturgy by priests, chanters, and choir, kissing the church icons, gifts of bread following the close of the service, and sugared wheat memoralizing dead parishioners. The Holy Week services are the focal point of the liturgical calendar. Even those who have not gone to church the rest of the year now come early to be sure of a place inside. On Great Friday, the flowered tomb of Jesus is carried three times around the inside of the church to the accompaniment of dirges. In many communities, the symbolic tomb is taken outside and around the block. Police hold up traffic and Americans gawk curiously at the procession. On Great Saturday night, the church is in black stillness. At midnight the priest lights the candles of those before him, and they in turn give light to their neighbors. The Resurrection song begins: "Christos Anesti"—Christ is Arisen.

It is remarkable not so much that the religion of the Greek immigrants left an imprint on their children and grandchildren, but that the American generations are in many ways more Greek Orthodox than their contemporaries among middle-class youth in urban Greece. The tie the Church has with its young people speaks not only to the appeal of the Orthodox heritage and a clergy responsive to youth, but also to the gallant efforts of their forebears to establish a Greek Orthodox presence in a strange land. During the 1950s, a major transmission of Greek Orthodox commitment to the American born occurred through the lay-founded and lay-directed Greek Orthodox Youth of America (GOYA). Although it was eventually replaced by an Archdiocesan department of youth ministry, GOYA served as the incubator for a generation of lay leaders now active in the Greek Orthodox community.[6]

For the immigrants of the early decades of this century, it was taken for granted that their church in America would be as much a replica as possible of what they knew in the old country. Greek priests in America, with their full beards, tall hats, and flowing robes, were objects of public attention. The male congregants stood on the right side of the church, women on the left. Today, the clergy dress in the manner of Roman Catholic priests and tend to be clean shaven. Bishops still grow beards, but in a much more trim style than that of the old country. Pews have been introduced and the custom of sexual segregation has vanished. The liturgy has been streamlined down to about an hour and half. Sunday schools, unknown in Greece, exist in practically every church community.

In the traditional Greek church service, a male chanter or *psaltis* assists the priest in the singing of the liturgy. Although never the object

---

[6]James Steve Counelis, "A New Church: The Americanization of the Greek Orthodox Church" (paper presented at the Bicentennial Symposium on the Greek Experience in America, University of Chicago, 1976), p. 26.

of adoration that a Jewish cantor might receive from a temple congregation, the *psaltis* is subject to the audial scrutiny of the worshippers. Over
the decades, the position of the *psaltis* has given way more and more to
mixed choirs with organ accompaniment. The choir group, made up of
American-born young men and women, is often the main youth activity
of the church community. The *psaltis* is still indispensable, however, for
baptisms, weddings, and, especially, funerals. Regrettably, few if any of
the American born move into the role of *psaltis*. Were it not for re-
plenishment from among the new immigrants, the psaltic tradition in
this country would die.

The process of Americanization of the Church is nowhere more
evident than in steps to introduce English into the service. The language
question has become one of the most divisive in the Greek Church in
America. As early as 1927, a Boston bishop held that the Greek Orthodox could be considered faithful even if they did not know Greek.[7]
But this was a cry in the wilderness at the time. Archbishop Athenagoras
was a conservative on the language issue. In avoiding a fight with community leaders, he may have lost an element of the youth.[8] Even Sunday
schools were required to use Greek as the language of instruction up
through the 1940s. Proposals for an English liturgy were seriously advanced in the 1950s, but Archbishop Michael authorized English only in
sermons. GOYA, however, was allowed to use English as its official language. In 1964, the clergy-laity congress allowed certain readings and
prayers in the liturgy to be repeated in English. In the important clergy-
laity congress of 1970, following the personal appeal of Archbishop
Iakovos, an English liturgy was permitted, depending upon the judgment of the parish priest in consultation with his bishop.

The progression to English would have been inevitable and relatively smooth had it not been for the large influx of immigrants from
Greece since 1966. Older traditionalists could now join forces with a new
constituency committed to the Greek language. The Greek Orthodox
Church was more ready, in effect, for English in 1960 than it is today.
Yet, despite obstinate resistance, the Church in America has begun to
adapt to linguistic change. In the late 1970s, most liturgies were still
predominantly but not exclusively in Greek. Language use varied
widely. Churches in the immigrant neighborhoods of the large cities in
the North and East offered their services entirely in Greek. Churches in
the metropolitan suburbs and in the West and South, those most likely to
be attended by the American born, had services increasingly in English.
In a manner of speaking, a kind of local option system was evolving.

---

[7]George Papaioannou, *From Mars Hill to Manhattan: The Greek Orthodox in America
Under Athenagoras I* (Minneapolis: Light and Life Publishing Co., 1976), p. 151.
   [8]*Ibid.*, pp. 142–43.

The Americanization of the Greek Church is also apparent in its aesthetic side.[9] Highly talented and professionally trained American-born musicians have composed church and choral music and organ works that blend non-Greek with traditional liturgical harmonies.[10] An American idiom is also found in the architecture of new Greek churches, several of which have received distinguished architectural awards: San Francisco's Holy Trinity, Milwaukee's Annunciation, Chicago's suburban Holy Apostles, Atlanta's Annunciation, and Oakland's Ascension. Greek-American theologians and church commentators are seeking to shape a religious tradition and organizational structure according to the needs of Greek Orthodoxy in America.[11] In church iconography, however, there has been a return to an older tradition. Newly commissioned icons are more likely to represent a more pure Byzantine style than older icons, which reflected the sentiments of nineteenth-century Western Romanticism.

The changing role of women in the church also reflects an Americanization process. Some church historians argue that an autonomous role for women is quite consistent with Byzantine tradition, a tradition that was only submerged during the subsequent Ottoman era. Although there are still a few communities where women cannot vote in parish assemblies, the overall pattern is clearly toward greater representation of women in leadership positions. Women have been increasingly elected to parish boards and also serve on the Archdiocesan Council, the highest lay body in the Church. The issue of ordination of women, however, is one that has not surfaced in the Greek Orthodox Church. Indeed, the move in that direction by the Episcopal Church has ruptured the formerly close ties between Episcopalianism and Greek Orthodoxy in this country.

Perhaps the ultimate in the Americanization of the Greek Orthodox Church is the growing number of non-Greeks who are joining it. Nearly all of this non-Greek infusion consists of people who become a

---

[9]A good discussion of the aesthetic aspects of the Americanization of the Greek Orthodox Church is Counelis, "A New Church," pp. 27–34. For a collection of primary sources reflecting the changing concerns of the Archdiocese from 1922 to 1972, see Demetrios J. Constantelos, ed., *Encyclicals and Documents of the Greek Orthodox Archdiocese of North and South America* (Thessalonica: Patriarchical Institute for Patristic Studies, 1976).

[10]The musical church works of Frank Desby, Tikey A. Zes, Anna Gerotheous Gallos, and Dino Anagnost are particularly to be noted. Counelis, "A New Church," p. 27.

[11]A partial list of Greek Orthodox theologians and writers who strongly reflect the American experience would include: Constantine Cavarnos, Anthony M. Coniaris, Demeterios J. Constanelos, Kimon Doukas, Alexander Doumouras, Stanley S. Harakas, Nikon D. Patrinacos, John Rexine, Katherine Valone, and Nomikos M. Vaporis. The *Greek Orthodox Theological Review*, published in the United States by the Holy Cross seminary, has become a recognized major journal in general Christian thought as well as in Eastern Orthodoxy. Insights on the contemporary church in America are to be found in the periodic writings of James Steve Counelis, Andrew T. Kopan, Harris P. Jameson, George Papaioannou, and Harry Psomiades.

part of the community through marriage. As early as 1926, it was estimated that one in five Greeks in this country entered a mixed marriage.[12] In the 1960s, mixed couples accounted for three out of ten church marriages, and by the mid-1970s the figure was about half. Although a nationwide occurrence, intermarriage is most frequent in the communities of the West and South. In Portland, Oregon, for example, of 163 church weddings between 1965 and 1977, there were only 37 in which both partners were Greek.[13] In most cases, the non-Greek spouse plays a minor role in church functions, but there are some who do become actively involved. Non-Greeks, in fact, increasingly have been elected to church boards in many communities. Such converts—a very, very few who learn to speak Greek—will become a new element in the impetus toward Americanizing the Church.

On social issues, the Church combines American pragmatism and traditional dogma. Birth control is not disapproved of, as it is in the Eastern Orthodox Churches of the old world, though one of the primary purposes of marriage still is procreation. Abortion is opposed, but tacit approval is given when medical advice holds that the life of the mother will be endangered by childbirth. The Church in America has not been prominent in the organized antiabortion movement. Divorce is permitted, but only after determination of just cause by an Archdiocesan ecclesiastical court. Homosexuality is regarded as immoral and perverse. Gambling is frowned upon, but many parishes resort to bingo games to raise funds. On race relations, Archbishop Iakovos has taken a strong civil rights position, even marching in the forefront with Martin Luther King, Jr., in Selma, Alabama, in 1965. There is little question, however, that the Archbishop's actions on civil rights were far in advance of the majority of his flock.

In many ways, the Greek Orthodox Church in America possesses the qualities of the "communal church" that Andrew M. Greeley has described and prescribed for the Roman Catholic Church in this country.[14] This is a church whose members affiliate selectively with traditions and who seek a sacramental ministry at such times in life when such a ministry seems appropriate—for some, every week, for others, only at times of passage, like baptism, marriage, and death. Like Greeley's communal church, the Greek Orthodox Church is not one in which important instruction is expected from the ecclesiastical structure on contemporary political and social issues.

The Greek Orthodox Church stands midway between what has been termed ethnic religion and mainline religion.[15] Its ethnicity is self-

[12]Saloutos, "The Greek Orthodox Church," p. 399.

[13]Thomas Doulis, *A Surge to the Sea: The Greeks in Oregon* (Portland, Oregon: privately printed, 1977), p. 87.

[14]Andrew M. Greeley, *The Communal Catholic* (New York: Seabury Press, 1976).

[15]Martin E. Marty, *A Nation of Behavers* (Chicago: University of Chicago Press, 1976).

evident, but its striving for mainline status is also to be recognized. This explains the benedictions given by Orthodox clergymen at national political conventions and presidential inaugurations, and the persistent efforts to be recognized as the "fourth faith" of the United States, side by side with Catholics, Protestants, and Jews. The move toward the mainline is also found in the acceptance by the Church of the legitimacy of other religions not on sufferance or tolerance, but as a tenet of its own religion in the pluralism of America.

Although neither in the state of disarray of many mainline churches, nor a victim of eroding ethnicism, the Greek Orthodox Church has been buffeted by religious currents with which it is only beginning to grapple. Several deserve special comment. One is the embryonic movement to return to an unadulterated Orthodoxy, an American equivalent of the higher spiritual tradition of Byzantium. In place of Americanized church activities, viewed as hollow in theological substance, the neo-Byzantists stress devotional observances—such as frequent and severe fasting—or even forms of lay monasticism, thereby placing Orthodoxy at the center rather than the margins of personal experience. A second is the charismatic movement with its emphasis on the gifts of the Holy Spirit.[16] Although the Church appreciates the religiosity of the charismatics, it is wary of what seems to be an almost Protestant evangelicalism. The charismatics have been contained within the Church up to now, but there is apprehension that their growth could introduce a subjectivism that temperamentally and sociologically would undermine what is essentially a sacramental church and an ethnic community. Though coming from two opposite directions, both the proto-Orthodox stirrings and the charismatics bring the Archdiocese into conflict with dissenting priests.

Another development on the religious front concerns relations between the Archdiocese and patriarchates in the old world and its sister Orthodox churches in the United States. The urgency in inter-Orthodox relations was caused in 1970, when the patriarch of Moscow granted autocephalous status to the main body of the Russian Orthodox Church in America, commonly known as the Metropolia. The establishment of a truly independent and canonically legitimate Eastern Orthodox Church in this country upset existing understandings between Orthodox bodies. The 1970 decree not only granted complete self-government to the Metropolia, but also established its claims to be the instrument of unity for all Orthodox Christians in this country, a sentiment expressed in its new name—the Orthodox Church of America. Although these claims are not recognized by the Greek Archdiocese or most other East-

---

[16]Eusebius A. Stephanou, *The Charismatic Renewal in the Orthodox Church* (Fort Wayne, Ind.: Logos Ministry, 1977).

ern Orthodox churches, a discordant note has been struck within Christian Orthodoxy. The actions of the Russians have also stimulated the latent issue of whether or not the Archdiocese ought to press for complete independence from the Ecumenical Patriarchate in Istanbul, and become itself an autocephalous church. There is little indication of such a step in the foreseeable future; it runs counter to spiritual and ethnic ties, and could well be the death knell of a precarious Patriarchate in a hostile Turkish environment. An important precedent has been set, however, in the way one major Orthodox body in this country has been ready to shed its immigrant origins.

The conflict and potential in the Greek Orthodox Church in this country arise from a clash of two cultures. The new culture emerged with the ascendance of the American born. Proud of its Greek ethnicity, it is nevertheless receptive to the vision of an open church, holding itself out to all baptized Orthodox. The old culture, fortified by recent immigrants, rejects these premises. It looks back to a church serving as the repository of the Greek language and national survival. It favors a fortress church amidst the battering of Americanism. The significance of the religious turmoil in the Church today can only be appreciated against the background of this cultural struggle. Archbishop Iakovos, himself a product of both cultures, has balanced the Church between these two contending forces, if not always happily, at least skillfully.

Lodges and Associations

Greek-American voluntary associations tend to fall into two groupings.[17] On the one side, there are those organizations that seek to perpetuate national and regional ties with the Greek homeland, while providing the opportunity for persons of the same place of origin to come together socially in this country. On the other side, there are those associations whose members seek to work out some relation between themselves and America. Whether or not English is the usual language in which the meetings are conducted is a fair measure of distinguishing between the two.

The leading Greek-American voluntary association is the Ahepa, ever since its inception over a half century ago. The organization has a membership of around forty thousand in good standing, including

[17]Studies of Greek-American voluntary associations are: Mary B. Treudly, "Formal Organization and the Americanization Process with Special Reference to the Greeks of Boston," *American Sociological Review*, 15 (February, 1949), 44–53; Constantine Yeracaris, "A Study of the Voluntary Associations of the Greek Immigrant of Chicago from 1890 to 1948, with Special Emphasis on World War I and the Post-War Period" (unpublished master's thesis, University of Chicago, 1950); and Robert James Theodoratus, "The Influence of the Homeland on the Social Organization of a Greek Community in America" (unpublished doctoral thesis, University of Washington, 1961).

female and youth auxiliaries. A much larger number of Greek Americans have been initiated into the lodge at one time or another and are considered to be permanently part of the "Ahepa family." With about 430 chapters, mostly active, the Ahepa has grassroots nationwide. The association has its national headquarters in Washington, D.C., with its own building and paid permanent staff. In its first decades, the lodge served to Americanize many Greek immigrants through its official use of the English language, promotion of loyalty to the United States, and quasi-Masonic rituals. In recent decades, when the demographic balance has shifted to the American born, the Ahepa has been in the forefront of supporting Hellenic ethnicity and has often spoken for the Greek-American community at large.

The Ahepa, in addition to generating many local philanthropic activities, raises money at the national level for worthy causes. Among its continuing good works have been disaster relief in Greece, funding hospital and health care facilities in Greece, and the establishment of an extensive scholarship program for Greek-American youth. Its most recent major project has been to foster research and treatment of "thalassemia" (also known as Cooley's anemia), a genetic blood deficiency that afflicts perhaps as many as one in nine Greeks and other peoples from the Mediterranean region.

The Ahepa is most vibrant during its annual conventions attended not only by chapter elected delegates, but also by thousands of others who look forward to the premier social event in Greek America. National offices are hotly contested at convention time, and elections revolve around a two-party system whose origins in the lodge go back to the 1920s. Though substantive differences between the two parties are not always easy to discern, members feel strong allegiance to one or the other. On more than one occasion, fractious infighting has caused the lodge embarrassment when grievances between factions have been brought into open court litigation. Yet, somehow, even though it has never settled down in harmony—some would say because of this—the Ahepa continues to attract a sizeable portion of the Greek-American middle class.

The longtime rival of the Ahepa, the more traditionalist and Greek-speaking Gapa, has faded as the original cohort of early immigrants passed on. Gapa still exists, however, and hopes to get a second wind with the recent arrivals from Greece. If new immigrants do join voluntary associations, though, they are more likely to become members of existing *topika somateia*, associations based on common origin from a region or even a village in the old country. It is hard to convey the loyalty the Greek has for his or her place of birth, a devotion that far surpasses the hometown identity of most Americans. A roster of the regional associations reads like a Greek gazeteer: Arcadian, Athenian, Cassian, Cephalonian, Chian, Cretan, Elian, Epirotic, Euboean, Kasterlorizoton, Kasterian, Laconian, Lemnian, Macedonian, Messinian, Rhodian, Thessalian, Thracian, and Zakinthion. And these are only the larger regions. If the village associations were also counted, the list would be almost endless. By and large, however, the regional associations do not carry well into the American-born generations. Old country localisms tend to be worn down into a common Greek-American identity.

Along with the vast number of unlettered Greek immigrants, there existed early on a small coterie of Greek university students and professionals. Never fully at ease with their American colleagues and socially distant from the main body of their co-ethnics, they gathered together and formed their own associations. They sought both to raise the cultural level of the Greek immigrants principally through public lectures and to bring the Hellenic heritage to the general attention of the American community. In 1911, Aristides E. Phoutrides, a Harvard undergraduate, and other Greek students from the Boston area founded Helicon, the first Greek-American intellectual association.[18] In 1918, in New York City, the Hellenic University Club (known as the Greek-American Intercollegiate Club until 1945) was established by Dr. George N. Papanicolaou. A group of Chicagoans formed the Hellenic Professional Society of Illinois (originally called the Greek Professional Men's Club) in 1924. All three of these pioneer associations have continued to thrive into the present. An outlet for the Greek-speaking intelligentsia of New York has been the Filiko society, founded in 1933 by Maria Vryonidou. More consciously Hellenic than Greek American, Filiko still holds its public lectures only in the Greek language. This stricture led in 1958 to the formation of the Parnassos Society of New York, whose intent was to extend appreciation of Greek culture beyond the Greek-speaking world.

By the 1950s Greek-American professional associations existed in most major cities. If there was a sufficiently large Greek-American concentration, one could also find Hellenic professional associations for doctors, lawyers, or educators. What all such voluntary associations shared in common, however, was that the immigrant founders were being gradually supplanted by American-born university graduates. Mention must also be made of the Greek student organizations that come and go on many large campuses. Though theoretically open to both Greek nationals studying in the United States and Greek-American students, they tend to be dominated by one or the other. Greek nationals, usually more politicized, and Greek-American students tend to move in different circles.

One must understand Greek-American voluntary associations as part of the general rule that people are at their most involved when

---

[18]A detailed account of the founding of Helicon, the conflict in this country between the supporters of the demotic versus puristic forms of the Greek language, and the remarkable Aristides E. Phoutrides, whose life was cut short in his mid-thirties, is Nikos I. Rozakos, *Modern Greek Renaissance in Boston* [*Neoelliniki Anagennisi sti Bostoni*] (San Francisco: Wire Press, 1975).

acting in contact with those they know intimately rather than for abstract causes. This is also how we are to understand the petty but intensely personal politics of Greek-American organizations. *"Nenikikamen"*—we are victorious—was the battle cry of the ancient Athenians and Spartans returning home from their Persian wars. *"Nenikikamen"* was the happy cry of the majority Ahepa party after winning the lodge offices in the 1977 convention held in New Orleans.[19] There is probably no place in Greece where such victory exaltations still prevail.

The Greek Press in America

The first Greek newspaper in the United States, *New World* [*Neos Cosmos*] of Boston, appeared in 1892.[20] Since that time, well over a hundred Greek newspapers in America have appeared at one time or another.[21] An informed American observer of the early immigrant community maintained that the Greeks published more newspapers proportionate to their numbers than any other nationality in this country.[22] The golden era of Greek journalism in America was the time between World War I and the Depression. The influence of the Greek language press was remarkable because so few of the early immigrants brought with them the habit of reading newspapers. Reading a newspaper regularly was something they learned to do in the United States.

Greek newspapers have been published in many cities, but two New York dailies—the conservative *Atlantis* and the liberal *National Herald*—have dominated the national scene from their inception. It was only in 1972 that the *Atlantis* finally succumbed. Its publisher, Solon J. Vlastos, nephew of the newspaper's founder, was forced to stop seventy-eight years of continuous publication in the face of rising costs and union disputes. Thus the *National Herald*, with a circulation of around twenty thousand, stood alone as the only Greek language daily in the United States. In 1977, however, another Greek language daily, *Proini*, began publication in New York City. Whether *Proini* would be able to develop a national readership in the manner of the *National Herald* remained to be seen.

Greek weeklies, biweeklies, and monthlies are also found in a few of the larger cities. In a special category are periodicals such as *Campana* and *Satyros*, which for many years successfully upheld a Greek journalistic tradition of iconoclastic and satirical news. The longterm viability of

---

[19]*Hellenic Times*, Sept. 29, 1977, p. 14.

[20]Bobby (Charalambos) Malafouris, *Greeks in America 1528–1948* [*Hellines tis Amerikis 1528–1948*] (New York: privately printed, 1948), p. 227. *New World* [*Neos Cosmos*], under the editorship of Constantine Fasoularides, came out for only a few months in 1892.

[21]S. Victor Papacosma, "The Greek Press in America" *Journal of the Hellenic Diaspora*, 5, no. 4 (winter, 1979), pp. 45–61. On the Greek-American press, see also Malafouris, *Greeks in America*, pp. 227–48.

[22]Henry Pratt Fairchild, *Greek Immigration to the United States* (New Haven: Yale University Press, 1911), p. 209.

the Greek language press in the United States, however, is problematic. It is not uncommon for a Greek language newspaper to receive a letter in English from a son or daughter asking that a subscription be canceled because an aged parent has died or is no longer able to see well enough to read the paper. It cannot even be assumed that the new influx of immigrants will assure another reading generation of Greek newspapers published in America. Different media circumstances preclude a recapitulation of the golden age of Greek journalism that followed World War I. Eight different Athens and Thessalonica newspapers are flown to New York and Chicago daily. There is a growing number of Greek radio programs in America, from an estimated 30 in 1955 to over 160 by 1979. Greek television programs also appear regularly on ultrahigh frequency channels in the very same cities where local Greek newspapers must make a go of it. The electronic media relentlessly draws both readers and advertisers away from the Greek press.

Faced by diminishing numbers of Greek newspaper readers, the press has searched for a wider audience among the American born. The clearly dominant trend in Greek-American journalism has been the replacement of Greek language newspapers by either bilingual or fully English papers. A gauge of the language preference of readers of Greek-American newspapers can be derived from reported circulation figures in the late 1970s. Of the Greek-American readership, slightly over half read papers published solely in English; about a third read bilingual papers (usually more English than Greek), and the remainder completely Greek.[23] In 1922, the *American-Hellenic World*, the first Greek-American newspaper in English was published. Under the editorship of Demetrios A. Michalaros, it came out regularly for several years in Chicago.[24] This was definitely a very exceptional press venture and it

---

[23] *Editor and Publisher International Year Book* (New York: Editor and Publisher, 1976), p. 336.

[24] On the *American-Hellenic World* and the early Greek press in Chicago, see Andrew T. Kopan, "Education and Greek Immigrants in Chicago, 1892–1973: A Study in Ethnic Survival" (unpublished doctoral thesis, University of Chicago, 1974), pp. 139–44. Kopan states the *American-Hellenic World* started publication in 1922. Another researcher, however, places its beginning in 1925, and notes *The Democrat* (city unidentified) which appeared in 1923 and billed itself as "The First Greek Newspaper Published in English." Papacosma, "The Greek Press," p. 58. A subgenre of the early Greek press in America consisted of periodicals representing sectors of the immigrant business community. Because they represented efforts to present a good image of the Greek immigrant rather than serious journalism, such periodicals typically contained articles in both English and Greek. One example was *The News of the Bootblacks Association of Chicago*, which appeared on a monthly basis during 1923 and 1924.

An English-language monthly, the *Hellenic Spectator*, was published in Washington, D.C., in the early 1940s. The import of the *Hellenic Spectator* was not in its durability or circulation—it came out for only a few issues and had a limited readership—but in the fact that its editor, Constantine Poulos, was an American-born Greek. This appears to be the first Greek-American periodical edited by a member of the second generation. See Louis Adamic, *Commonweal Magazine*, 33 (January 31, 1941), pp. 366–68, reprinted in Melvin Hecker and Heike Fenton, eds., *The Greeks in America 1528–1977* (Dobbs Ferry, N.Y.: Oceana Publications, Inc., 1978), pp. 88–92.

would not be until more than a generation later that the shift to English would gain momentum. Supporters of the Greek language regarded such tendencies as anathema. Even as late as 1962 when an American-born columnist—writing in Greek, moreover—stated that the use of English was inevitable, he was assailed by traditionalists with a particularly harsh epithet, "janissary," the historical referent being Greek boys kidnapped by Turks who were raised in the Islamic faith to serve as Ottoman soldiers against Greeks.

One outcome of the shift to English in the Greek-American press has been, paradoxically enough, a narrowing of coverage to include only events in Greece or Cyprus and the Greek-American community. Where the Greek language press served as the principal source of outside information for the immigrant reader, the second- or third-generation Greek American will follow the general news scene through American newspapers. There are about a dozen Greek-American weeklies or biweeklies printed mainly or solely in English. Some are rather anemic in their content, but a few of the more interesting ones warrant mention: the *Hellenic Chronicle*, published in Boston, has by far the largest paid circulation of any Greek-American newspaper in the country (over thirty-five thousand subscribers); the *Hellenic Times* of New York gives candid and insightful accounts of Greek-American voluntary associations; the *Hellenic Journal* of San Francisco offers its reader sophisticated reviews of modern Greek literature and arts; Chicago's *Greek Star*, Republican oriented and founded in 1903, is the oldest continuing published Greek-American newspaper; and the *Greek Press*, Chicago's Democratic paper, presents extensive coverage of the Greek-American social scene.

One can get an idea of Greek-American newspaper coverage and the interests of the Greek-American community from looking at the content of representative issues during 1978.

Lead stories: U.S. arms embargo against Turkey lifted; Greece ready to enter European Common Market; Greek Americans lose good friend in death of Hubert Humphrey.

Feature stories: the U.S. Postal Service issues a commemorative stamp to honor the late Dr. George N. Papanicolaou; Greek Letters Week to be observed at Hellenic College; the Ahepa to raise $300 thousand to build a surgical theater for Evangelismos Hospital in Athens; the Parthenon Dancers tour America; East Marion, an unincorporated community near the northeastern tip of Long Island, becoming a summer resort for Greek Americans of New York City. Short biographies of Telly Savalas, baseball player Milt Pappas, and Dionysios Solomos, the national poet of Greece.

Letters to the editor: Columbia University professor Edward Malefakis demolishes a critic who in an earlier letter opposed establishment of a modern Greek studies program at Columbia (the first writer favored a grandiose center at George Washington University devoted to the "complete Hellenic Ideal").

Numerous obituaries. Favorable review of *Midnight Express*, a film portraying brutal conditions in Turkish prisons.

Calendar of events: The Philoptochos charities of Brooklyn and Staten Island are sponsoring a benefit for the Greek Children's Cardiac Center at New York Hospital; the Hellenic Council on Education of Chicago will host a cheese and wine party at DePaul University; there will be an exhibit of Byzantine style icons by the contemporary artist Stathis Trahanatzis at the Greek Orthodox church in Belmont, California; the film *Phaedra* to be shown in the New Zorba Room, Olympia Restaurant, Lowell, Massachusetts. Full page advertisement in Greek by Olympic Airways: "Come Back to Greece Before They Are Gone"—photograph of old man and woman in village waiting for visitor.

Classified ads: counseling and representation in all matters before immigration and naturalization authorities; Greek teacher will tutor your child at your home; hot dog pushcart for sale—owner returning to Greece.

Language and Schools

It was always true that the unlettered Greek immigrant could bask in a kind of reflected glory coming from the esteem in which classical Greek culture was held among the highly educated in this country. But the cultural links with ancient Hellas were tenuous at best, and became even more so as the immigrants grappled with the practical affairs of meeting their bills. Even for their better-situated children, the immigrants typically viewed education as something that should lead to a comfortable living rather than as learning for its own sake.

There was one feature of their culture that the immigrants strenuously tried to pass on to their children—the Greek language. Along with the Greek Orthodox faith, the Greek language had formed the fundamental constituent elements of modern Hellenic nationalism. But matters were complicated because virtually two different languages had developed in Greece itself. One was *katharevousa* or puristic Greek, an aritificial form largely the inspiration of the early nineteenth-century philologist and nationalist Adamantios Koraes, based on classical Attic Greek and fenced off from changes in the living language or foreign intrusions. The other was the demotic or spoken language of the people, the same vernacular brought over by the Greek immigrants to this country. Symbolically, the puristic language harkened to an idealized classical Hellene, while demotic represented the language of the common, actual people of Greece. To this day in Greece *katharevousa*—though fighting a rearguard action—is still a status symbol of the social superiority of those who are able to use it. Though the Greek Orthodox Church in America was for too long a time committed to *katharevousa* in its language maintenance programs, the demotic is now the form used almost exclusively in the United States.

The immigrants' confrontation with the English language was one of shock. They faced a language with hardly any cognates in ordinary speech—what did it matter that scientific terms were based on Greek roots?—as well as a different alphabet. Few were able to attend night classes where English was taught. Those who started in the service trades and later moved on into their own small businesses learned the new language by trial and error. Those working in the factories and labor gangs often did not learn English adequately, their co-workers being fellow Greeks or other immigrants. Women, especially in the Greek colonies of the North and East, could live in this country for more than a half century and still never learn more than a handful of English phrases. Many American-born children would not hear English regularly spoken until they entered the first grade, thus making the initial months of public school a time of trauma. Some immigrants forbade the use of English in the home. The typical conversation between the generations, as the children grew older, was for parents to address their offspring in Greek and be answered in English.

Between Greek and English there developed an overlap that native speakers on both sides were aware of but could do nothing to prevent.[25] English syntax often prevailed among the American born when they spoke Greek, and even crept into the language of the immigrants themselves. Many words were coined from English—*banka, keki, gasolini, grosaria, polismanos, tseki, vakasio* (respectively, bank, cake, gasoline, grocery, policeman, check, vacation). Some would humorously call this hybrid language "Grenglish." More poignantly, many of the immigrants came to realize that after decades in this country they were unable to speak either Greek or English correctly.

Whatever their own language problems, the immigrants went to great lengths to see that their own children would learn Greek.[26] Two forms of organized education developed in this effort. One was the full-time day school. A handful of these appeared before World War I with the idea to establish a replica of the primary school in Greece. This conformed with the early immigrants' notion that they and their families would soon be returning to Greece for good. The language of instruction was Greek, with English taught as a foreign language! In time, however, as the need for state accreditation arose, English became the main language of instruction, though the Greek language—along with

[25]On spoken Greek in the United States, see the studies by Paul David Seaman, *Modern Greek and American English in Contact* (Paris: Mouton, 1972); and Panos D. Bardis, *The Future of the Greek Language in the United States* (San Francisco: R and E Research Associates, 1976).

[26]All researchers interested in the Greek educational system in this country must refer to Kopan, "Education and Greek Immigrants." Annual statistics on the number of Archdiocesan parochial schools, Greek language schools, and the students enrolled therein are to be found in the yearbooks of the Greek Orthodox Archdiocese of North and South America.

Greek Orthodoxy and Greek history—continued to be heavily stressed. Also the day schools eventually came under Archdiocesan governance and evolved into a parochial school system. The Greek-American community, however, never developed an extensive day school system. Not only did budgetary problems overwhelm, but, especially before 1960, it was felt that the Greek-American schools might not properly prepare children for American higher education. In the late 1970s, there were eighteen day schools under the Archdiocese—mostly in New York and Chicago—serving about 5,000 students, the usual grade range being from kindergarten through the eighth grade. Belying the earlier skepticism as to the quality of the Greek day schools, graduates in recent years have placed uncommonly high in citywide school examinations.

How to teach their children Greek has been a perennial concern for immigrant parents; it is still a concern of second-generation parents. The Greek day schools reached only a small segment of the younger generation. Afternoon Greek language schools actually had much greater impact on Greek-American youth. Usually held somewhere on the church premises, these schools are what Greek Americans usually refer to when they say they went to "Greek school." Such schools have existed for decades in most communities large enough to maintain a Greek Orthodox church. Greek classes in the early years were usually given by the priest himself, but the rule today is more for such instruction to be offered by trained language teachers. In 1978 there were close to four hundred afternoon Greek schools functioning under the Archdiocese with an enrollment of over thirty thousand students, an increase of more than 20 percent from 1970. Beyond the Archdiocesan schools, there existed independently run Greek schools in major cities along with an extensive, if informal, system of private tutors in the Greek language. Over the years the Greek schools and teachers have helped tens of thousands of children to become at least acquainted—and often learn quite well—the language of their parents and grandparents. To be sure, attendance at Greek school was often accompanied by much dragging of feet, partly alleviated by parental bribery. But it seems to be one of those laws of hindsight that nearly every adult who resented Greek school as a child looks back upon the experience as worthwhile and rewarding.

A new development in Greek language education in America comes out of the Bilingual Education Act passed in 1968. Under provisions of this act, bilingual programs were to be established in public schools where a sufficient number of non-English speaking children warranted the special curricula. In the Greek-American case this has led to bilingual education in the public schools of those New York and Chicago neighborhoods where there are heavy concentrations of recent Greek arrivals. The goal of the bilingual program is to eliminate the educational handicaps faced by children who enter an English-speaking classroom without adequate knowledge of the language. Its pedagogical principle is that the schooling of the immigrant child will be facilitated by first teaching the child in his or her native language, and then weaning the youngster to a full English curriculum. The difference in Greek bilingual education is that, unlike the Greek day and afternoon schools, it is funded entirely by public tax money.

Bilingual education has generally received the enthusiastic support of the ethnic groups it serves, but Greek Americans have had a mixed reaction. When it was proposed in 1972 for the Budlong elementary school, located in Chicago's new Greektown area, an acrimonious dispute broke out. On the one side, supporting the bilingual approach, were liberal educators who wanted the schools to recognize and accept a larger responsibility for non-English speakers, the Hellenic Council on Education (consisting largely of second-generation Greek-American teachers and school administrators), the Greek ethnic press, and many of the immigrant parents in the neighborhood. On the other side, opposing bilingual education, were the large majority of second-generation Greek-American residents, as well as some of the new immigrants of the neighborhood, the Budlong parents association, and the parish board of the local Greek Orthodox church (whose own afternoon Greek school was just across the street from Budlong).

Although unable to stop the program at Budlong, the opponents of bilingual education raised some provocative points. They argued that the bilingual approach would retard the immigrant child's entry into the American mainstream, that it subjected Greek-American pupils to a questionable and unproved teaching method, that immigrant parents were pressured into accepting a program they did not understand, and that it would stigmatize Greek-American youth as being akin to the poverty stricken Spanish-speaking population. More cutting, the foes stated the number of children who would presumably benefit by a Greek curriculum was falsely inflated to increase the job opportunities for Greek-speaking teachers. In balance, it appeared that, if educational conservatives tended to overlook the numbers of non-English-speaking youngsters who had not made it during the sink-or-swim days of American pedagogy, it was also the case that some supporters of the bilingual program were just as likely to lose sight of the simple and only justifiable goal of bilingual education—to provide the English-language tool for learning, and doing so as rapidly as possible.

Culture and Hellenism in America

Stronger in sentiment than in learning, the society of the early immigrant Greeks did not possess a "high" culture. It lacked a leisure class that could validate intellectual pursuits, it had few books, little art, no theater, no symphonies, no opera or ballet. Yet somewhere between the Greek-language bound existence of the immigrant mainstream and the American scholarly world, there existed early on a handful of immigrant intellectuals and persons of letters whose work was published in the English language. Their premise was that Greek culture—ancient, Byzantine, and modern—was unfettered by nationality lines. They were, in a manner of speaking, Greek-American Hellenizers.

Some of the early Hellenizers were from among the few Greek immigrants who held university positions. Others did not hold academic posts and were, if men, often dependent upon benefactors within the emergent Greek-American bourgeoisie, or, if women, upon their husbands' earning abilities. But, whatever the source of their livelihood, their mission was to bring the Greek word to a larger American audience. It was a mission that was also to captivate some American-born Greeks.

What appears to be the first English edition in America of modern Greek short stories was published in 1920.[27] The translators were Demetra Vaka Brown who, born of Greek parentage in Asia Minor, later established a reputation as a Greek-American belletrist, and Aristides E. Phoutrides, the founder of Boston's Helicon society. The archetypical Hellenizer was Chicago's Demetrios A. Michalaros, who edited *Athene*, an "American Magazine of Hellenic Thought," published entirely in English. *Athene* came out as a quarterly from 1941 to 1967 and contained articles on all aspects of Greek history, pieces on happenings in the Greek-American community, as well as advertisements of the Greek merchants who supported it. Painstakingly and lovingly edited by Michalaros, *Athene* was pathbreaking in that it regarded the culture of the Greeks in the United States as a continuing and dynamic part of the Hellenic tradition.

The *Charioteer*, "A Review of Modern Greek Culture," has been published off and on by the Parnassos Society of New York since 1960 and offers translations of modern Greek literature along with articles covering the historical range of the Hellenic experience. The *Coffeehouse*, a lively but occasional publication since 1975, presents contemporary Greek poetry and short fiction in English translation. The *Journal of the Hellenic Diaspora*, published since 1974, has evolved into a high quality review of modern Greek literature and critical commentary on current Greek issues.[28]

[27]*Modern Greek Stories*, trans. Demetra Vaka and Aristides E. Phoutrides (New York: Ams Press, 1920).

[28]A full listing of the various Greek-American cultural periodicals that have appeared over the years is hard to come by, but in addition to those discussed in the text mention can be made of *Argonautes* (in Greek) which came out in three volumes in 1959, 1963, and 1967; *Trireme* (in Greek), irregularly published in the late 1960s; and *Pilgrimage* (in English) with several issues in 1975 and 1976.

Another development has been the appearance of what might be termed middle-brow illustrated magazines. Many of these come and go, but one that has had an impact on the Greek-American scene is the bimonthly *Greek World*, "The Magazine for the Friends of Greece," which started publication in 1976. Under the energetic hand of Emmanuel Plaitakis, who came to an untimely death in 1978, *Greek World* developed a successful formula by dealing in about equal measure with events in Greece and in Greek America.

The most ambitious publication effort to project Hellenic culture to a wide audience was *Greek Heritage*, "The American Quarterly of Greek Culture." The periodical was first published in 1963 and came out regularly for five years before it succumbed to publishing costs (it never carried advertisements as a matter of policy). *Greek Heritage* represented the epitome of the Hellenizing spirit of this country. The first edition was introduced with: "We wish . . . in this periodical to emphasize the still *living* heritage of the Greek way of life, and in no chauvinistic sense, for it has long since passed national boundaries and become the environment of modern man . . ."[29] *Greek Heritage* was a hardcover periodical, exquisitely illustrated, with an almost coffee-table-book format, which carried translations and articles covering the whole gamut of the Hellenic culture.

What made *Greek Heritage* sociologically interesting was that its founding impetus was the product of the second generation. Its publisher was American-born Christopher G. Janus, a wealthy Chicago financier. The editor was Kimon Friar (who came to this country at age three), indisputably the leading Greek American of Hellenic letters. His English translation in 1958 of Nikos Kazantzakis's *The Odyssey: A Modern Sequel* was hailed as one of the literary events of the decade.[30] Friar was that special kind of Greek American who was intellectually more at home in his ancestral land than he was in the United States. Yet he evaded both the national parochialism of Greece and the assimilative processes of America. Kimon Friar is a celebrant of the highest form of the universality of the Greek word.

The focal point of Greek-American cultural interest has definitely shifted in recent decades. Where formerly there was a somewhat affected and strained focus on classical Hellas, the contemporary awareness is much more in tune with the literature of modern Greece. This shift has almost been entirely due to the increasing availability of English translations of modern Greek writings, for not many American-born Greeks comfortably read novels or poetry in the original Greek. The beginnings of the new mood can be traced to the translations of the

---

[29]*Greek Heritage*, 1 (winter, 1963), p. 102.
[30]Nikos Kazantzakis, *The Odyssey: A Modern Sequel*, trans. with an introduction and synopsis by Kimon Friar (New York: Simon and Schuster, 1958).

novels of Nikos Kazantzakis in the 1950s. These also stimulated interest in other Greek writers, notably the poets Constantine P. Cavafy, a product of the Greek diaspora in Alexandria, Egypt, and George Seferis, who won the Nobel literature prize in 1963.

In the late 1960s and through the 1970s, English translations of modern Greek writers quickened in pace. Much of the recently translated literature is of the "social protest" variety, an outcome of the repression suffered in Greece during the 1967–74 rule of the colonels' junta. The poet Yannis Ritsos has become something of a cult figure in certain Greek-American circles. The appearance of high quality Greek-American book publishing firms in the 1970s has been one important instrument in introducing Greek authors to an English reading audience.[31] Yet all of this must be put into perspective. Certainly there is new interest in Greek-American literature. But it would be fair to say that the main body of the Greek immigrants and their American-born children and grandchildren remain largely unaware of the modern Greek literary scene.

Modern Greek studies are beginning to take root in more structured academic settings. The driving force behind such efforts has been due to Greek-born scholars who have settled in this country, second-generation Greek-American professors, and modern Greek literary critics of non-Greek origin. The first formal effort in this direction was the Center for Neo-Hellenic Studies founded in 1965 at the University of Texas by George G. Arnakis. Essentially a one-man enterprise, it was problematic that the Neo-Hellenic Center would continue following Arnakis's death in 1976.[32] Hopes for developing a nationally based and sustained interest in modern Greek society and culture came a long way toward realization with the formation of the Modern Greek Studies Association (MGSA) in 1968. By the late 1970s, the MGSA had a membership of around four hundred, most of whom were of Greek descent and held university positions allowing them to engage in research on modern Greece. The symposia of the MGSA—held every two years and dealing with themes such as modern Greek literature, the Greek War of Independence, forces shaping modern Greece, the impact of the 1940s on Greek society—have become the center of attraction for Greek scholars in this country. The audience in attendance at the MGSA symposia usually draws widely from the general Greek-American community.

Breaking away from the traditional offerings in classical Greek found in most universities, the seventies have witnessed a growing in-

---

[31]Greek-American publishing houses that appeared in the 1970s include Caratzas Brothers, the Pella publishing company, and the Wire Press.

[32]The history and intent of the Center for Neo-Hellenic Studies is given in George G. Arnakis posthumously published *Greek Essays from Texas* [*Hellinika Dokimia apo to Texas*] (Austin, Texas: Center for Neo-Hellenic Studies, 1978), pp. 65–73.

struction in the modern Greek language and even some courses dealing with contemporary Greece. Major efforts to implement a modern Greek program have been pursued in such universities, among others, as Harvard, Columbia, Princeton, Ohio State, Kent State, Illinois at Chicago Circle, Minnesota, and Queens College of the City University of New York. More limited programs, too often dependent upon the energies of a single faculty member, appear at many other colleges and universities throughout the country. All endeavors to introduce or expand modern Greek offerings face the problem of raising funds from outside donors and persuading straitened university administrators to release money or teaching time. Most likely, modern Greek studies will be regularized at a few universities while maintaining a tenuous and sporadic existence on many other campuses.

Greek-American studies as distinct from modern Greek studies can hardly be said to exist as a separate subject field.[33] Several books came out just before World War I describing the early immigrant settlements. Over the next half century a handful of articles dealing with Greek Americans appeared in professional journals or edited volumes. Across the decades there have also been accounts rendered in Greek by travelers from Greece or immigrant commentators.[34] It was only in 1964 that the first full-length scholarly history of Greek Americans appeared, Theodore Saloutos's monumental *The Greeks in the United States*.[35] Since that time more works have appeared on the subject: a score of published monographs and articles in social science journals, a dozen or so doctoral dissertations, and a few histories of local Greek-American communities.[36] Almost without exception, this literature has been written by immigrant or second-generation Greek Americans.

[33]Greek-American studies have not made any significant entrance into the undergraduate curriculum. Only two professors have ever taught a course on the topic. Charles C. Moskos, Jr., has given "The Sociology of Greek Americans" at Northwestern University in 1974, 1977, and 1980. Alice Scourby offered a course on "Greek-American Communities" in 1978 at Queens College of the City University of New York.

[34]The most comprehensive of the secondary sources in the Greek language is Malafouris, *Hellines tis Amerikis 1528–1948* [*Greeks in America 1528–1948*]. Malafouris's book is often drawn upon, though not as often cited, by researchers of Greek America. Although not presented as a scholarly contribution, Malafouris's work is of special value in that it put into print information on Greek-American history and institutional life gathered at a time when many of the pioneer generation, the same group as Malafouris himself, were still alive. The volume concludes with a collection of photographs and capsule biographies of the Greek-American businessmen and professionals, immigrants all, who contributed financially to its publication.

[35]Theodore Saloutos, *The Greeks in the United States* (Cambridge: Harvard University Press, 1974).

[36]The major studies on Greek Americans, whether published or in doctoral dissertation form, are listed in the selected bibliography in the back of the book. For more extensive bibliographical listings of primary and secondary sources, see Evan C. Vlachos, *An Annotated Bibliography of Greek Migration* (Athens: National Center of Social Research, 1966); Michael N. Cutsumbis, *A Bibliographic Guide to Materials on Greeks in the United States, 1890–1968* (New York: Center for Migration Studies, 1970); and Saloutos, *The Greeks in the United States*, pp. 389–400.

An era of self-reflection within Greek America may have been ushered in by the MGSA symposium on "The Greek experience in America" held at the University of Chicago in 1976. Never before had a scholarly conference been held dealing solely with the Greek-American experience. Funded by Greek-American donors and a grant from the Illinois bicentennial commission, representative speakers came from history, sociology, psychology, education, philosophy, and literature. Also in 1976, the Maliotis Cultural Center was established on the Hellenic College/Holy Cross campus in Brookline, Massachusetts, to present cultural work pertaining to the Greek-American as well as Greek and Orthodox heritages, such as lectures, films, art exhibits. In 1978 the Greek Theater of New York and the *Journal of the Hellenic Diaspora* announced a playwriting competition on the Greek experience in America to be produced in both Greek and English versions. In 1978, as well, the National Endowment for the Humanities allocated $797 thousand, contingent upon matching funds, to produce a documentary television series on the Greeks in America.

If one can hazard a single generalization about Greek Americans in the contemporary period it is that they lend themselves less to stereotype than in times past. The Greek-American experience today is an increasingly diverse one. It consists of a declining cohort of older immigrants. It includes the adult children of the older immigrants and their own children. It is the still evolving history of the new immigrants from Greece. Between, and to a lesser degree within, each of these groups there are major differences in class position, loyalties to the old country, commitment to Greek Orthodoxy, language use, life style, and politics. Yet in some important ways these differences ought not obscure the larger steadiness of the Hellenic presence in America.

Throughout Greek America a set of themes keeps recurring: the persistencies and changes in Hellenic culture over the generations, much of which is captured in Greek-American fiction; the uneasy ideological juxtaposition of the majority of political conservatives and the smaller number of radicals, about which little has been written; and the entrance of the Greek-American mainstream into the American middle and upper-middle classes, a topic we will discuss more directly in the next chapter. Brushing aside questions of how one measures what is "typical," generalizations can be made about Greek-American life. But it is important to understand the Greek experience in America as more than an episode between the adjustment of the immigrants and the assimilation of their children and grandchildren. By bending where they had to, Greek Americans yielded to American ways without losing their distinctive ethnic identity.

Greek-American Themes

ACROSS THE GENERATIONS

If the Greek family in America could not exactly replicate that of the old country, it was not for lack of trying.[1] Husbands insisted on their moral authority over their spouses, though the formal submission of the wife could mask her practical dominance in household affairs. Mothers and fathers tried to enforce a strict disciplinary code over their children, though this could be softened by frequent parental indulgences, or subverted by clandestine activities with American friends outside the home. Thus, along with what can be fairly called a kind of peasant family structure, every recollection of early Greek immigrant family life notices the dislocation with traditional patterns.

[1]On the Greek-American family, see James W. Kiriazis, "A Study of Change in Two Rhodian Immigrant Communities" (unpublished doctoral thesis, University of Pittsburgh, 1967), pp. 107–42, 268–301; Phyllis Pease Chock, "Greek-American Ethnicity" (unpublished doctoral thesis, University of Chicago, 1969), pp. 36–136; Chrysie Mamalakis Costantakos, "The American-Greek Subculture: Processes of Continuity" (unpublished doctoral thesis, Columbia University, 1971), pp. 259–336; Nicholas Tavuchis, *Family and Mobility Among Greek-Americans* (Athens: National Center of Social Research, 1972); Constantina Safilios-Rothschild, Chrysie Mamalakis Costantakos, and Basil B. Kardaras, "The Greek-American Woman" (paper presented at the Bicentennial Symposium on the Greek Experience in America, University of Chicago, 1976); and George A. Kourvetaris, "The Greek American Family," in *Ethnic Families in America,*, eds. Charles H. Mindel and Robert W. Habenstein (New York: Elsevier, 1976), pp. 168–91.

Although parental discipline was firm by American standards and great store was placed on proper behavior, this was rarely to the point of smothering initiative. Hitting and spanking were common, but never really severe. Both parents were physically affectionate toward their offspring with much kissing of young children. In the earlier immigrant families, however, fathers were often much older than mothers, which gave a distinctive cast to the family constellation. Children were included in adult activities and age segregation was alien to the Greek immigrant mind. The family system of the new Greek arrivals shares much in common with that of the old immigrants, for example, formal patriarchy and parental sacrifice. But important differences are to be noted, the central one being that the wives are in the same age bracket as their husbands and are much more likely to be employed outside the home. Moreover, partly reflecting value changes in contemporary urban Greece, divorce does not carry quite the stigma that it did for the earlier immigrants. Yet, for early and recent Greek immigrants the primary joys of life are bringing children into the world and raising them, the satisfaction of seeing them married, and the gratification that they are well educated and financially secure.

Until about ten years of age, restrictions placed on girls and boys did not greatly differ in the early immigrant Greek family. But in their teens, sons would be granted more independence, while daughters were much more restricted. A second-generation woman, writing anonymously in 1950, bitterly comments:

> To be born a woman and intelligent is definitely risky. But to be born a sensitive, intelligent woman and to be born to Greek Americans—that is little short of a calamity. Because to Greek Americans the concept of equality of the sexes is so completely demoralizing that the superior woman is beaten before she begins! I spent my childhood and adolescence in constant inner and often outward rebellion at the deference accorded to the male members of my family even when they were patently in the wrong. Again and again I was told, "You must give in. You are a girl." But no one ever took the time to explain why the woman must always give in. To this day, no one ever has.[2]

Despite or, better, because of its very "old-fashionedness," the immigrant Greek family was tenacious. The unstated premise of the immigrant parents was: "We will sacrifice for you, our children, and be repaid by your success and sense of obligation." Though somewhat eroded over the generations, this premise still has some power among American-born Greek parents. That there may be something to this formula is attested to by the unusual closeness between the generations, a closeness

---

[2]"The Forgotten Generation," *Athene*, 10, no. 4 (winter, 1950), 22.

all the more noteworthy when one considers the remarkable class mobility between the immigrants and their grown children. Indeed, an important study of the Greek-American family found that class mobility strengthens intergenerational cohesiveness; that is, ties are closest in those extended families where American-born children have advanced highest on the social ladder.[3]

A generalized respect for elders is ingrained in both Greek and Greek-American cultural norms. This is complemented by the notion that grandparents are expected to "spoil" their grandchildren. The *papou* and *yaya* are regarded as extremely benign figures in Greek-American family life. Aunts and uncles are also looked upon with warmth by nieces and nephews. In America as in Greece filial loyalty is especially stressed. Although there is no statistical proof, it is commonly held among Greek Americans that second-generation children are much more likely to look after aged parents—including letting their parents move in with them—than is the usual practice in American society. On this point, a second-generation woman once ruefully remarked: "We are the last generation to take care of parents, and the first whose children will not."

To grow up a second-generation Greek American was to be raised in a hybrid environment; on the one hand, there were Greek parents, relatives, family friends and immigrant priests, on the other, American schools, non-Greek friends, and popular American culture. It also meant being part of a family system which contrasted its higher morality and sense of obligation with that of the *amerikanoi*. One might also grow weary of the constant reminders of the glorious Greek heritage, but it helped allay feelings of self-doubt in the Anglo-conformity of American life. Rather than conveying a negative concept of the ancestral culture, Greek immigrant parents were much more likely to assert that anything Greek was best. Though there were always exceptions, a sense of social inferiority was not a characteristic of American-born Greeks.

To be sure assimilative processes were always at work. Even though most second-generation Greek Americans were familiar with the Greek language, and many could speak it quite well, English became the language of American-born Greeks in their own homes as well as on the outside. While vestiges of patriarchy persisted, egalitarian relations between the spouses became more the mode along with more equal treatment of sons and daughters. Ties with *koumbaroi*—either best men at weddings or godparents—were not as strong as within the immigrant generation. Divorce shifted from a terrible calamity to an undesirable but sometimes necessary resolution of marital problems. Female liberation, incomprehensible to the immigrants, largely bypassing the second

---

[3]Tavuchis, *Family and Mobility Among Greek Americans.*

generation, has come to influence many women in the third generation.[4] Yet, one informed observer of sex roles in both Greece and this country has made the point that young middle-class Greek Americans are more likely to adhere to a conventional sexual code than do their counterparts in contemporary urban Greece.[5]

In certain discernible ways, however, old country values have permeated the American-born generations.[6] The traditional *philotimo* has been transfigured but is still recognizable in the appreciation of the grand gesture, displays of personal generosity, and a demeanor that mixes respect for those higher in the prestige ladder with an inner sense of low social distance. It also seems that most Greeks and Greek Americans intuitively identify and understand authority while also seeking to manipulate it.[7] Much like in the old country, Greek Americans stress observable conduct and results rather than intentions and effort. Even the immigrant parental admonition to both sons and daughters to "marry a rich Greek" was internalized more than many would like to admit.

The immigrants could be embarrassed by their failures with the English language, their awkwardness with their children's American friends; but most of all they feared the prevailing ethos of romantic love, especially because it could lead their children to marry outside the community. Although arranged marriages, the traditional manner of betrothal in Greece, were to become virtually an extinct species in this country, the immigrants fervently hoped—and often schemed accordingly—that their offspring would marry other Greeks. But because parental discipline was less strictly enforced for boys than for the

---

[4]Safilios-Rothschild, Costantakos, and Kardaras, "Greek-American Woman," p. 22.

[5]Statement made to the author by Constantina Safilios-Rothschild, 1978.

[6]Although little has been written on the Greek-American personality, the literature on the Greek personality is quite extensive. Good summaries on Greek character development and value orientations are: Vasso Vassiliou, Harry C. Triandis, George Vassiliou, and Howard McGuire, "Interpersonal Contact and Stereotyping," in *The Analysis of Subjective Culture*, ed. Harry C. Triandis (New York: Wiley-Interscience, 1972), pp. 89–115; and Harry C. Triandis and Vasso Vassiliou, "A Comparative Analysis of Subjective Culture," *Ibid.*, pp. 299–335.

Psychiatric observations of newly arriving Greek immigrant wives have pinpointed a "Persephone Syndrome"—neurotic symptoms of anxiety and depression brought about by the geographical separation of grown daughters in America from their mothers in Greece. Extreme mother-daughter attachment regarded as normal in Greece becomes pathological when the daughter is, in a manner of speaking, "abducted" to the United States by her husband. Nicholas Dunkas and Arthur G. Nikelly, "The Persephone Syndrome," *Social Psychiatry*, 7 (1972), 211–16. See also Dunkas and Nikelly, "Group Psychotherapy with Greek Immigrants," *International Journal of Group Psychotherapy*, 25, no. 4 (October, 1975), 402–9.

[7]A comparative study of Greek and American school children found the Greek personality to be much less empathetic and much more competitive than the American counterpart. K.V. Roe, "A Study of Empathy in Young Greek and U.S. Children," *Journal of Cross Cultural Psychology*, 8, no. 4 (December 1977), 493–502.

more cloistered girls, this meant brothers more than their sisters would have opportunities to find their spouses from among the *xenoi*—the outsiders. The 1950 recollections of the second-generation woman cited above are again instructive.

> One of the sorest spots in Greek-American social relations was the problems of "going-out." I belonged to the generation which was not allowed to go out as our non-Greek friends were. That the girls were not allowed. The boys went. Poor parents. They knew that propinquity was nine-tenths of love and they feared for the honors of their girls. And well they might, considering the ignorance in which they allowed their daughters to grow up! But boys will be boys. They did not want to run the risk of being faced with a shot-gun and dragged to the altar just for taking a girl to the movies once or twice. So they went out with non-Greek girls and the propinquity worked. They married! In spite of parental protest and maternal maledictions and general tearing of hair.[8]

The Greek-American community has had to change its position on intermarriage in the face of its frequency. The initial edict of the immigrant parents was to tell their children that all Greek spouses were better than all non-Greek. Though less common today than in the past, a too typical reaction for immigrant parents confronting intermarriage was to break social relations with the errant child, and then to relent once grandchildren arrived. The next line of defense, typical of the second generation, is to acknowledge that there are equal measures of good and bad in all nationalities, but the sharing of a common Greek background makes for a better marriage. Whatever the personal merits of a non-Greek son/daughter-in-law, even second-generation parents would find themselves resorting to defensive praise when relating their children's outmarriage to oldtimers. The final argument, a common recourse for the third generation, is that if one does marry a non-Greek, then one must be sure that the spouse is able to adapt to the family kinship system and willing to become Greek Orthodox.

The intersect between ethnicity and family structure is a complex one. It is generally agreed, however, that those immigrant parents who displayed a more open attitude toward American influences were more successful in passing on Greek ethnicity than those parents who tried to resist totally all American encroachments.[9] Efforts to rear children as

---

[8]"The Forgotten Generation," p. 22. It has been suggested that the dating restrictions imposed on second-generation Greek-American women may have allowed them to escape the adolescent popularity game. As a result they could develop their talents and ambitions more freely, allowing for subsequent high achievement. Safilios-Rothschild, Costantakos, and Kardaras, "The Greek-American Woman," p. 35.

[9]Clinical studies of mentally disturbed second-generation Greek-American children found the children came from families where an extremely traditionalist Greek form of child rearing was attempted. John Papajohn and John Spiegel, *Transactions in Families* (San Francisco: Josey-Bass, 1975), p. 200; John Papajohn, "The Relations of Intergenerational Value Orientation Change and Mental Health in an American Ethnic Group" (unpublished paper, Brandeis University, 1977).

though they were living in Greece, more common among blue-collar than middle-class immigrants, could often lead to grief when the children were old enough to escape the confines of their home life. To pose the alternatives as all or nothing Greek, as many traditional parents were inclined, could lead some of their adult children to forsake their Greek background entirely. But the much more characteristic outcome has been one of continuing—though changing in form—Greek identity across the generations. The ethnic anchor of Greek-American family life has been characterized as primarily that of language maintenance among the immigrants and Greek Orthodoxy among the American born.[10] There is a clear tendency among the adult children of the immigrants in dealing with their own children to ease up on teaching Greek and concentrate more on instilling interest and pride in the Greek heritage and the Greek Orthodox faith. Indeed, for reasons not well understood, there is some evidence that some second- and third-generation Greek Americans are more committed to a Greek ethnic identification in this country than are some of the new arrivals from Greece.[11]

The contrasting forms of Hellenic ethnicity between the Greek immigrants and their American offspring can also be shown in an analogy drawn from two popular kinds of Greek cooking: the *souvlaki*, a skewered combination of grilled meats alternating with vegetables; and the *gyros*, a cone of blended meats rotating on an upright spit. The immigrant life style is akin to the *souvlaki*; an alternation, an often conscious separation, between old country habits in the ambiance of home or when with fellow Greeks and American behavior in the public workplace. American-born Greeks can be likened to the *gyros*; an inseparable blend of Greek and American cultures, a more constant presentation of self whether the setting is within the Greek community or in the larger society. Where the immigrant is sometimes Greek, sometimes American, the native born is truly Greek American.

One cardinal feature of Greek-American ethnicity is the trip back to the old country. The advent of relatively inexpensive air service has brought travel to Greece within reach of the Greek-American community. Greek-American newspapers often carry full-page listings of air excursions to Greece. Among American-born Greeks, a large number, perhaps a majority, have visited the ancestral homeland at least once. Although a few might be irritated at some of the petty annoyances of a real Greece no longer filtered through the nostalgia of their parents or grandparents, the more common reaction has been a surge in Greek

[10]Kourvetaris, *First and Second Generation Greeks* (Athens: National Center of Social Research, 1971).

[11]Costantakos, "The American-Greek Subculture," pp. 180–83. Other studies that explicitly look at ethnic maintenance across the generations are: Alice Scourby, "Third Generation Greek Americans: A Study of Religious Attitudes" (unpublished doctoral thesis, New School for Social Research, 1967); and Evan C. Vlachos, *The Assimilation of Greeks in the United States* (Athens: National Center of Social Research, 1968).

identification. For many of the new immigrants, regular trips to Greece provide not only a time for family reunions and respite from the work pace of America, but also the opportunity to bolster the Greek language competence of their school-age children. Yet for most immigrants the return trip to Greece leads to a recognition, often for the first time, that they are not as Greek as they thought and more American than they realized.

Greek-American folkways are an amalgam of old country customs and new world fashions. Greek music has a strong hold among many of the second and third generations, more so, some would say, than among some of the immigrants. The band at a Greek-American social function will alternate between Greek and American music, but the dance floor is most crowded when the Greek music is played. Although many old peasant superstitions such as fear of the evil eye have disappeared in America, Greek Americans, in comparison with other Americans of similar education and class background, seem to have a greater interest in fortune tellers, horoscopes, and the like. At organizational meetings when a schedule is set, the chair is likely to state this means "American not Greek time" to stress that punctuality is really expected.

If the generalization of an eating culture has any validity, it certainly applies to Greeks and Greek Americans. Food is one of the centerpieces of everyday life. Home menus—lamb dishes, olive oil and vinegar salads, *pastisio* (a mixture of ground meat, cream sauce, and macaroni), *tiropites* (a kind of cheese pie), and a multitude of Greek pastries— are a source of conversation and comparison as well as nourishment. The image of the immigrant mother with a spoonful of food following her child around is a recurring one. Even among the third generation, a survey found that over four out of five still regard Greek food as very much part of their diet.[12] One of the most practical ways for a non-Greek wife to ingratiate herself into a Greek-American family is to become adept at preparing Greek cuisine. Adaptations to American eating habits are made but with compromise. The turkey at a Thanksgiving dinner table is set along side feta cheese and kalamata olives. The current fashion of slimness and requisite dieting confronts the Greek-American craving for calorie-laden Greek food.

Greek immigrants are more likely to drink the "American highball"—bourbon and ginger ale—than ouzo or Greek whiskies, when visiting each other. Although the American style of drinking without food is increasingly common among the second and third generations, alcoholism is not regarded as a major problem within the Greek-

[12]Costantakos, "The American-Greek Subculture," p. 183. As early as the turn of the century, an American observer could say of the Greek immigrants: "They are not exceeded even by the Chinese in that loyalty to native food which I call the patriotism of the stomach." Edward A. Steiner, *On the Trail of the Immigrant* (New York: Fleming H. Revell Co., 1906), p. 290.

American community. One might be expected to get a little light headed at a dance or party, but losing control under the influence of alcohol is severely looked down upon. But there is the gnawing realization that as Greeks become more like the *amerikanoi*, alcoholism will rise.

No better illustration of the coexistence of Greek and American customs is found than in the Greek-American funeral. One is most often notified of a death by telephone, but usually someone in the extended family scans the daily obituaries of the metropolitan press to be sure no death is inadvertently overlooked. Before World War II, wakes were commonly held in the home of the deceased and, following the funeral, a memorial meal of fish was prepared at home by some of the female relatives for the mourners. Today, the wake is held at a funeral home, typically Greek-owned. Not to go to a Greek undertaker, in areas where one is available, is an unmistakable sign of assimilation. A Greek-American wake is well attended, more so than the funeral itself. Every relative and friend of the deceased is expected to make an appearance. In times past, all the women wore black, but now black is worn only by the women of the immediate family. Likewise, black ties for men are now worn only by close relatives. The black armband symbolizing mourning, still seen in Greece, has not been used in this country for well over a generation.

If the deceased was an old person, there will not be excessive gravity at the wake. Wailing is much more subdued than it used to be, and, if carried on at any length, is likely to embarrass most of the American born. Oldtimers visit among themselves in the back rows of the funeral parlor and, as Greeks will, discuss the symptoms of aging, boast a little about their children, and try to identify the less familiar faces among the younger people. The wake comes to an end when the priest arrives and offers prayers. The next day, there is a service at church, the interment at the cemetery, and a postfuneral meal at a restaurant. The entire funerary event remains—though now refracted through commercial establishments—a major manifestation of the collective consciousness of the Greek-American community.

The crucial question is always whether, as the old generation passes on, the new one will reform its associational ties along Greek-American lines. So far, in the main, it seems to be doing so.

THE GREEK IMAGINATION
IN AMERICAN FICTION

Out of the immigrant experience, there came a rivulet of poetry, satire, and light fiction. Written in Greek, possessing varying literary qualities, these works mainly mirrored the yearning for the old country and the encounter with the new. On rare occasions some of the writings

transcended the narrow immigrant milieu and, as in the poetry of An-
donis Decavalles, could be accepted by Athenian critics as representative
of the finest work in modern Greek literature. Some of the ferment of
contemporary Greek letters was brought to this country in the late 1960s
by writers escaping the Greek dictatorship. But our interest here is with
the writings that offered a peek into the minds of most immigrants with
their *nostalgia*—the Greek word is an exact cognate of the English—and
xenitia, the sense of sojourning in foreign parts. In time, with the advent
of second-generation authors writing in English, Greek-American literature came to reflect the new consciousness of the move toward assimilation while still being half persuaded that Greeks were unassimilable.

By the 1970s, Greek-American literature had developed sufficiently to become the subject of informed scholarship. Our understanding of the Hellenic word in the United States, whether written in English
or Greek, is especially indebted to two Greek-American literary critics.
M. Byron Raizis has for some time performed the essential task of relating Greek-American writers to each other and to the literary scene in
Greece. Alexander Karanikas has given us *Hellenes and Hellions*, a complete survey of Greek characters in American fiction from the early
nineteenth century to the present.[13] A work of monumental authority,
Hellenes and Hellions promises to be a model for other scholars who can
expand our knowledge of the ethnic experience by uncovering the literary images of America's diverse nationality groups.

Of all the Greek-language fiction writers in this country, none war-
rants our attention as much as Theano Papazoglou Margaris. Fleeing the
Turkish eradication of Greeks in Asia Minor, she arrived in America as a
young woman in 1922. She settled in Chicago where she married and
became a mother. Since the 1930s she has written essays, prose sketches,
a play, and columns for Greek newspapers. But Margaris is best known
for her short stories now collected in six books. One of these, *The Chronicle of Halsted Street* [*To Chroniko tou Halsted Street*], received a Greek state
prize for literature in 1963, the first time the award went to a Greek
writer living outside of Greece.[14] Although Margaris "writes like a next-
door neighbor or friend who dropped by for a cup of coffee and small
talk,"[15] her work demonstrates analytical intellect, photographic realism,
and a Chekhovian concern for the human condition. Most of her stories
deal with the dissipation of the strong Greek atmosphere that used to
characterize individuals and neighborhoods in this country, or the emo-

[13] Alexander Karanikas, *Hellenes and Hellions: Modern Greek Characters in American
Fiction 1825–1975* (Urbana: University of Illinois Press, 1980).

[14] Theano Papazoglou Margaris, *The Chronicle of Halsted Street* [*To Chroniko tou Halsted
Street*] (Athens: Fexis, 1962).

[15] M. Byron Raizis, "Suspended Souls: The Immigrant Experience in Greek-
American Literature" (paper presented at the Bicentennial Symposium on the Greek
Experience in America, University of Chicago, 1976), p. 27.

tional anguish of the immigrant caught between two worlds. Margaris's work forms a portion of American literature, albeit in a language that prevents it from having other than a restricted readership.

"The Suspended Ones," a story from *The Chronicle of Halsted Street*, grasps the immigrant's quandary as to what is his *patrida*—homeland.[16] The protagonist, Leo, formerly Leonidas, has toiled for years in the Midwest. Now at age forty-nine, having resolutely avoided the temptation to set roots in America, Leo decides he is still young enough to return to his ancestral village and start life anew. He takes leave of his Greek-American friends after an emotional farewell party. The friends receive a few postcards from Leo, followed by a four-month silence. They assume he has forgotten them and they begin to forget him. Then one day, with no advance warning, Leo suddenly appears in their usual meeting place, a neighborhood café. To their astonished questions, Leo answers: "Over there, boys, I felt more like a stranger than here! . . . Over here I have you guys! . . . We speak the same language, you know what I mean. I had nobody in my village." Even Leo's mother could not recognize the graying "foreigner" who had replaced the young darkhaired man she had missed all those years. Leo's problems, though, did not end with his return to America.

> Six months later, Leo left again for Greece. Now everything appeared ugly to him here. He would stay over there for good this time. But the other day we got a letter saying that he's coming back again. To stay here definitely, that's what he says!

Margaris evokes the Greek immigrant's dilemma by amending, in effect, Thomas Wolfe: you can't go home again and, as well, you can't really find a home where you are.

Poised between the claustral immigrant milieu and the horizons of American literature, the novels of the children of the immigrants present an expansion of the picture of Greek-American life. At least fifteen novels by second-generation Greek Americans with Greek-American settings have been published over the past three decades. The best of them gain their strength from authentic knowledge of the immigrant world while managing to keep a measure of distance. Portraying a slice of the Greek experience in America, these works of fiction are dominated by a theme and countertheme. The theme claims that Greeks seek to preserve their national identity in a new land. The countertheme responds that the individual struggling against his or her environment must give way, at least partly, to the inexorable processes of assimilation. This view of the cultural and generational dialectics of ethnicity appears in nearly all serious Greek-American fiction.

[16]The synopsis of Margaris's "Suspended Ones" is adopted from Raizis, pp. 32–33.

The first novel depicting the immigrant Greek is *Gold in the Streets* (1945) by Mary Vardoulakis.[17] It starts in the early 1900s in Crete. George Vardas has weighty problems on his mind—the dowry of his two sisters, a bitter land dispute with a cousin. He hears that in America a man can go to work in the factories and come home rich. Vardas leaves his native land to go to the mill town of Chicoppee, Massachusetts. There Vardas and other Greeks labor at the looms. Despite language difficulties, long working hours, and hostility from Polish immigrant workers, the desire to return to Greece begins to recede. In time Greek women also arrive. Vardas marries another Cretan and they both know that America is to be their permanent home, the place where they will raise their children. Vardas and his bride will set up housekeeping in Hartford where the pay is better. The novel ends on an open note:

> The knowledge that he was free to move from one place to another now, free to search for whatever America might hold for him, was the ringing, overpowering thought in his mind . . . We haven't seen half the streets.[18]

Following Vardoulakis's pathbreaking novel, Greek-American fiction has ranged over the gamut of the ethnic experience. *The Octagonal Heart* (1956) by Ariadne Thompson deals with the life of a wealthy Greek family in St. Louis around the time of World War I.[19] Tom T. Chamales's *Go Naked in the World* (1959) is about the conflict between domineering Peter Stratton, a theater chain owner, who lives, according to the book's jacket, in the "plush decadent glitter of Chicago's North Shore," and his son, Nick, a returned World War II veteran and aspiring novelist.[20] Chamales's assault on Greek-American philistinism is unrelenting. Thalia Cheronis Selz's novella, *The Education of a Queen* (1961), is a sensitive portrayal of the maturation of a young Greek-American woman.[21] *All I Could See From Where I Stood* (1963) by George Christy tells of growing up Greek in a small town in Western Pennsylvania.[22] Daphne Athas's *Entering Ephesus* (1971) is a somewhat surrealistic account of a Greek-American family that goes from wealth to poverty.[23] *The Wing and the Thorn* (1972) by Roxanne Cotsakis is set in Georgia and offers an almost ethnographic account of Greek-American folklore, church ceremonies, and household practices.[24] H.L. Mountzoures's *The Bridge* (1962) records the collapse of a Greek-American family in a New En-

[17]Mary Vardoulakis, *Gold in the Streets* (New York: Dodd, Mead, 1945).

[18]*Ibid.*, p. 255.

[19]Ariadne Thompson, *The Octagonal Heart* (Indianapolis: Bobbs-Merrill, 1956).

[20]Tom T. Chamales, *Go Naked in the World* (New York: Scribner, 1959).

[21]Thalia Cheronis Selz, "The Education of a Queen," *Partisan Review*, 28, nos. 5 and 6 (1961), 552–73, 669–87.

[22]George Christy, *All I Could See From Where I Stood* (Indianapolis: Bobbs-Merrill, 1963).

[23]Daphne Athas, *Entering Ephesus* (New York: Viking Press, 1971).

[24]Roxanne Cotsakis, *The Wing and the Thorn* (Atlanta: Tupper and Love, Inc., 1952).

gland coastal town with the mother losing her mind and the children placed in foster homes.[25] Yet at the end of the novel, the long journey to manhood of Phillip Neros ends with an oblique affirmation of his Greekness.

Making up a separate type unto themselves are the books of Charles E. Jarvis: *Zeus Has Two Urns* (1976), and *The Tyrants* (1977).[26] Jarvis's works are what can best be called Greek-American historical novels. Set in "Cabot City" during the Depression years, Jarvis describes the personalities, thinly disguised by name changes, and events that shaped the Greek community of Lowell, Massachusetts—with its ethnic infighting, church squabbles, and eventual political movement into the Democratic Party of Franklin Delano Roosevelt. *The Tyrants* concludes when an unprecedented Irish-Greek electoral alliance upsets the long mayoral rule based on French-Canadian and Yankee voters. On the eve of the election, the Greek community leader exclaims: "Our greatest moment has come! We will no longer be the damn Greeks, the stupid Greeks. We will be a force to be reckoned with . . ."[27]

Greek-American fiction has its fullest expression in the works of Harry Mark Petrakis. Petrakis's parents came to the United States from Crete in 1916. His father, a Greek Orthodox priest was assigned in 1923 to a large parish in Chicago where he served until his death almost three decades later. When his family moved to Chicago, Petrakis was less than a year old. As a young man, he worked in many jobs—steel worker, baggage handler, real estate salesman, owner of a lunchroom, speech writer—and overcame a penchant for gambling. But it was Chicago's Greektown that left upon him an indelible imprint. Petrakis describes his formative years:

> My earliest memories, tangled and ambulatory, had to do with what was almost totally Greek. Greek parents, Greek language, Greek food, Greek school, and Greek Church. There were artifacts that belonged to the new land—candy and baseball, ice cream and movies. For the most part these existed as a kind of exotic bazaar outside the gates of the real city in which I lived.[28]

In a succession of novels—*Lion at My Heart* (1959), *The Odyssey of Kostas Volakis* (1963), *A Dream of Kings* (1966), and *In the Land of Morning* (1973)—Petrakis would make Greektown his own special province.[29] He

[25]H.L. Mountzoures, *The Bridge* (New York: Charles Scribner's Sons, 1972).

[26]Charles E. Jarvis, *Zeus Has Two Urns* (Lowell, Mass.: Ithaca Press, 1976); *The Tyrants* (Lowell, Mass.: Ithaca Press, 1977).

[27]*Ibid.*, p. 158.

[28]Harry Mark Petrakis, *Stelmark: A Family Recollection* (New York: David McKay, 1970), p. 26.

[29]Harry Mark Petrakis, *Lion at My Heart* (Boston: Little, Brown, 1959); *The Odyssey of Kostas Volakis* (New York: David McKay, 1963); *A Dream of Kings* (New York: David McKay, 1966); *In the Land of Morning* (New York: David McKay, 1973).

describes it as a grimy place crammed with windbags, adulterers, errant offspring; yet here too are found people's priests, sacrificing parents, and dutiful children. Although Petrakis has received literary awards and recognition, his writings have also raised the ire of some touchy Greek Americans who felt they were maligned as a group. In this sense, portions of Petrakis's ethnic audience have reacted similarly as have Irish Americans to James T. Farrell, Jewish Americans to Phillip Roth, or Italian Americans to Mario Puzo. Yet for all their exaggeration, Petrakis's central figures are accurately observed creations. It would be hard to come up with a more succinct characterization of Greeks—in American and in the old country—than that given in *In the Land of Morning*: ". . . a vibrant and passionate people, warm, generous, sensitive to honor and to pride, easily slighted, mordantly vengeful."[30]

Like many Greek-American novels, Petrakis's first book, *Lion at My Heart*, involves a clash between the first and second generations, which is muted until one of the grown children decides to marry a non-Greek. The anger of Angelos Varinakis, a widower, knows no bounds when he hears that his son, Mike, will marry Sheila Cleary. Mike confides to Tony, his brother who is caught in the middle: "That old country crap is for the birds. If you love a girl, it don't make any difference whether she is a damn Greek or not."[31] The more Angelos draws into his Greekness, the more Mike rejects everything Greek. As Mike later tells Tony:

> "Ever since we were kids we eat and sleep and grow on the glory of Greece. All around us we got nuts . . . haughty as hell because two thousand years ago they knocked hell out of some Persians and knocked hell out of each other and a guy named Socrates got poisoned and a guy named Odysseus got lost."[32]

Angelos remains bitterly unreconciled to his son's marriage; he even takes perverted satisfaction when he believes his curse caused the stillborn child of Mike and Sheila. The novel ends when Tony, who escapes the steel mills of his father and brother by becoming a teacher, sets out on his own marriage to a Greek American. Always supportive of his brother and sister-in-law, Tony still feels strongly for his father, but sees the crumbling of the old Greek ways.

Some of Petrakis's best works are his short stories in which he deftly sketches characters who while unmistakably Greek are in some ways agents of the human condition as well. In "Pa and the Sad Turkeys," three partners, who are not above stealing from one another, run a lunchroom sinking into insolvency.[33] To cut corners one of the partners,

[30]*Ibid.*, p. 122.
[31]Petrakis, *Lion at My Heart*, p. 9.
[32]*Ibid.*, p. 41.
[33]Harry Mark Petrakis, "Pa and the Sad Turkeys," in his *Pericles on 31st Street* (Chicago: Quadrangle Books, 1965), pp. 71–84.

half-knowingly, buys some spoiled turkey from his supplier, Anastis. After one of the other partners eats the turkey and collapses—"It would have been worse if it was a customer"—from food poisoning, Anastis, the original purveyor, is forced into eating some of the tainted turkey himself. In "Dark Eye," Petrakis writes of the break between the generations.[34] A practitioner of the shadow puppetry of the *karaghiozi*, he tries, as tradition demands, to pass the art on to his young boy in America. But, to the father's disgust, the lad can never overcome a fear of the "huge dark eye" of the silhouetted cardboard puppet. Years later, the now grown son is cleaning out the remaining possessions of his deceased father. He comes across the cardboard figure and throws it into a fire. In a mixture of remorse and relief, he watches it burn, the flames finally consuming the staring eye.

Petrakis not only portrays Greek-American figures with their immigrant sentiments regarding humaneness and suffering, but also draws upon classical Greek themes involving doomed protagonists. It is significant that Petrakis has lately turned to Greece itself for artistic inspiration. His novel, *The Hour of the Bell* (1976), set in the early 1820s, is a historical recreation of the beginnings of the Greek war for independence.[35] Mercifully free of national chauvinism, it is intended as the first of a trilogy. Petrakis has recollected that as a child he was nostalgic for a Greece he had never been to. But by focusing the creative energies of his middle years upon his ancestral homeland, he has come full circle in his own life.[36]

As must be true for every group, Greek Americans are much more likely to see a movie than read a novel about themselves. Movies most always have a greater audience than do books. Five feature films have dealt explicitly with Greek-American material. Three of them need only be mentioned in passing: *Beneath the Twelve-Mile Reef* (1953), a pot boiler about Greek spongers in Tarpon Springs, Florida; *Go Naked in the World* (1961), an unhappy film translation of the Chamales novel; and *A Perfect Couple* (1979), a comedy-romance directed by Robert Altman, set in contemporary Los Angeles involving a Greek-American male of a father-dominated wealthy family and a female member of a rock group.

It has been the tale of a Greek immigrant, however, that has most successfully brought to the screen the emotional force of the lure that

[34]Harry Mark Petrakis, "Dark Eye," in his *The Waves of Nights* (New York: David McKay, 1969), pp. 171–84.

[35]Harry Mark Petrakis, *The Hour of the Bell* (Garden City, N.Y.: Doubleday & Company, 1976). Athena G. Dallas-Damis, *Island of the Winds* (New Rochelle, N.Y.: Caratzas Brothers, 1976) is another example of a second-generation Greek American using the Greek Revolution of 1821 as the inspiration for a historical novel.

[36]"Nostalgia is something I have always known. Although I have never been to Crete, the island where my father and mother were born, the constellations of my childhood shimmered with stories of that tragic and lovely land . . . I knew the myths that were steeped in blood." Petrakis, *Stelmark*, p. 11.

was America. Elia Kazan wrote the screenplay and directed *America, America* (1964), the fictionalized account of his uncle's obsession and eventual success in getting to the United States.[37] It starts just before the turn of the century and carries young Stavros from his home village in Anatolia, to Constantinople and finally to New York. Along the way Stavros is deceived and in turn deceives, in a journey marked by treachery and guile. Finally arriving at Ellis Island, his name suitably Americanized by an immigration official, "Joe Arness" starts life in the new world as a shoeshine boy. To relate the bare bones of the plot cannot convey the cinematic imagery and character portrayals in what is the most powerful film statement ever made on the drama of those who longed for these shores.

The other important Greek-American movie is *A Dream of Kings* (1969), a flawed film version of the Petrakis novel. Set in Chicago's Greektown, it depicts Leonidas Matsoukas who, despite his faults, has never cheated in gambling, from which he earns an uncertain living. Matsoukas, however, has become fixated with the idea that he must take his ailing son back to Greece where the Aegean sun can work its curative powers. Desperately he resorts to using loaded dice in a big game. Found out, beaten up, Matsoukas loses the last shreds of his personal honor. Where *America, America* portrays a Greek who will stop at nothing to come to the United States, the Greek-American protagonist in *A Dream of Kings* will do anything to return to Greece.

If Greek-American characters in fiction often behave like rogues, they nevertheless possess the qualities of bravery and quickness of wit, qualities that Greeks seem to admire more than principled behavior. Such were Homer's Odysseus and the heroes of the Greek Revolution. Such are Matsoukas in *A Dream of Kings* and Stavros in *America, America*.

IDEOLOGY IN GREEK AMERICA

One may safely conclude that the Greeks of this country furnish the best material for good American citizenship, for their record stands high not only in commercial and social lines, but also in matters of morality. The Greek believes in family and home life and reputation, and as such he is mindful of the honor and reputation of his neighbor. He has no criminal or anarchistic tendencies whatever. His loyalty and allegiance to his adopted country are beyond question.[38]

So ended a full page advertisement taken out in a Chicago daily in 1925. Addressed to the American public, the advertisement was paid for

---

[37]Elia Kazan, *America, America* (New York: Stein and Day, 1962) is the screenplay for the film of the same title.

[38]*Chicago Daily Journal*, December 31, 1925, no page indicated. The lengthy statement entitled "Hellenic Element in United States Makes Rapid Progress" was written by William J. Russis.

by Greek business executives and professionals. It seems that much of the early immigrant bourgeoisie's desire for acceptance into American society and pride in conventional moral standards has been passed down the generations.

We do have one important source of data that allows for an attitudinal comparison of one major segment of Greek-American youth with their non-Greek peers. The American Council on Education (ACE) conducts a nationwide survey of entering college freshmen each year. In 1972 the ACE included, on a one-time-only basis, an item allowing for ethnic self-identification. Thus we have a singular opportunity to contrast the social attitudes of Greek-American college students—virtually all of whom can be presumed to be of the second or third generation—with that of other American students. Compared to the national norm, as reported in Table 4-1, Greek Americans are markedly more conservative in their political views, less sympathetic with criminal rights, less concerned to meet people of different backgrounds, and much more likely to regard higher education in instrumental terms. It appears that the college offspring of the Greek immigrants are in many ways more typical of what we think of as "middle Americans" than are even the main body of college students.

TABLE 4-1

SOCIAL ATTITUDES OF COLLEGE FRESHMEN:
GREEK AMERICANS, NATIONAL NORM, AND JEWISH AMERICANS (in percents)

Agree With Statement:	Greek Americans (1972)	National Norm (1972)	Jewish Americans (1969)
Political preference is middle of the road or conservative	73.5	64.8	45.2
Too much court concern for rights of criminals	62.2	50.3	33.6
Very important to have friends from different backgrounds	56.8	63.3	76.8
Chief benefit of college is to increase earnings	71.4	59.7	38.7

National data, based on a sample of approximately 188,900, is reported in American Council on Education, *The American Freshman,* 1972. Jewish-American data, based on sample of approximately 10,600, is reported in David E. Drew and the American Council on Education, *A Profile of the Jewish Freshman*, 1970. Greek-American data, based on a sample of approximately 530, obtained from a special ACE run requested by writer.

Another study of the ACE data singled out Jewish American students; it is instructive, as also shown in Table 4-1, to compare their attitudes with those of Greek Americans. The contrast is striking. On all items, the Jewish students are less conservative, are more concerned with criminal rights, place a higher value on meeting people from different backgrounds, and are most committed to the intrinsic value of a college education. The comparison is worth lingering over. Greek Americans occupy a position about as much to the right of the student political spectrum as do Jews to the left. The differences between Greek-American and Jewish students occur despite the fact that the immigrant experiences of Greeks and Eastern European Jews shared some important parallels—entry into America around the turn of the century, strong communal identity in an urban milieu, and subsequent advancement into the middle class. Yet in much the way that the well recognized phenomenon of Jewish liberalism has been carried over into this country, the less known, but equally strong, hold of Greek immigrant conservatism has been transmitted. Both Greek and Jewish American-born generations have, each in their own way, been true to the values of their forebears.

The ACE surveys of college freshmen, which have been conducted since 1966, have consistently shown that the higher the class background of the students, the greater the tendency toward liberal values. Among Greek Americans however, the pattern does not hold. Unlike American students in general, and Jews in particular, Greek Americans become more conservative as they become wealthier. Students of Greek parentage have little social consciousness or class guilt. In this one important respect, Greek-American youth remain loyal to the immigrant heritage and class aspirations of their families.

The Conservative Ethos

The general picture of social conservatism, even a trace of anti-intellectualism, drawn from the college survey data is supported by the observations of most who have looked at Greek-American life.[39] As imprecise as the term *conservative* is, it does characterize the ideological bent of most Greek Americans. To call Greek Americans conservative, however, refers not to party identity, not to a coherent body of ideas, but rather to an attitude of mind—a powerful sense of conventional mores, a distaste for confrontation politics, a wish to enjoy the fruits of one's labor, a betterment through individualistic actions, and a suspicion of collective steps for social improvement. Greek Americans search not for a better world, but for a better life.

A historically specific combination of cultural values and Greek

---

[39]On Greek-American conservatism, see Alice Scourby, "Third Generation Greek Americans"; Nicholas P. Petropoulos, "Social Mobility, Status Inconsistency, Ethnic Marginality, and the Attitudes of Greek-Americans Toward Jews and Blacks" (unpublished doctoral thesis, University of Kentucky, 1973); and Marios Stephanides, *The Greeks in Detroit* (San Francisco: R and E Research Associates, 1975).

New York city mayoral candidate Mario H. Cuomo, speaking at a Greek Independence Day celebration, hailed "the middle-class morality of Greek Americans—the sense of family and work—which is the glue that keeps the city and state together." *New York Times*, May 19, 1975, p. 31.

regionalism also contributed to the core conservatism of Greek Americans. The immigrants who came to the United States before World War I—and to some degree those of later times—were products of a cultural milieu and educational system which understood society in excessively nationalistic terms. As a result, they were not concerned with social differences within their immigrant community and, by the same token, did not identify with non-Greeks of the same class position in the broader society. It is also important to remember that the majority of those Greeks who came to the United States were from the Peloponnesus, the region which in modern Greek history is the most conservative on social and political matters. Indeed, it would not be too far afield to propose that Greek-American culture is an overlay on a Peloponnesian-American base.

The most apparent explanation of Greek-American conservatism is that many Greeks have done well in the United States. By the end of World War II, a sizeable number of the immigrants had become small business entrepreneurs. Their deepest persuasion was that their children in commerce, the corporate world, and the professions, or through marriage, would do even better in this country. Since the fifties most of the second generation, in fact, has become well situated in the middle and upper-middle classes. And it is into the hands of the middle-class American born that the Greek Orthodox Church and Greek-American organizations are passing. It also appears that second- and third-generation Greek Americans who remain in the working class are less likely to participate in communal activities than middle-class Greek Americans of the same generations.[40] The ideological tone of Greek America comes with the mutual reinforcement of the bourgeois orientation of the older immigrant generations and the self-selection into Greek-American institutional life of the conservatively inclined among the American born.

No better example of the ideological main currents of Greek America was there than the community's reaction to the 1967 military seizure of power in Greece. It is arguable that many Greeks heaved a sigh of relief when the colonels first took over, but there is no question that the military regime was supported by a large majority of Greek

[40]Data from the national survey of college freshmen collected by the American Council on Education (ACE) in 1972 are informative on the question of Greek-American participation in communal institutions by class background. Although the correspondence is by no means perfect, the ACE data consistently show that university students come from higher socio-economic levels than do junior college students, as one would expect. Thus the kind of institution of higher education can be used as a loose surrogate measure of class background. Among Greek-American freshmen, 78 percent of those enrolled in universities claimed to attend church regularly, compared to 47 percent of those in junior colleges. For the total national sample, however, the opposite pattern prevailed. University students were less likely to attend church regularly than junior college students.

Americans. Elias P. Demetracopoulos, a Greek national who became something of a legend in his one-man lobby against the Greek dictatorship in Washington, has remarked: "Greek Americans are not my cup of tea. Eighty percent of them backed the junta."[41] Indeed, for many older people the Greek regime—with its clamping down on disturbances, its anti-hippy stance—was doing what ought to be done in this country. Speaking on their behalf, a sixty-eight-year-old immigrant was quoted as saying: "America is a great country with many good things, except for one thing, it gives too much freedom."[42] It ought also be remembered that the well-born Greek elite has customarily looked down on Greek Americans and their peasant background. The junta, partly composed of Greeks of more modest origins than Greece's traditional ruling class, struck a responsive chord among self-made Greek Americans.

Yet acquiescence, when not outright support, of the Greek military regime was almost as evident among the American born. A part of this was because the second generation preferred not to get involved with Greek domestic politics. But as the American liberal establishment made opposition to the Greek dictatorship a cause, many Greek Americans defensively rallied around the junta. In an effort to refurbish their image, mainline Greek-American organizations have since argued that their accommodation to the junta was only a way of keeping lines open to the ancestral homeland. During the six-year rule of the military regime, however, their sentiments seemed as much genuine as expedient. Following the massacre of students at the Athens Polytechnic in November, 1973, support for the junta noticeably weakened in this country. But one must admit that widespread opposition to the Greek dictatorship never appeared within the Greek-American community.

The Greek-American Left

To describe only the dominant conservatism of Greek Americans is to give an incomplete picture of the ideological currents running through Greek America. Coexisting with the main body of Greek Americans there has long been a Marxist element. Starting in the 1920s, a number of Greek workers' clubs and labor union locals appeared, the most im-

---

[41]Cited in Russell W. Howe and Sarah H. Trott, *The Power Peddlers* (Garden City, N.Y.: Doubleday, 1977), p. 461. Other antijunta commentators have consistently noted the general support given the Greek dictatorship by the Greek-American community. See, for example, George D. Anagnostoupoulos, "A Protest Letter to Greek Newspapers," *Journal of the Hellenic Diaspora*, 2, no. 1 (January, 1975), pp. 77–78; Stephanides, *The Greeks in Detroit*, p. 89; Stephanos Zotos, *Hellenic Presence in America* (Wheaton, Ill.: Pilgrimage, 1976), p. 123.

[42]Quoted in *The Orthodox Observer*, July 7, 1976, p. 6. It should be noted that the quotation was prefaced by an editorial plea for "law-and-order" Greek Americans to be more supportive of civil liberties and minority rights.

portant being the Greek furriers of New York City. These organizations, whose hard core were members of the communist party and others sympathetic of the Soviet Union, gained modest ground in the Depression years and continued to show vitality through World War II. But the "old" Greek-American left was to suffer mightily in the years following the war, a victim of sectarian infighting and repressive legislation of the Smith Act.

Since the 1960s, however, and particularly since the 1967 military takeover in Greece, the Greek-American left has again come to represent a distinctive component in Greek America. To somewhat oversimplify, the "new" Greek-American left draws from three identifiable groups: a segment of the new immigrants of working-class background, some Greek-born university students and intellectuals, and a scattering of second-generation academics. No one quite knows the relative weight each carries. Collectively they bring together a constituency that strives to politicize Greek-American activities and to move the community toward identification with anti-American or anti-capitalist movements within Greece.

It should not be surprising that some of the new immigrants bring to this country a leftist ideology. The passions and injustices of the Greek civil war (1944–49) still lie close to the surface. Moreover, even though the communist party itself was illegal and ballots were often rigged in favor of the government, Marxist-tinged parties polled an average of close to twenty percent in Greek elections held during the 1950s and 1960s. The United States' backing of the Greek junta (1967–74) and its favoring of Turkey during the Cyprus crisis caused many Greeks to move toward anti-Americanism. In the 1977 election, the most free ever held up to that time in Greece, more than one in three Greek voters chose anti-American leftist parties representing Kremlin-aligned communists, the Greek variant of Eurocommunists, and the socialists led by Andreas Papandreou (himself a former Greek American). Indeed, the recent immigrants seem not to have carried political identities over to America reflective of the leftist composition of the contemporary Greek electorate. Yet surely the new arrivals are coming out of a less conservative country than did their predecessors. Perhaps too they are entering an America less confident of its own national superiority.

Writers, intellectuals, and artists, always the first victims of authoritarian rule, were immediately affected by the Greek military coup of 1967. Many went into exile in the United States and elsewhere during the Greek dictatorship, and, when parliamentary democracy was restored in 1974, not all returned home. Moreover, many Greek-born intellectuals who had come to America before the coup later identified with anti-junta groups. It was through such opposition to the military regime that some Greek intellectuals in this country began to revive

Greek-American leftist activities and thought. Greek-American social scientists of the left have also become part of a serious scholarly undertaking to reinterpret the Axis occupation, the Greek civil war, and the dominant role of the United States in contemporary Greece. This has had the positive effect of shifting Greek historiography away from a chauvinistic to a more international point of view. But it could also lead to a rendering of Greece in strained Marxist terms as typical of third world developments. Greek-American leftists also seem unable to bring themselves to the stage where they will concede that the parliamentary government of the post-junta period during the late 1970s was the most democratic in all of Greece's history, and, in fact, one of the most democratic in the world.

The long term direction of the Greek-American left is not easy to predict. Almost certainly it will continue to exert influence but its limitations appear as evident as its potenial. It will be difficult for leftist intellectuals to pass on to their children a commitment to radical ideas and an affiliation with Greek-American life where the communal structures of Greek Orthodoxy predominate. Equally problematic will be the linkage of the Greek intelligentsia with the main body of Greek immigrants. To be sure, when a Mikis Theodorakis is on concert tour in the United States, sell-out audiences of mainly new Greek arrivals will cheer his leftist lyrics. But among the mass of Greek immigrants, both new and old, there has been an obstinate refusal to resign their children to the working class. Their indifference to Marxist ideologies is mainly a recognition of the irrelevance of leftist thought to the life the immigrants must now lead in their new home. Socialist ideology plays little part in the things Greek immigrants are really interested in—raising dutiful children, making money, buying property, and going on holidays to Greece.

There are two competing Hellenic traditions in contemporary Greek life: a sixty-year-old tradition in the belief of socialism and rejection of capitalism; and a 600-year-old tradition, developed out of the necessities of the Ottoman era and later emigration, of self-reliance, of getting around government controls, of using every device of Greek ingenuity to take advantage of opportunities as they appear. In Greek America the older tradition has proved to be stronger.

The will to achieve has been the subject of some controversy in the social science literature. But if psychological factors emphasizing achievement do help explain upward mobility, such an explanation certainly fits the Greek experience in America. A well known study by Bernard C. Rosen in 1959 found that Greek Americans had the highest achievement motivation compared to white Protestant Americans and a sample of other ethnic groups in America.[1] The utility of such a cultural predisposition toward success, a cardinal tenet of Greek immigrant folk wisdom, is supported by U.S. census data. A careful analysis of the 1960 census revealed that second-generation Greek Americans possessed the highest educational levels of all, and were exceeded only by Jews in average income.[2] The same pattern was confirmed in the 1970 census, which showed that among twenty-four second-generation nationality groups, Greeks trailed only Jews in income levels and continued to rank first in educational attainment.[3]

Making It in America

In appraising the social status of second-generation Greek Americans one can consider native white Americans as the "norm." According to the 1970 census, Greek American men and women were 70 percent more likely to have completed college than the native white population.[4] With reference to income levels, Greek Americans enjoy earnings 31.6 percent higher than the native white average.[5] It is true that Greek Americans are concentrated in metropolitan areas where average income exceeds that of the nation as a whole. If we compare their salaries with those of other urban whites in New York, Chicago, Boston, Detroit, and Los Angeles, their proportional income

[1]Bernard C. Rosen, "Race, Ethnicity and the Achievement Syndrome," *American Sociological Review*, 24, no. 1 (February, 1959), 47–60.

[2]Leonard Broom, Cora A. Martin, and Betty Maynard, "Status Profiles of Racial and Ethnic Populations," *Social Science Quarterly*, 12, no. 4 (September, 1971), 379–88. In actuality, the U.S. census does not enumerate Jews as a separate ethnic category, nor does the study cited above. When I refer to Jewish income levels, the reference is to those classified as "Russians" by the census. My switching of labels, while presumptuous, is defensible, inasmuch as the large majority of Eastern European Jews entered the United States as immigrants from Russia, and the bulk of "Russians" counted by the census were in fact Jewish. Of course, non-Jewish Russians are also included in the Russian ethnic category of the census.

[3]U.S. Bureau of the Census, *Census of the Population: 1970*, Subject Reports, National Origin and Language, Final Report PC(2)-1A.

[4]*Ibid.*, pp. 21, 114.

[5]*Ibid.*, pp. 51, 161.

declines but still comes out to be around 15 percent higher.[6] The educational and income data remain incontrovertible: second-generation Greek Americans have done uncommonly well.

The profile of a generally successful second generation of Greek Americans can only be appreciated in the context of where their forebears entered the social ladder. We turn once more to the 1970 census. Table 5-1 gives the school attainment of Greek male immigrants, forty-five years and over, and male Greek Americans of the second generation, ages twenty-five to forty-four; figuratively speaking, an educational contrast between "fathers" and "sons." (To put the educational standing of Greek Americans in perspective, Table 5-1 also presents data for comparable age groupings of native white Americans. Where almost two-thirds of the immigrants stopped their education at primary school, over half of the seond generation went on to college. There has been tremendous intergenerational mobility between those who came to this country as immigrants and those born in America.

TABLE 5-1

"FATHERS AND SONS"—EDUCATIONAL LEVELS OF NATIVE AMERICAN WHITES, GREEK IMMIGRANTS, AND SECOND-GENERATION GREEK AMERICANS BY AGE GROUPS, 1970 (in percents)

Educational Level	Native White Males (45 years and older)	Native White Males (25–44 years old)	Male Greek Immigrants (45 years and older)	Male Second-Generation Greek Americans (25–44 years old)
8 Years or Less	33.6	13.4	65.8	5.1
Some High School	21.9	17.4	11.1	13.1
High School Graduate	26.9	36.5	14.6	31.1
Some College	8.3	13.9	3.7	19.0
College Graduate	9.3	18.8	4.8	31.7
Total	100.0%	100.0%	100.0%	100.0%

Source: U.S. Bureau of the Census, *Census of the Population: 1970*. Subject Reports: Educational Attainment, Final Report PC(2)-5B, pp. 3–6; National Origin and Language, Final Report PC(2)-1A, p. 115.

Whether their immigrant fathers remained in the working class or became proprietors, the second generation—and even more so the third—are likely to be employed in the corporate world, public agencies, teaching, and the professions. Even though a significant number of the

[6]*Ibid.*, pp. 314, 326, 338, 350, 374.

American born still manage their own businesses, they make up a declining proportion within the Greek-American community. Evidence from two quite different Greek communities in the mid-1970s illustrates this pervasive occupational shift. In Warren, Ohio, over 80 percent of the immigrant Greek men worked as laborers, mainly in the steel mills, yet only about a quarter of the second generation were still in blue-collar jobs.[7] In Albuquerque, New Mexico, over 90 percent of the immigrant Greeks ran their own businesses, mainly bars and restaurants, but only a quarter of the American born were similarly self-employed.[8] In both communities, despite the contrasting social bases of the immigrant cohort, over a third of the second-generation men were professionals. Although we do not have such precise information for the large Greek-American communities, and though the upward movement is probably not as pronounced as observed in Warren and Albuquerque, the clear trend across the generations is away from the working class, away from the small entrepreneur, and toward white-collar and upper-middle class vocations.

Along with the social ascent of the main body of Greek Americans, quite a few have made a major name for themselves on the American scene. To try to list Greek Americans who have left a significant mark on their society is to risk inadvertently leaving out equally deserving names. But the following can serve as a partial roster. Among the immigrant generation, there have been Dr. George N. Papanicolaou, developer of the "Pap smear" used to detect cervical cancer; Dr. George Kotzias, the neurologist who pioneered in the treatment of Parkinson's disease; Dimitri Mitropoulos, world-renowned symphony conductor; Dimitri Tselos, a leading art historian; George Mylonas, the archeologist who has been active in the excavations at Mycenae; the Skouras brothers—Spyros, Charles, and George—of the movie industry; Thomas A. Pappas, director of the Exxon industrial complex in Greece; Charles Maliotis, industrialist and benefactor of the Greek-American community; the sculptor, Polygnotos Vagis; the artist, Lucas Samaras; and Jim Londos, the world-champion wrestler.

To list second-generation Greek Americans of prominence would be too lengthy for our purposes here. A representative sampling would include the following: Elia Kazan (regarded as second generation in that he came to America at age four), who, in addition to his illustrious career as a director of Broadway stage plays, has been one of the world's leading film directors. After forty years as a director, Kazan turned his genius to writing novels. In theater, film, and television, one may include John Cassavetes, actor and film director; Alexander Scourby, drama

[7]James W. Kiriazis, "A Study of Change in Two Rhodian Immigrant Communities" (unpublished doctoral thesis, University of Pittsburgh, 1967), pp. 338–39.
[8]Survey conducted by the author in 1977.

actor of the New York stage; Andrew Sarris, film critic; Theodore Kalem, drama critic; Ike Pappas of CBS news; and Anthony D. Thomopoulos, president of ABC entertainment. Greek Americans who have served in the government include: Peter G. Peterson, secretary of commerce; John N. Nassikas, chairman of the national power commission; Thomas Karamachines, chief of operations, CIA; Achilles N. Sakellarides, inspector of economic and military assistance programs for the state department; Eugene T. Rossides, assistant secretary of the treasury; and Andrew E. Manatos, assistant secretary of commerce. In industry there have been William Tavoulareas, president of Mobil Oil; Thomas Phillips, chairman of Raytheon corporation; and Louis Anderson, general manager of the Onassis shipping organization.

American-born Maria Callas, the embodiment of the prima donna, was acclaimed during the peak of her operatic career as the world's leading soprano. Second-generation Greek Americans who are highly regarded in the art world include Theodoros Stamos, William Baziotes, Peter Voulkos, and Harry Bouras.[9] Several thousand Greek Americans hold academic positions in American universities and colleges and to mention even a few would be invidious. In education administration, however, special note must be made of Matina Souretis Horner, president of Radcliffe College.

With two or three exceptions, Greek Americans have not been superstars in sports. By most accounts the first baseball major leaguer of Greek descent was Alex Kampouris, who played for the Cincinnati Reds in the 1930s. Since that time a number of Greek Americans have played regularly in the major leagues including Gus Niarchos, Harry Agganis, Gus Triandos, Alex Grammas, and Milt Pappas. Lou Tsioropoulos was a regular starter on the Boston Celtics basketball team. The most prominent Greek-American sports figure has been Alex Karras. An all-pro defensive tackle during his football career, Karras has turned sports broadcaster and remains something of a celebrity. Reflecting the assumption that persons are Greek whose last names end in an "s" preceded by a vowel, Karras tells a delightful story. "When I was with the Detroit Lions I never pushed hard against Johnny Unitas because I thought he was a Greek. Then I found out he was a Lithuanian and I knocked him on his ass."[10]

---

[9]An excellent overview and interpretation of Greek-American artists is Thalia Cheronis Selz, "Greek-Americans in the Visual Arts" (unpublished paper, 1976). During the immediate post-World War II period there was a group of Greek-American artists—immigrant and American born—who lived in the Chelsea district of New York City and interacted with each other on an almost daily basis. This group consisted of Constantine Abanavas, Nassos Daphnis, Theo Hios, Michael Lekakis, Charles Nagas, and Theodoros Stamos.

[10]*New York Times*, December 26, 1975, p. 61.

Greek Americans have only in the past decade or two made major entry into the entertainment world. George Maharis and George Chakiris have played leading roles in several movies. The considerable acting talents of Helen Kallianiotes and Elaine Giftos are beginning to receive critical attention. But without dispute one name towers above all Greek-American celebrities—Telly Savalas. Starting his film career portraying "heavy" villains, Savalas has achieved genuine international recognition both as actor and entertainer. Long active in the Greek-American community, Savalas, true to form, played a Greek-American character in the title role of *Kojak*, the long-running television series. The viewing audience might wonder why the main character's name was Hungarian or Slavic rather than Greek. (Greek Americans also noticed the picture of Savalas's immigrant father on the wall of Kojak's office, a photograph that looked like some in their own family albums.) George Savalas, Telly's brother, also played a Greek-American role in the series, that of detective Stavros.

Another television series, though short lived, with a Greek-American character in the title role was the *Andros Targets*. "Mike Andros," an investigative reporter, was loosely modeled after Nicholas Gage, who covered crime syndicate mostly for the *New York Times*. Gage, who came to this country from Greece as a child, has also headed the Athens bureau of the *New York Times* and written *The Bourlotas Fortune*, an epic novel of Greek shipowners.[11]

A list of well known Greek Americans cannot omit Jimmy "the Greek" Snyder (Synadinos), the Las Vegas odds maker and regular on the lecture circuit. Carrying on a long Greek tradition of interest in gambling, Jimmy Snyder might remind one, at first glance, of Nick "the Greek" Dandolos, who dominated the American gambling scene of a half-century ago. But where Nick wagered his own money—and lost as many fortunes as he won—Jimmy makes a regular and comfortable living by telling other people how to bet *their* money. This surely must represent ethnic progress of a sort.

But ultimately to point with pride to the contributions persons of Greek descent have made to American society—as scientists, creators of art, businessmen, sports figures, media celebrities—is faintly self-denigrating. It assumes that native American opinion has the right to pass judgment as to whether or not Greeks really merit acceptance and respect. It is the acknowledgment that such ethnic boasting is a form of indulgence, that some now react against inflated claims of "the Greeks as

[11]Nicholas Gage, *The Bourlotas Fortune* (New York: Holt, Rinehart and Winston, 1975). The Greek-American Gage clan, many of whose men own pizza parlors in Worcester, Massachusetts, is intimately portrayed in Joan Howard, *Families* (New York: Simon and Schuster, 1978), pp. 98–112.

worldbeaters." Such acknowledgment may be the true sense of Greek-American security and accomplishment.[12]

GREEKS IN AMERICAN POLITICS

By the end of the 1940s, most Greek Americans were voting for the Democratic Party. During the Depression, the New Deal recovery measures of Franklin Delano Roosevelt appealed to the large majority of both working class and small businessmen alike. In sharing well in the general prosperity following World War II, Greek Americans strengthened their Democratic Party loyalties. Harry Truman's anti-communist intervention in the Greek Civil War further solidified these ties. During the Eisenhower years and especially during the 1960s, however, Greek Americans began to support the Republican Party. There were several reasons for this movement: it reflected antagonism toward social disturbances and the weakening hold of Democratic city machines as Greek Americans moved to the suburbs; and Spiro T. Agnew appeared on the national Republican ticket in 1968 and 1972. But most important it was an outcome of the social ascent of second- and third-generation Greek Americans, groups that were more likely to vote along class lines rather than according to tradition. Democratic voting still exceeded what might be predicted on an economic basis alone, but this seemed to be mostly a matter of party identification lag.[13]

The Greek ethnic presence in American politics is not in its electoral strength, but in the visibility of second-generation Greek Americans in positions of high office. Even though the mainstream of the Greek-American population tends to be socially conservative, the anomaly exists that most Greek Americans holding major electoral positions reflect the liberal wing of the Democratic Party. Paul L. Sarbanes, the

[12]Lest one think Greek Americans have contributed only positively to American society, a few mentions must be made on the other side of the ledger. The introduction of race-based "scientific" anti-semitism in the United States has been attributed to Thomas T. Timayenis, a Greek writer and teacher, who immigrated to America in the 1880s. John Higham, "Anti-Semitism in the Gilded Age," *Mississippi Valley Historical Review*, 43, no. 4 (March, 1957), pp. 559–78. George Lincoln Rockwell, founder of the American Nazi Party, was slain by a disgruntled aide, Greek-American John C. Patler (originally Patsalos). Michael Thevis ran a $100 million pornography business out of Atlanta, Georgia, until his conviction for transporting obscene materials across state lines in 1974. *Newsweek*, May 22, 1978, p. 34. John Grammatikos was indicted in 1979 for heading what federal officials said was "the largest drug-smuggling ring operating between the United States and the Mideast." *New York Times*, April 4, 1979, p. B4. And so on.

[13]Survey data collected during the 1970s report the party identification of Greek Americans as follows: 48 percent Democratic, 24 percent Republican, and 29 percent Independents (total adds to 101 percent due to rounding computations). This corresponds almost exactly with the national distribution. Mark A. Siegel, "Ethnics: A Democratic Stronghold?" *Public Opinion*, Sept./Oct., 1978, p. 48.

Maryland Democrat, was elected to the U.S. Senate in 1976. The son of an immigrant café owner, Sarbanes graduated from Princeton, received a law degree from Harvard, and was a Rhodes scholar. Paul E. Tsongas, the Massachusetts Democrat, was elected to the U.S. Senate in 1978. The son of an immigrant tailor, Tsongas graduated from Dartmouth and received a law degree from Yale. In the ninety-sixth Congress five Greek Americans held seats in the House of Representatives: John Brademas (D.-Ind.), the majority whip and also a former Rhodes scholar; Gus Yatron (D.-Penn.), the only Congressman who used to be in the ice cream business; Nicholas Mavroules (D.-Mass.), former mayor of Peabody and the son of immigrant parents who worked in the mills of that city; L.A. "Skip" Bafalis (R.-Fla.), the only truly conservative Greek American in Congress; and Olympia Bouchles Snowe (R.-Me.), who came up through privation (her childhood years were spent in the Greek Orthodox orphanage in Garrison, N.Y.) to become in 1978 the youngest woman ever elected to the House. Other Greek Americans who held Congressional seats in the 1970s, along with Sarbanes and Tsongas, were Peter N. Kyros (D.-Me.), and Nick Galifianakis (D.-N.C.). Galifianakis made a strong bid for the Senate in 1972, but his campaign problems began with his unadulterated Greek name. He tried to finesse the issue by telling voters it began with a "gal" and ended with a "kiss."

At the state level, Democrat Michael S. Dukakis served as governor of Massachusetts from 1974 to 1978. Other Greek Americans who ran for governor in general elections were Republican Nicholas L. Strike of Utah in 1972, Democrat Harry V. Spanos of New Hampshire in 1976, and Democrat Michael J. Bakalis of Illinois in 1978. The number of Greek Americans who serve in state legislatures or on the judicial bench are too many to be counted reliably. Several dozen Greek Americans have been elected mayors and one, George Christopher of San Francisco, was even born in Greece. Greek-American mayors of some of the larger cities in the 1970s included Lee Alexander of Syracuse, New York, George Athanson of Hartford, Connecticut, Helen Boosalis of Lincoln, Nebraska, and John Roussakis of Savannah, Georgia. Over a score of second-generation Greek Americans have been chosen mayors in the mill towns of New England, a delayed culmination of the aspirations of the early Greek immigrants who toiled there.

The mushrooming number of Greek-American elected officials is all the more remarkable when we remember that with only a few minor exceptions—the new Greektowns of New York and Chicago, some of the New England mill towns, Tarpon Springs, Florida—there is no sizeable Greek ethnic bloc that can propel them into office. Greek-American candidates must pitch their campaigns to the general electorate. Where the candidate's Greekness does matter, however, is in the capacity to raise substantial money from fellow Greek Americans. Any serious candidate of Greek descent running for office can expect to tap the Greek-American community—well-to-do immigrant businessmen are the best touch—directly for campaign funds, at least for starters. It has been estimated that Sarbanes raised $200,000 from Greek-American contributors across the country during his Senate race, or roughly 25 percent of his campaign budget.[14]

The absence of a "Greek vote" which can be "delivered" by one or another communal leader has been a fortunate circumstance. For this allows the Greek-American candidate to reap financial contributions with few strings attached—except to remain on good personal terms with the donors—while allowing him or her free rein in drawing up the campaign strategy. It has also meant that Greek Americans who have been elected to high office are not regarded as politicians constrained to a parochial ethnic base. In effect, Greek-American candidates can run for office in a manner not all that different from native white Protestants. This leads us to discuss the person of Greek ancestry who was elected Vice-President of the United States.

When Spiro T. Agnew was first nominated for Vice-President, it was widely remarked that his name was not exactly a household word. Actually, it depended about whose household one was talking. For the fact of the matter was that, well before the 1968 Republican national convention, the political rise of Agnew on the Maryland scene had been carefully noted among most Greek Americans across the land. After all, Agnew was the first person of Greek descent to be elected governor in the United States. Even his first name—which sounded either alien or comical to the American ear—had a familiar ring to an ethnic group in which there was probably a Spiro in every family tree. Agnew's subsequent election and reelection to the Vice-Presidency and his emergence as a leading contender for the 1976 Republican presidential nomination seemed the epitome of the ethnic dream of success in American society. Dare we fantasize, a Greek in the White House! What more fitting capstone for an ethnic group that had played by the rules and, by and large, had made it in American society.

Yet from the beginning, Greek-American identification with Agnew presented problems. He was Greek only on his father's side, his last name had been Anglicized from Anagnostopoulos, he spoke no Greek, and he was Episcopalian rather than Greek Orthodox. Although his was the extreme case of the assimilated ethnic, Agnew's Greekness was probably more accepted by the immigrant Greeks than by the American born. For most of the immigrants, paternal blood descent was a sufficient condition of Greekness. There was also the immigrant's em-

---

[14]Michael Kiernan, "The Anatomy of Marlyand's U.S. Senate Race—1976," *Washington Star*, October 26, 1976, pp. B1, B4.

pathy with Agnew's father, Theophrastos, a small lunchroom owner, who during his life has been an active Ahepan and a pillar of the Greek-American community of Baltimore. And if one's son wasn't very Greek but nevertheless Vice-President of the United States, what Greek immigrant would say this was such a bad trade-off? Much more for the American-born generations, where to be Greek was less an issue of blood and more a matter of choice, Agnew's Greekness was a matter of argument. Yet there remained the core truth that Agnew's urban conservatism was in accord with the ideological predispositions of the Greek-American mainstream, whether immigrant or American born. In Agnew, that is, we seemed to have found someone who not only could be called a Greek, but also someone who articulated how most Greek Americans felt about law and order, family integrity, and the up-by-your-own bootstraps mentality.

It seemed especially heartening that Agnew was becoming more Greek *after* he became Vice-President. His 1971 visit to his father's birthplace, the village of Gargaliani in the Peloponnesus, was exhaustively covered in the Greek-American press. (That the Agnew trip implied American governmental support for the Greek junta was somehow overlooked in all the commotion.) He was courted by leading Greek-American organizations and reciprocated these attentions. Agnew's lately found ethnic identity seemed that much more genuine inasmuch as it had no obvious self-serving purpose. This was very heady stuff for the Greek-American community. What was better validation of the Vice-President's own ethnic heritage than his demonstrating more pride in his Greek background than ever before in his career?

It was a shock to the Greek-American community when Agnew resigned from the Vice-Presidency in 1973 after pleading no contest to charges of evasion of income taxes. Yet the findings of a survey of Greek Americans conducted shortly after Angew's resignation and public humiliation revealed an ambiguous diversity of opinion.[15] Some retreated to the ready rationale that, after all, Agnew was never really a Greek anyway. Others took refuge in the traditional plaint of America's tribal groups when one of their own has been caught with his hand in the till: "He may be an s.o.b., but at least he's *our* s.o.b." The reaction most often reported, however, was dismay with what was seen as Agnew's betrayal of his middle-class constituency. There was no uniform closing

---

[15]Theodore A. Couloumbis, John A. Nicolopoulos, and Vassilis Pantazoglou, "Impact of the Agnew Resignation on the Greek American Community," *Athens News*, November 7, 1973, p. 5. See also Nikos Petropoulos, "Greek-American Attitudes Toward Agnew," *Journal of the Hellenic Diaspora*, 2, no. 3 (July, 1975), 5–25. A general discussion of the Greek-American electorate during the Agnew era is Craig R. Humphrey and Helen Brock Louis, "Assimilation and Voting Behavior: A Study of Greek Americans," *International Migration Review*, 7, no. 1 (spring, 1973), 34–45.

of Greek-American ranks in support of the former Vice-President. Rather, Agnew quickly became a nonperson in the Greek-American community.

The trend in Greek America during the sixties toward the Republican Party, symbolized by the Agnew Vice-Presidency, was abruptly reversed by tragic events in Cyprus. On July 15, 1974, a coup led by Greek mainland officers and abetted by the Athens junta overthrew the government of President Makarios. On its part, the United States government reacted indifferently to the ouster of Makarios, and may have even given signals that it approved of the turn of events. This further poisoned relations between the American government and democratic forces in Greece and Cyprus. Charging that the Greek-engendered coup threatened the security of the Turkish Cypriot minority on the island, Turkey launched an invasion. By August, 1974, after violating numerous cease-fire agreements, Turkey had gained control of 40 percent of the land area of Cyprus. In more starkly human terms, about 180,000 Greek Cypriots, close to a third of the total Greek population on the island, had become refugees. The reaction of the Greek-American community was immediate. Large sums for refugee relief were raised. Whatever their previous stand on the Athens junta, all elements in Greek America were equally angered by the "tilt" toward Turkey brought about by President Ford and Secretary of State Kissinger. The Turkish invasion of Cyprus generated a political mobilization of the Greek-American community never before seen.

Greek-American pressure was exerted on Congress to prohibit the transfer of American arms to Turkey. The principle of the "rule of law" was invoked, as the Turkish use of American military weapons on Cyprus clearly violated U.S. laws banning their employment for other than defensive purposes as well as a specific agreement between Washington and Ankara against shipment of such weapons without U.S. consent. The efforts of the Greek-American community became so well orchestrated that *Time* magazine in 1975 wrote that "one of the most effective lobbies in Washington today is that of Greek Americans."[16] Congressmen of Greek descent served as the nucleus of the opposition to Turkish arms, but they were greatly assisted by others, notably Senator

[16]"New Lobby in Town: The Greeks," *Time*, July 17, 1975, pp. 31–32. Mass media identification of a so-called Greek Lobby placed the Cyprus issue in the minefields of ethnic politics and thus obscured the broader moral and legal implications. An excellent and dispassionate analysis of the political mobilization of the Greek-American community is Sallie M. Hicks, "Ethnic Impact on United States Foreign Policy: Greek Americans and the Cyprus Crisis" (unpublished doctoral thesis, American University, 1979). An extremely hostile view of Greek-American influence on Congress is found in Russell W. Howe and Sarah H. Trott, *The Power Peddlers* (Garden City, N.Y.: Doubleday, 1977), pp. 406–68. A critique of the establishment orientation of Greek-American political efforts is A.A. Fatouros, "The Turkish Aid Ban: Review and Assessment," *Journal of the Hellenic Diaspora*, 3, no. 2 (April, 1976), 5–25.

Thomas Eagleton of Missouri and Congressman Benjamin Rosenthal of New York. Congress did impose an embargo on arms to Turkey in February, 1975. Yet, even though under the terms of the 1975 legislation the embargo could only be lifted after substantial progress had been made toward a Cyprus settlement, the restrictions were subsequently modified to allow Turkey to receive large sums in military credits. The mobilization of the Greek-American community was impressive in its own right, but its successes were also in large part due to factors independent of ethnic politics. Opposition among Greek Americans to military aid for Turkey coincided with the new Congressional mood to reassert its foreign policy prerogatives.

That the partial embargo was implemented over the strenuous opposition of Ford and Kissinger and much of the national press was a stunning achievement for a community heretofore not organized for political action. The so-called Greek Lobby consisted at the start of the Greek Orthodox Archdiocese and the Ahepa. In the wake of the Turkish invasion other important groups appeared. Based in Washington was the American Hellenic Institute–Public Affairs Committee (AHI-PAC). In actuality, AHI was more of an association promoting trade between Greece and the United States, while PAC acted more in a lobbying capacity on the Cyprus question and sought as well to encourage Greek Americans to become politically involved. The United Hellenic American Congress (UHAC), headquartered in Chicago, had strong Archdiocesan links and served as the major umbrella organization by coordinating Greek-American political efforts. The Hellenic Council of America, based in New York, primarily enlisted professional and academic Greek Americans for the cause. Local "Justice for Cyprus" committees were particularly effective in letter writing campaigns. All of these organizations also sought—beyond their immediate concern for the tragedy of Cyprus—to foster and articulate a collective sense of the Hellenic presence in America.[17]

A contentious people, the Greek Americans in their effort on the Cyprus issue were not innocent of infighting and backbiting. Yet, the overall picture was one of a degree of communal unity unprecedented since the days of the Greek War Relief in World War II. The difference, however, is that during World War II the activities of the community corresponded to American national goals, while the Cyprus cause put Greek Americans in opposition to Administration policies. It was a sign of Greek-American maturity, however, that the efforts of the 1970s were based on the wisdom of working within the American political system. The political mobilization of the Greek-American community brought

[17]The American Hellenic Institute and the United Hellenic American Congress were headed by second-generation Greek Americans: Eugene T. Rossides, and Andrew A. Athens, respectively.

about by the Turkish invasion of Cyprus never was meant to test dual loyalty. Rather, the issue was posed as the parallel of Hellenic interests and American legal morality.

The opposition to Ford-Kissinger—the names became joined by a hyphen—was so deep in the Greek-American community that there would have been enthusiastic endorsement for whomever the Democrats nominated. The unknown Jimmy Carter may not have been the first choice, but Greek-American organizations rallied strongly behind him. Even Republican Greek-American newspapers endorsed Carter's candidacy. A Carter strategist estimated that 87 percent of the Greek-American vote went for the national Democratic ticket.[18] Though this estimate may be inflated, the Greek-American vote was particularly significant in Ohio, which Carter carried by only 6,500 votes. The true measure of the Greek-American impact on the 1976 election was a more subtle one. Because the Kissinger policy in the eastern Mediterranean had alienated Greeks, Turks, and Cypriots all at the same time, the Cyprus issue became a test case in the fight for open government in American foreign policy. Greek Americans, that is, were the first to puncture the myth of Kissinger's infallibility, perhaps setting in motion enough erosion of the Republican position to make the difference in a close election. In Nicosia, the capital of Cyprus, Greek Cypriots danced in the streets when Carter's victory became known. They praised Greeks in America for making the victory possible.

But false hopes were raised. With growing disappointment the Cyprus situation remained unresolved. By 1978, moreover, the White House had reneged on its campaign promises and succeeded in having Congress lift the arms embargo against Turkey. The Carter administration had adopted a position no different from that of the one it had replaced. It remained to be seen how Greek Americans would continue to press for justice on the Cyprus issue and whether American foreign policy would stand by its own laws.

In Greek-American discussion it is common to contrast the perceived weak Greek political influence on foreign policy with that of strong Jewish influence in support of Israel. Indeed, the Jewish precedent was frequently cited as the appropriate model for Greek-American efforts in behalf of Cyprus in Washington. It was thus something of a reversal to read a 1977 letter in the *New York Times* defending Jewish pressure against Carter's Middle East policies: "We [American Jews] were only acting in the American tradition, just as the American Greeks attacked American foreign policy on the Cyprus issue."[19] Such testament is a fitting footnote on the Greek-American entrance into the political system.

---

[18]"Greek-Americans Score Big in Carter/Mondale Campaign," *Greek World*, Nov.–Dec., 1976, p. 11.

[19]*New York Times*, November 13, 1977, p. E16.

GREEKS AND RESTAURANTS:
AN AMERICAN PHENOMENON

The first recorded Greek-owned restaurant was the "Peloponnesos," which began operation in 1857 and was located at 7 Roosevelt Street on the lower East Side of Manhattan.[20] The proprietor was one Spyros Bazanos, a native of Sparta. Another Greek restaurant on the same street, founded in the 1880s, was described by an American commentator as "a poor, forlorn affair; yet to the lonely immigrant it meant comradeship and a breath of home. This the [Greek] peddlers made their rendezvous. Here they found cooking and manners of home."[21]

It was from such inauspicious beginnings that Greeks were to make their major mark on the public mind of America. By 1913 there were an estimated six hundred Greek-owned eating establishments in Chicago and two hundred in New York, mainly of the "chop-house or third-rate" variety.[22] By the end of World War I, the expression became popular that "when Greek meets Greek they start a restaurant."[23] In point of fact, because of the necessity to pool resources, a Greek would often go into partnership with a fellow Greek. Squabbles between business partners became part of the Greek-American scene, but somehow most of the restaurant owners made a go of it. During the 1920s there were several hundred or more Greek-owned restaurants in most of the large industrial cities of the North—over eight hundred in Chicago alone. The relative number of Greek-owned restaurants in the smaller cities and towns was, if anything, even greater.

Some Greeks went into the restaurant business because of the new health laws in the early decades of this century that restricted or forbade food carts. A more important reason was the collapse of the confectionery or sweet shop business in the 1920s. The changeover to manufactured candies and, later, the appearance of candy stands inside movie theaters was the death knell for most small Greek confectioners.[24] Many of them converted their businesses to lunchrooms and eventually restaurants. One reliable estimate places the total number of Greek-owned restaurants and lunchrooms—serving their customers American menus, of course—at around seven thousand on the eve of the Depression.[25]

[20]Bobby (Charlambos) Malafouris, *Greeks in America 1528–1948* [*Hellines tis Amerikis 1528–1948*] (New York: privately printed, 1948), p. 276. My own sense of Greek-American history makes me skeptical that a Greek restaurant in this country could appear as early as 1857. It is possible that the restaurant identified by Malafouris may have been an eating establishment catering to Greek sailors coming to the port or New York. More plausible is that the Greek restaurant Malafouris locates on Roosevelt Street is the one described beginning operation in the 1880s on the same street. Thomas Burgess, *Greeks in America* (Boston: Sherman, French & Co., 1913), p. 26.

[21]*Ibid.*, p. 26.

[22]*Ibid.*, p. 37.

[23]J.P. Xenides, *The Greeks in America* (New York: George H. Doran, Co., 1922), p. 81.

[24]Theodore N. Constant, "Employment and Business of the Greeks in the U.S.," *Athene*, 7, no. 2 (summer, 1946), p. 40.

[25]*Ibid.*, p. 41.

A few of the Greek immigrant restaurateurs even managed to develop chains. In New York the big restaurant names were Foltis, Stavrakos, and Litzotakis; in the Carolinas and Virginia it was Lambropoulos.[26] John Raklios, who owned twenty-five restaurants in the Chicago area, became a legend in the Greek immigrant community. Losing all in the Depression, Raklios was not only financially ruined but also sent to debtor's prison. Entering the county jail, Raklios dreaded the ultimate humiliation—dish washing. Grasping the last shreds of his dignity, he requested of the warden: "Please don't make me a pearl diver."[27]

The thirties were a time of severe trial. Even by extending their already excruciatingly long hours, many restaurant owners could not make ends meet and went under. The Depression not only reduced the number of patrons who could afford to eat out, but also a rival in food service arose from an unexpected quarter. The restaurants had to compete with the introduction of lunch counters in drugstores, department stores, and five-and-ten-cent chain stores. But the economic prosperity engendered by World War II revived the fortunes of the restaurant owners. Through the 1950s and 1960s the Greek restaurants continued to expand.

By the late 1970s, Greeks had become a prominent mainstay of the American restaurant scene. One can only estimate the number of Greek-owned restaurants in the United States. The U.S. census enumerated a total of about 113,000 restaurants and lunchrooms in 1975.[28] On inspecting the roster of the National Restaurant Association one finds that 20 percent of its membership have identifiable Greek names. Whether Greeks would be more or less likely than others to join a restaurant association can be debated either way. But if one projects the restaurant association figures to the total number of independently owned eating establishments in this country, one would come up with about 23,000 Greek-owned restaurants and lunchrooms. In other words, there is one Greek-owned restaurant for about each ten thousand people in America.

Since not many of the children of the restaurant owners are likely to want to take over the family business, most restaurant ownership continually passes over into the hands of newcomers from Greece. The older restaurateurs were succeeded by later immigrants after World War II and since 1965. Finding it easier to deal with a Greek employer, often a relative, many of the new immigrants naturally gravitated toward the restaurant business. Indeed, one can detect a note of envy among some Greek-American academics—immigrant and American-born alike—

[26]Theodore Saloutos, *The Greeks in the United States* (Cambridge: Harvard University Press, 1974), p. 271.

[27]*Ibid.*, p. 272.

[28]National Restaurant Association, *Washington Report*, March 8, 1977, p. 3.

when they compare their earnings with those of the modestly educated immigrants who prosper in their resturants.

Granting that there will be new immigrants willing to undertake the long hours, risks, and worries of running a restaurant, there are storm clouds on the horizon of Greek restaurant ownership in this country.[29] Fast-food franchises, the scourge of the small restaurant owner, are cutting into the market at an alarming rate. But if some of the restaurant owners have their backs to the wall in the battle against fast-food service, we have good reason to expect that most will survive as did their predecessors who left their push carts in the 1910s, converted their confectioneries in the 1920s, and struggled with the lunch counters of the chain stores in the 1930s and 1940s. The Greek restaurateurs' response to the fast-food franchises of the 1970s has proceeded on several fronts: more full-menu American restaurants serving alcoholic beverages, Greek cuisine restaurants, night clubs with entertainment, and, taking the fight to the enemy on its own grounds, the development of fast-food operations serving Greek specialties.

Greek restaurant owners will also benefit from a fundamental shift in American eating patterns. Whereas in 1960 only 20 percent of the American food budget went to eating out, this increased to 30 percent in 1975, and to a projected 36 percent by 1985.[30] These cheerful statistics for restaurant owners reflect broad demographic trends—more working women, more single person households, smaller families—as well as a cultural change in American society toward more eating out. The "greasy spoon" restaurant—the maliciousness of the pun was always evident to Greek Americans—will be consigned to the ashcan of history. The Greek in the food service of the future will still live up to the description of Greek-owned restaurants given by B. Malafouris more than a generation ago.

> It is a business in which the purchase of raw materials is a daily indispensability, it is a small factory whose primary product is food to be served, it is more than a business, it is an art. The restaurant entrepreneur is also one imbued with psychological and social perception for he must be in contact with the low and the high of a many faceted American society. The greater part of the success of the Greek restaurant entrepreneur is due precisely to this psychological quality. In all locales, the Greek restauranteur brings to his establishment that characteristic cordiality of traditional Greek friendliness to guests . . . It is this sentiment combined with the business acumen of the Greek restaurant entrepreneur that has come to stereotype Hellenism in America.[31]

[29]Despite arson being a taboo topic in Greek America, more restaurants have burned down over the decades than probability statistics would predict. Fire insurance may have been the recourse of several failing Greek-owned enterprises. Following an outbreak of arson in Greek-owned restaurants during the mid-1970s, Chicago firemen began referring to "Greek lightning."

[30]National Restaurant Association, *Washington Report*, July 18, 1977, p. 5.

[31]Malafouris, *Greeks in America*, p. 275. (translation C.C.M.)

IMAGES OF GREEK AMERICANS

Any full description of an ethnic group should report how they are regarded by the larger American society. A generation ago radio listeners regularly heard Joseph Epstein play "Mr. Parkyakarkas," a buffoonish Greek restaurant owner, on the Eddie Cantor and Jack Benny shows. George Givot told Greek dialect jokes during the 1930s and 1940s in a comedy act that played in vaudeville, night clubs, and occasionally on radio.[32] More recently, Anthony Quinn, of Irish-Mexican descent, became almost a Greek film stereotype playing the title role in *Zorba the Greek*, a Greek guerrilla in *The Guns of Navarone*, Matsoukas in *A Dream of Kings*, and "Onassis" in *The Greek Tycoon*. Only in the past few years has Telly Savalas eclipsed Quinn as the Greek prototype in the mass media.

But what do Americans really think about Greek Americans? No conclusive data of this sort exist. In an effort to begin to answer the question, six hundred Northwestern undergraduates (the inevitable captive audience of the introductory sociology class) were surveyed in 1976 and 1977 as to what came to mind when they thought of Greek Americans. Almost all answered according to three basic groupings, although respondents could mention as many images as they wished. The largest number, 61 percent, mentioned either Greek-owned restaurants or Greek cuisine. Fifty-four percent described family-centered lives, close ties with relatives, big weddings, and membership in the Greek Orthodox Church. And 41 percent imagined Zorba-like dancers and warm but emotional personalities. Thus to the outsider Greek Americans present a montage of restaurant owners, strong and extended families, and a Mediterranean joie de vivre. Actually, much of this view is not all that far fetched, although the real social mosaic of Greek Americans is, of course, vastly more complicated.

What was perhaps most interesting is what did *not* come out in the survey—significant negative stereotypes of Greek Americans. (Though how is one to classify the 6 percent who mentioned long unpronounceable names, the 4 percent who thought big noses synonymous with Greek Americans, and the 2 percent who mentioned pederasty!) Also revealing is that a quarter of the surveyed students could report no image whatsoever of Greek Americans. On the whole, then, it appears that Greek Americans suffer no serious social stigma. Yet, what is one to make of an alleged story reported in *Time* magazine? It seems that when a friend of President John F. Kennedy remarked that his brother Teddy "looked like a damn Greek god"—an intended compliment—the President replied with a wicked grin: "Are you sure you don't mean he looks like a goddamn Greek?"

[32]Breaking the pattern of Jewish comics playing Greeks roles, a comedian of Greek descent, Peter Marsekas, whose professional name was Peter Randall, used Greek dialect jokes in his act which played in vaudeville, theaters, and night clubs during the 1940s and 1950s. *Hellenic Times*, January 5, 1978, p. 5.

Those of us born between the two world wars occupy a special place in Greek America. Perched between our immigrant parents who came over in the early decades of the century and our own mostly middle-class and suburbanized progeny, we are the middle generation—the only group that can touch upon both the historical beginnings and the contemporary range of the Greek ethnic experience in this country. No single family memoir could capture the many different ways Greeks have encountered America, but a personal vantage can help trace the connections between societal forces, communal factors, and individual biographies.

The vagaries of Balkan history intertwine with my family origins. My parents were born Ottoman subjects of Greek ethnic stock in what is today Albania.

During the Ottoman period Argyrocastro, in northern Epirus (my father's birthplace in 1898), was a regional center of moderate importance in the western reaches of the empire. In the decades following the collapse of the Ottoman Empire, Argyrocastro declined into a backwater town. But during my father's youth Argyrocastro, with a population of about twelve thousand, was considered an important center for that part of the world. Along with commercial establishments of all kinds, the town had schools, newspapers, and even a telegraph line. Automobiles were not unknown.

The villages surrounding Argyrocastro were predominantly Greek Orthodox. In the town itself, however, Albanian Muslims outnumbered Greek Christians by about three to one. Christians dominated the commerce of the city, but Muslims owned most of the real estate. Many of the Christians spoke Albanian, but they identified with other Christians in "liberated Greece" across the border to the south. This was the type of environment in which my father grew up.

Growing Up Greek American: A Family and Personal Memoir

For a period during 1914 Argyrocastro was the nominal capital of the "autonomous government of northern Epirus," which sought to distance itself from the newly created Albanian state in anticipation of eventual union with Greece. History was not to be kind to the Hellenes;

the entire region of northern Epirus was destined to remain outside the Greek nation. False hopes were raised in the winter of 1940–41 when the Greek army thrust back an invading Italian force and occupied most of southern Albania. (As a six-year-old my memory of the Greek liberation of Argyrocastro is more vivid than that of Pearl Harbor Day a year later, because of my father's joy.) Northern Epirus was to be controlled by the kingdom of Italy, the monarchial regime of the Albanian chieftain Zog, fascist Italy, Nazi Germany, and the rigidly communist state of Enver Hoxha. Although my parents always identified as Greek, it was ironic that my family could never harken to a Greek homeland.

All sides of the Moskos family were Greek Orthodox and identified as Greek. Yet my father's mother, Helen, spoke only Albanian, and it was Albanian that was the language of the home. My father's father, John, was bilingual, speaking both Greek and Albanian fluently. Owing to the beneficence of Epirotic philanthropists, who made their fortunes and residences abroad, a free Greek school system had been established in the towns of Epirus even though the region was Ottoman. My father had eight years of formal schooling, which gave him a sound background in arithmetic, reading and writing Greek, and a smattering of French. Greek history and patriotic songs were also taught in school, but with the understanding that such seditious learning be kept under wraps outside the classroom to avoid antagonizing the Turks. Remarkably for that time period and locale, girls also attended the free Greek schools, a privilege not accorded girls in the Muslim schools of Argyrocastro or, for that matter, Greek girls in most of "liberated Greece" either. Thus my father's three sisters, unlike their mother, were literate.

My father's father was a shoemaker, as was his father before him. This was the same trade his sons—my father and my two uncles—would follow in the United States. (Yet when the generations-long Moskos tradition of cobbling was to disappear with his American-born sons, there was neither regret nor nostalgia on my father's part.) My father's first and only job in Argyrocastro, however, was not in shoemaking. At age fifteen he obtained employment in the Greek-managed telegraph office. But in 1916, when Italy occupied northern Epirus, the Greek-speaking telegraph employees were abruptly replaced by an Italian staff. My father was now eighteen years old and without a job or a future. His own father's marginal shoemaking business could not afford another hand. His two older brothers and a maternal uncle were already in Chicago. The decision to emigrate to America was inevitable.

An agent in Argyrocastro arranged for passage and an Italian passport. The ticket was purchased with the severance pay my father received from the Greek management at the telegraph office. First he traveled by stagecoach to a port on the Adriatic, then by local ships to Naples via Corfu and Patras. At Naples he boarded the Italian ocean liner *Caserta*. The crossing was stormy. But he was not concerned with the waves, but with the German submarines lurking underneath. In December 1916 my father—who was born under Ottoman rule, who spoke Albanian as his first tongue, who was ethnically Greek, who was presumably recorded as an Italian immigrant, and who was to become an American citizen—arrived at Ellis Island.

But to arrive at Ellis Island was not the same as to be admitted to the United States. All arrivals first had to pass a physical examination, a requirement many did not anticipate. Denial of entry was indicated by the examiner placing a chalked "X" on one's back. The fear of U-boats during the crossing was nothing compared to the stark terror of that cursed "X." A compatriot of my father, a man who had been his companion all the way from Argyrocastro, was one of the unfortunates. Rather than admit complete defeat, he changed his destination to South America. My father was never to know whether his fellow *argyrocastritis* ever found a new home. Happily my father passed the examination in routine fashion.

After being processed through Ellis Island my father took a train to Chicago. The next day he was shining shoes in his brothers' stand. Soon he decided that he needed a more suitable first name. His baptismal name—Photios—sounded too foreign to American ears. Slips with appropriately American-sounding first names were placed in a hat. "Charles" was drawn, and this was the name under which he became a U.S. citizen in 1925.

My father's uncle Constantine and two older brothers, Evangelos and Spiros, had arrived in America several years before my father. Although they were good men, he felt they would always be stuck in old country provincialism. Learning only the rudiments of English, they found their companionship among fellow Epirots in Chicago. The larger Greek-American community, not to mention American society, were beyond their understanding. Evangelos, the oldest brother, had assumed the mantle of family head in the traditional style. (My grandparents in Argyrocastro had died in the 1918 influenza epidemic.) At times my father would chafe under Evangelos's heavy patriarchal hand. There was the time when Evangelos forbade the purchase of a suit, cut to the latest fashions of 1919 America, which had caught my father's eye. In disgust, my father ran off to Wichita, Kansas. He stayed there several months, shining shoes, until a chastened Evangelos brought him back to Chicago. But my father had made his point—he would not be a bumpkin in Chicago. Yet whether out of fear or respect, my father would never smoke in front of Evangelos.

In 1919 the three Moskos brothers opened up their first shop with shoe repair services as well as a shoeshine stand. In the mid-1920s Evangelos and Spiros, feeling that they had accumulated enough money, returned to the old country. They left the shop in my father's hands. All my father's business activities in Chicago were located in the near North Side, the area immortalized in Zorbaugh's *The Gold Coast and the Slum*. Whatever the sociological cachet of the area, the work hours were excrutiatingly long. My father worked twelve hours daily. Sundays offered a respite when the shop was open for only four hours.

Upon returning to Argyrocastro my uncle Spiros invested his earnings wisely in a tannery. He rebuilt the family home—with running water, no less—and enjoyed the role of comfortable burgher until World War II. Evangelos, on the other hand, found his American savings insufficient to sustain an appropriate life style. In 1927 he returned to America illegally—having neglected to acquire American citizenship during his first sojourn—for a second try. My father turned the shop over to Evangelos and set up his own place of business. Evangelos was finally turned in to the immigration authorities by a fellow Greek with whom he had argued and was deported in 1930. My father's efforts to bribe the immigration officers on his brother's behalf were unsuccessful.

In 1929 my father opened up a shoe repair shop in the art deco Michigan Square Building, one of the last large buildings to go up in Chicago before the Depression. The building faced prestigious Michigan Avenue and the landlord allowed a shoe repair store on the back of the building facing Rush Street. It was my father's intention—in which he succeeded—that the Michigan Square store would not be an ordinary immigrant's hole-in-the-wall shop. Its well-appointed fixtures included an elevated shoeshine stand made of marble and semienclosed booths for "while-you-wait" service. Others in addition to my father included another shoe repairman, a hatter, a clothes presser, and two shoeshiners. Except for some of the shoeshiners, all the employees were Greeks. During the Depression and the war my father made a good though not munificent living. He was now solidly ensconced in the lower middle class. His working hours also became more reasonable. My father's week at the shop was down to a mere sixty hours, or ten hours a day with Sundays completely off.

My father's maternal uncle, Constantine Zisos, had been the first of the family to arrive in America. Coming to Chicago about 1905, he worked continuously at only one place, the Armour packinghouse. After twenty-five years of labor at Armour, he was summarily laid off in 1930. Speaking only a few words of English and without the wherewithal to earn a living, Constantine became his nephew's charge. My father paid his uncle's modest living expenses and used him as a handyman in the shoe repair shop. My great-uncle suffered a stroke in 1935, which led to his moving into our home. He lived with us as an invalid until his death ten years later.

Like most Greek immigrants, my father had originally intended to make his fortune and then return home to lead a leisured and respected life. Again as in the case of most of his fellow immigrants, circumstances did not work out as they had been originally planned. Although life in America could be hard, it did have its compensations. My father enjoyed himself at amusement parks and on Lake Michigan cruises. Introduced to baseball, he became a Cubs fan. He liked American dancing and often went to the great ballrooms of that era, the Aragon and Trianon. He enjoyed big city life.

My father became active in the Ahepa, the lodge whose membership consisted largely of Greek small business entrepreneurs. A nationwide fraternity, the Ahepa sought to transcend the homeland regionalisms within the Greek immigrant community as well as to work for the acceptance of Greeks by the larger American society. In addition to the Ahepa, the Greek immigrant scene was enlivened by a multitude of organizations, the *topika somateia*, whose constituency came from one particular region in the old country. It was at an affair sponsored by one such organization that my father met Rita Shukas. She was to become his wife and my mother.

My mother's father, Harry Shukas, was born in 1887 in the village of Chatista in northern Epirus, a day's walk from Argyrocastro. Chatista was an entirely Greek-speaking village; and, unlike the Moskos side of the family, the Skusases were never exposed to the Albanian language. The dance at which my parents met was sponsored by the Chicago diaspora of Chatista. By the 1930s there were more *chatistanoi* in Chicago than in the old country. Thus, although my parents met and married in America, theirs was an Epirotic union.

Around the turn of the century Chatista was a village of some four hundred people. Many of the men earned a living by making barrels and working as itinerant carpenters. Most of the villagers supplemented their incomes by grazing animals as well. Harry Shukas's father was a shepherd but also served a term as *muktar*, or village headman. My great-grandfather died a violent death, murdered by an Albanian Muslim in a revenge killing. Despite the backwardness of the village, it did have a primary school supported by local assessments and Greek Epirotic philanthropy. My grandfather completed that school with six years of education.

At age fourteen, like many of the young men of the village, Harry Shukas went to Constantinople to seek his fortune. He stayed there eight years, working in stores owned by relatives. My grandfather would later wax elegiac over the Constantinople of his youth. He readily adapted to urban ways and took pleasure in the cosmopolitan character of the city. Quick-witted and now in command of Turkish, he saw himself becoming an established merchant in his own right. But my grandfather's optimism for a future in Constantinople was cut short by the Young Turk revolt of 1908. With the old Ottoman order teetering, my grandfather was prescient enough to see that the new Turkish nationalism would soon turn against the non-Turkish minorities, especially the Greek merchant community. When the new government changed the draft law to include—for the first time—non-Muslim men, this was cause enough for my grandfather to make a hurried departure from Constantinople. He had decided to go to America.

First, however, Harry Shukas returned to Chatista to marry a comely village girl, Alexandra Soulios. My grandmother's physiognomy was definitely Oriental, revealing some Mongol ancestry somewhere in the family lineage. Her father was a small merchant who rotated between Chatista and Constantinople. He was pleased to give his daughter's hand to the ambitious young man who seemed to have a bright future wherever he went. To avoid the Turkish draft, my grandfather left for the United States in 1910. His new bride, already pregnant with my mother, remained behind.

My grandfather's destination in America was Chicago, where some fellow *chatistanoi* had already settled. He first worked as a busboy. Soon he moved on to waiting tables at downtown Loop hotels. By 1913 he had saved enough money to open, with a partner, a short order restaurant and ice cream parlor in Maywood, a nearby Chicago suburb. In 1915, only five years after his arrival in America, Harry Shukas set up his own Parkview Sweet Shop facing Garfield Park on Chicago's West Side. With its walnut booths and marbletop soda fountain, the store was an original edition of the classic sweet shop. My grandfather was to stay with that store until his retirement forty years later.

For the first couple of years the sweet shop barely broke even. In 1917 my grandfather received his draft notice. He was desperate that he would lose the store. Fortunately, and to his everlasting gratitude, a fellow *chatistanos* volunteered to manage the store during his army stint. While in the service he was stationed at Camp Grant near Chicago and never left the state of Illinois. The army perfectly matched my grandfather's talents to an appropriate job—operating the post canteen. He claimed never to have held a rifle in his hands.

In 1917 my grandfather sent for his wife and the daughter he had never seen. With the money in hand, Alexandra Shukas and her seven-year-old daughter walked the several days it took to cross the Albanian border. They then made their way to the Greek port of Patras to embark for America. They arrived in Chicago in 1918 with no idea that my grandfather—now in the army—would not be able to meet them. Although my grandmother was to spend close to a half-century in this country, she never really learned English. But because her husband tutored her, she did become literate in Greek. She was to become a charming mixture of Balkan provincialism and Chicago savvy.

In the 1920s my grandfather's business prospered. The Shukas family filled out with the arrival of two sons, Tom and Peter. My grandfather bought the building the store was in and moved his family into the flat above. This flat was within reaching distance of the Lake Street elevated train, and the family grew up with the rumbling vibrations of the "L." In 1927 Harry Shukas went into partnership with a German-American friend, Schwanke, and they built a magnificent block-long apartment building. The building was lost in the Depression, thus ending my grandfather's hopes to make it really big. Schwanke tried to persuade my disconsolate grandfather to pick up the pieces and go to Oklahoma with him to try their luck in the oil fields. But my grandfather thought it better to stay with the Lake Street sweet shop, which at least offered a familiar living. What would a Greek know about oil? (Schwanke did go to Oklahoma and did strike it rich!)

Because she came to America at a young age, my mother's English was unaccented and her ways were not foreign. Yet she was raised in the conventional style of the Greek-American middle class of her time. My grandfather's intentions did not include continued schooling for my mother and she dropped out before finishing high school. Her parents assumed that the proper roles for a young lady were limited to being a dutiful daughter, a competent housewife, and a devoted mother. Rita Shukas was to live up to all these expectations, but she was always a woman of her own mind. She did not work outside the home anytime in her life.

My parents were married in 1933. Their courtship was romantic dating in the American manner. Their wedding, however, was old country. My father's best man, a leading confectioner in the Chicago Greek community and a prominent member of the Ahepa, arranged for the Greek Orthodox bishop of Chicago to perform the nuptials. After renting a series of apartments, my parents bought their own two-building flat. We always lived on the West Side within walking distance of my grandparents. I was born in 1934 and my brother, Harry, in 1936.

Neither of my parents could be described as intellectual. I doubt if either had ever read a book in their lifetimes. My mother enjoyed crime magazines. My father was an avid reader of newspapers in both Greek and English. Yet it was expected that their sons would do well in school and surely go on to college. Even if they had had daughters, they would have had the same academic expectations. Although I have never been able to pin it down precisely, my parents passed on something which fostered learning. Perhaps it was their belief that there was more to life than making money, or the respect they had for the opinions of their children. Perhaps it was a sense of her own educational deficiencies that led my mother to project high academic achievement for her sons.

It was my mother's presumption that one would get a better education in a Catholic parochial school than in the public system; I therefore started school at Our Lady of Angels. Even though I was the only non-Catholic in my classes, the sisters never tried to convert me. Probably they felt that Greek Orthodox was close enough. I was treated with affection and learned my three R's and a lot of religion as well.

My Chicago neighborhood was lower middle class and overwhelmingly Italian and Irish Catholic. Ours was one of the few Greek families around. I was certainly aware of ethnic categories, as were most people I knew. Of course it was before the word "ethnic" was in vogue. In those days one would be asked more directly, "What is your nationality?" After all, everybody—except the Indians—had to come from somewhere else. Perhaps because I was always short for my age, occasionally I would be called a "Dirty Greek" and would have to prove myself. Yet such taunts seemed to be generated more by a spirit of schoolboy macho than any real maliciousness. Besides, it was a cardinal tenet in my family upbringing that Greeks were better than "Americans"—which referred, depending on the context, to all non-Greeks or to Protestant Anglo-Saxons. Not only did we Greeks have a tradition going back to classical times, but even in the United States was it not self-evident that we were more likely to advance, less likely to get into trouble, and had a family life superior to most?

But there was a defensive side to our ethnic smugness—a hyperawareness of every Greek who could be singled out for achievement. (To this day I still have the habit of scanning movie and television credits for Greek surnames.) To grow up Greek in the 1930s and 1940s meant that household names included Dimitri Mitropoulos, Jim ("the Golden Greek") Londos, and Dean Alfange, the New York political figure. We were attuned to the careers of obscure film personalities like George Coulouris and Katina Paxinou. We identified with Babe Didrikson Zaharias, one of the greatest women athletes of modern times, who by marrying a Greek wrestler, George Zaharias, acquired a Greek sounding name. There was also the vague sense that Prince Phillip, the Duke of Edinburgh, came from a Greek family. A much admired figure in Greek-American circles during World War II was Cedric W. Foster, the radio commentator and well known philhellene. All this was in the era before the advent of Greek-American celebrities and political figures on the national scene. It was a time before movies such as *Never on Sunday* and *Zorba the Greek* gave being Greek a certain trendiness.

To be Greek American in Chicago meant identifying with one of the Greek Orthodox churches in the city. Our own church was the Assumption on the West Side supported mainly by members of the Greek business community. Saint Andrew on the North Side was regarded as the church of "rich Greeks." Holy Trinity was the more traditional immigrant church in the old Greektown near the Loop. (My present church, Saint Demetrios, is located in Chicago's new Greektown on the Northwest Side.) Saints Constantine and Helen on the South Side was noted for its magnificent edifice capped by a dome resembling that of the glory of Greek Orthodoxy—Saint Sophia in Constantinople.

Years later, when the neighborhood changed, Saints Constantine and Helen became Islamic following its purchase by the Black Muslims, who made it their showpiece mosque. I always thought that there was something historically correct for a vacated Greek church to become Muslim rather than be turned over to another Christian body. The transformation of the old "Saint Connie's" from Orthodox to Islamic, like that of the original Saint Sophia, seemed to recapitulate in the American context the Ottoman heritage in Greek life.

Politics—either Greek or American—were a conversational staple in my family circle. The monarchist versus republican schism which had characterized Greek political life since the turn of the century divided the Greek-American community until World War II. My own family was staunchly on the republican side. A small communist group existed in the Chicago Greek community, some of whom were family acquaintances. I remember these communists as engaging individuals, but also noticed that my parents and grandfather treated them with amused condescension. Although as a boy I was certainly aware of Greek politics, I was not that interested except in the irredentist Epirotic cause. It was my family's political view of America which naturally had the most meaning to me.

The politics of my family were consonant with the small shopkeepers we were. All my family—down to the present generation—has consistently held conservative social views. In his later years my father became a great supporter of Spiro Agnew, as much for the vice-president's political philosophy as for his Greek background. My family saw advancement in individual terms, not through organized collective action. Social altruism in a liberal sense was an alien concept. Responsibilities extended to self and family. If people took care of their own, there would be no social problems. With diligence, some innate talent, and a little luck, the American Dream could be realized. An added ingredient would be the esteem accorded by the Greek-American community.

In 1945 our family moved to Albuquerque, New Mexico, to find a better climate for my hay fever. My father tried his hand in the restaurant and bar business, but soon decided to keep to his old trade. He opened up Albuquerque's finest shoe repair shop which he operated until his retirement. We chose Albuquerque for our new home because of the presence of a Greek community with its own church. The Greek population, large for a Rocky Mountain city, was the legacy of an Ahepa tubercular sanitorium which had attracted Greeks from around the country to Albuquerque. The sanitorium had closed by the time we arrived, its failure being locally attributed to the excessive demands and idiosyncracies of its patients.

The focal point of the Albuquerque Greek community was Saint George's church. The older men, who mainly ran restaurants and bars, found election to the church board and Ahepa offices a means of acquiring some recognition and status in a familiar environment. The older women, almost all housewives, took part in various auxiliaries. The younger American-born generation belonged to church youth groups; most served in the choir or as altar boys. Efforts to maintain a Greek language school were more sporadic. Social life centered on namedays, baptisms, and major religious holidays. Extravagant formal weddings to which the whole Greek community was invited were major events. The community would be periodically rent by disputes arising out of bruised egos and personality clashes. Such disputes became especially bitter when the qualifications of the priest were questioned.

The Greek community was extremely alert to any straying from proper bounds. The rare divorce was always cause for gossip. One of the more memorable scandals involved a young woman who gave birth to a child out of wedlock. Suitably penitent, she sought readmission to the church youth group. Despite the pleas of the priest and the choir director we self-righteously refused to accept her back. If there was a generation gap in those days, the young seemed more prudish.

In the late 1940s and early 1950s I knew each of the several-hundred members of the Greek community in Albuquerque. The community ranged from the old bachelors who went to the pool halls near the railroad station to the main body of small business people, to a few who had become prosperous through real estate investment. Few of them had anything in common with the pristine Hellenes in classical Greece whom one read about. Rather, they were more Byzantine, more complicated, more like the forceful characters in a Harry Mark Petrakis novel.

There was George Ades, warm hearted but hot tempered, who had arrived when New Mexico was still a territory and was probably the first Greek there. He married into an old-line New Mexico family—descended from the *conquistadores*—and learned to speak Spanish himself. There was Theo Karvelas, compact and bald, who was the only adult immigrant in Albuquerque with an American high school diploma, acquired in night school back in Pittsburgh. Karvelas, the intellectual of the Greek community, was a major influence in my life. There was Father Silas Koskinas, gentle and ascetic, who was later raised to the bishopric. There was Father Peter Remoundos, a bear of a man, who tempered religious solemnity with perceptive wit. In what was the most appropriate eulogy I ever heard, Father Remoundos captured the essence of Greek Americana by pronouncing a local chef "an artisan with the ladle and the knife."

Even though the Greek community was a vital part of my growing up, it was not everything in my life. I was active in student politics in junior and senior high school. Albuquerque was divided into two basic ethnic groups, the Anglos and the Spanish (the term "Mexican" was pejorative and "chicano" had not yet come into fashion). A Greek was obviously neither. What successes I had in high school politics could be largely attributed to the fact that I could make appeals to both groups. My closest friends were non-Greeks, boys who like myself fell between the *pachucos* (Spanish toughs) and *stompers* (Anglo toughs) on the one hand and the country club set on the other. My youth in Albuquerque was a combination of family-centered Greekness and an *American Graffiti* existence of drive-ins and popular culture.

Ethnicity has always been the basic reality in my family's social world. The group consciousness which resulted from their ethnic background has been felt in all contexts of their lives. While one can argue that ethnic differences reflect root economic realities, it is equally true that class differences are outcomes of basic affiliations. Even to become Americanized—as American-born Greeks have become—seems to speak both to a partial absorption into class-based groups *and* an evolving ethnic adaptation which is still discernible from the broader American culture.

In my adult years when traveling abroad, I found that my Greek heritage often led to some of my most interesting encounters. For example, I attended the 1970 meetings of the International Sociological Association in Bulgaria, where I was presenting a paper on the collapse of Greek democracy. Several Greek communists, former guerrillas who had fled to Bulgaria in 1949 and definitely nonacademics, made special efforts to hear the paper. While taking polite exception to some anti-Stalinist passages, they allowed that it was a creditable study. They approached me at the end of the session and suggested we have dinner together. We met at a restaurant and, after exchanging pleasantries, they told me the purpose of the meeting. They were disturbed that their children raised in Bulgaria might lose their Greek identity. What could I as a "Greek sociologist" suggest to prevent such an outcome? What lessons for them might be drawn from the Greek experience, particularly in America? I was forced to tell them that the primary vehicle for Greek ethnic maintenance in the United States was the Greek Orthodox Church. They sighed and sadly shook their heads. This was a price too dear to pay. There must be another way. We left shaking hands and promising to stay in touch. But inwardly we knew that there was nothing more to be said.

In 1971 I was able to make a short trip to Jerusalem from Cyprus where I was doing some research. While in Jerusalem I visited the Church of the Holy Sepulcher, the holiest spot in Christendom. Inside the church is a small room, the site where tradition holds Jesus was buried and rose. It is a place that for centuries has been under Greek Orthodox custody—ever on guard against the encroachments of other Christian bodies. I entered the room and was alone except for a frail, octogenarian monk seated on a stool keeping vigil. We began to talk in Greek. He asked from where did I come. Evanston, Illinois, I replied. On similar queries I had always responded Chicago, but for some reason Evanston came to my lips this time. He leaped up, embraced and kissed me! His brother, whom he had not seen for sixty years, had settled as a young man in Evanston where he operated an ice cream parlor for many years. It was as if God, he said, had sent me in his brother's place. From somewhere deep in his cassock he pulled a tattered envelope with his brother's return address on it. Would I look up his brother when I returned home and tell him that all was well and that they would meet in the next world? When I did get back to Evanston I learned that the old monk's brother had died a few months earlier.

I returned permanently to the Chicago area—whose Greek community had been replenished by large numbers of new immigrants—when I took a position at Northwestern University. Much of my family life has a pleasant déjà vu. I was married by the priest who baptized me. In the preferred Greek fashion my *koumbaros*, or best man, was the son of my parents' *koumbaroi*. I was exceedingly fortunate to marry a modern woman who knows how to handle a traditional man. My wife Ilca, German born, has to my embarrassment and pride even learned to speak Greek better than I. My father lives with us and wears his years well. My brother is managing editor of the *Albuquerque Tribune*; his wife is a third-generation Greek American. My grandparents Shukas lived into ripe old age, staying close to and, finally, moving in with my uncle, a pharmacist, and his family.

Although the fates have smiled on me, there have been losses, too. My mother died too early, at age forty-three, and was never to see her sons grow to maturity. My uncles in Albania died in penury, a condition in which my father's sisters continue to live. Much of my father's time is spent attending the funerals—a reminder that we must all make that crossing over the Styx—of his rapidly diminishing group of friends. Wars took their toll. My uncle, Peter Shukas, was killed in World War II, and my cousin and godson, James Shukas, died in Vietnam.

It seems fair to say that if the family did well in America, America did well by it.

All told, more than seven hundred thousand Greeks have crossed to these shores at one time. About two out of three of these Greek arrivals made America their permanent home. The initial mass influx of Greeks during the first two decades of this century coincided with the full force of American industrialization. Besides the majority working in manual jobs, a significant portion of the early immigrants catered to the needs of a swelling urban population by becoming proprietors of their own businesses. Since the reopening of the immigration doors in 1966, new concentrations of Greeks have arrived, mainly settling in our large northern cities. Most of the newcomers make up a service labor force, but many have also become entrepreneurs. Despite the renewal of immigration from Greece, about three in four Greek Americans are native born. The progeny of the early immigrants have moved, in the main, into middle-class vocations and into the suburbs. Although processes of assimilation have been undeniable, there has been a persistent attachment to "Greek identity," however hard to define that sentiment might be, well into many of the second and third generations. This, in broad strokes, is the social-demographic portrait of Greek America.

The Sociology of Greek Americans

If we can locate one dominant characteristic of the Greek-American experience it would be in the course of "embourgeoisement." A very few years after the start of the mass migration, there also began within the Greek immigrant colony that process of internal social stratification that is characteristic of American society as a whole. The beginnings of a Greek-American middle class can be detected by, say, 1910. Certainly by the 1920s there was a considerable number of Greeks who had become owners of small businesses. Many Greeks did not succeed in their run for the golden end of the rainbow, to be sure, but the overriding trend beginning with the early immigrants and continuing across the generations has been that of a social ascent with few parallels in American history.

This advancement was largely due to the entrepreneurial ability of many of the early Greek immigrants, a phenomenon consistently noted by every American observer of the Greek colony during the early years of this century. How could a large component of an unlettered and rural migrant group display such an affinity for business after arrival in this country? To answer this question we must turn to the village life of Greece at the end of the nineteenth century.

Unlike peasants in most other Eastern European societies of that time, the Greek peasant participated directly in a market rather than a subsistence economy.[1] There was little of the peasant's traditional linkages with the soil through communal usages; land and agricultural products were commodities to be bought and sold. In the villages, selling and buying were familiar endeavors, and negotiation in the marketplace meant that cleverness and luck took priority in determining success over the "humdrum routines of everyday work and directness of simple honesty."[2] Even though late nineteeenth-century Greek society was overwhelmingly rural, the cultural hegemony of its urban merchant class—both in the Greek state and in the Greek diaspora—fostered an individualistic outlook on economic activities which even permeated the countryside. The Greek villager was already eager to emulate consumer and city life styles. Ostensibly peasants, Greek migrants were mentally primed before their departure to take advantage of capitalistic opportunities as they might appear in the new country. There can be little doubt that a satisfactory explanation of the genesis of Greek-American entrepreneurialism requires serious consideration of the cultural variables unique to Greek society and economy at the turn of the century.[3]

American industrial expansion and urbanization at the time of the Greek mass migration was a necessary condition for the appearance of a Greek-American bourgeoisie. Once enough of the first arrivals demonstrated that it was possible to move from manual labor to operation of a business, others followed in their steps, often by first working in the stores of relatives or fellow villagers. While this could sometimes lead to exploitative relationships, it also meant that a "greenhorn" would acquire the requisite know-how before setting out on a business of his own. It also helps explain why the early Greek shopkeepers concentrated on a narrow, but familiar, range of enterprises: confectioneries, bootblack

[1]This interpretation of values and economy in rural Greece during the nineteenth century comes from Nicos P. Mouzelis, *Modern Greece: Facets of Underdevelopment* (New York: Holmes and Meier, 1978), especially pp. 93–104; and William H. NcNeil, *The Metamorphosis of Greece Since World War II* (Chicago: University of Chicago Press, 1978), especially pp. 8–30.

[2]*Ibid.*, p. 13. It has also been argued that the formalistic qualities of Greek Orthodoxy—attentiveness to religious rules rather than moral issues—facilitated the emergence of a Greek commercial ethic as early as Ottoman times. Mouzelis, *Modern Greece*, p. 159.

[3]Greek immigrants to Australia during the late nineteenth and early twentieth centuries also entered the economy as manual laborers, but many soon moved into their own small businesses and formed a shopkeeper class. Mick P. Tsounis, "Greek Communities in Australia" (unpublished doctoral thesis, University of Adelaide, 1971), pp. 54–61. The Greek immigrant entrepreneurial tendency has also been documented in Canada. Peter D. Chimbos, "Ethnicity and Occupational Mobility," *International Journal of Comparative Sociology*, 15, nos. 1–2 (March–June, 1974). pp. 57–67.

and shoe repair parlors, dry cleaners, florists, produce stores, coffeeshops, and restaurants. Another explanation for the emergence of Greek businesses was the willingness of the immigrant shopkeeper to work achingly long hours and spend little on personal needs. After all, the typical immigrant of the early years was single and had neither the diversions nor expenses of family life. In a fundamental sense, if there was excessive exploitation, it was often of self.

The petty bourgeois component of the early immigrant Greeks deeply affected the future direction of the Greek-American community. The ethnic identity of Greek Americans, unlike that often described for other European ethnic groups, has not been strongly linked with working-class affiliation. On the contrary, the middle class always served as the reference point for Greek immigrants. Individual striving was considered more important than group betterment. Even in their communal organizations, Greek Americans have preferred to present a face of decorum in their relations with the general public and in their dealings with political leaders. They have been leery of collective efforts for public funds or of ethnic associations that depend on the state system. They do not feel the need to do as other minorities, whose social experience is different from theirs. Greek Americans tend to interpret the opportunities and risks of American society from a petty-bourgeois point of view. That their judgment has been sound, at least up to this point, reinforces the initial predisposition toward individualism.

If their inclinations lead Greek Americans to be wary of collective public actions, they also reflect an ingrained skepticism toward the "helping professions" that have become part and parcel of social service bureaucracies. Sociologists, psychologists, marriage counselors, and social workers are appropriating many of the family functions. Whether they are filling a vacuum or contributing to the problem has been argued both ways.[4] But to the degree that some professional approaches ignore the love and discipline that are the family's real glue, they deflect away from an understanding of the traditional strengths of the Greek-American family, which rest upon the obligation for the older generation and responsibility for the younger. Certainly the plight of some Greek Americans, especially among the new immigrants and the aged among the earlier arrivals, can be relieved by outside professional help and welfare assistance. It has long been true that a combination of complacence and shame has kept deprived Greeks from receiving the proper attention of the Greek-American community.[5] The appearance of

---

[4]Critiques of the "helping professions" now constitute a body of literature. Representative writings include: Christopher Lasch, *Haven in a Heartless World* (New York: Basic Books, 1977); Ivan Illich, ed., *Disabling Professions* (London: Marion Boyers, 1977); and Willard Gaylin, *Doing Good: The Limits of Benevolence* (New York: Pantheon Books, 1978).

[5]Hanac Staff, *The Needs of the Growing Greek-American Community in the City of New York* (New York: Hellenic American Neighborhood Action Committee, 1973).

Greek-American welfare agencies in the 1970s thus breaks the old pattern of neglect. But welfare organizations by definition depend upon people who are understood as lacking or deficient. There is no easy answer as to when the boundary is crossed between a "labeled" dependent population and a group objectively defined in real need. Perhaps the Greeks' pride in self-reliance that causes them to see recognition of need as a sign of personal failure will serve to keep the distinction in proper perspective.

GREEK-AMERICAN STUDIES: CONTRASTING PERSPECTIVES

Few subjects are as likely to stir up passions among Greek Americans than talking or writing about themselves. The understanding one has about Greek America almost always has prescriptive implications. In attempting to deal with this complex subject, this book has divided the Greek-American experience into five more or less distinct stages: (1) a time of false starts in the period before 1890; (2) the era of mass migration from 1890 to 1920; (3) the formation of Greek-American institutions from 1920 to 1940; (4) an era of consolidation from 1940 to 1965 within Greek America; and (5) the contemporary period since 1965 of increasing Greek-American diversity. No historical divisions, of course, can be so tidy as indicated here. Basic social patterns overlap across several of the periods, and in each there were counteracting tendencies against prevailing trends. Still each of these historical stages had certain dominant qualities that serve to mark one from the other.

In the contemporary period it becomes especially difficult to make generalizations about Greek America because of the diversity hidden by that term and because perhaps there is no such thing as *one* Greek America. Nevertheless, specifying certain paradigms, even if competing, will facilitate the development of Greek-American studies. Such an effort, at the least, does help us master our conceptual bearing, making it easier to grasp the Greek-American experience. The contending views about Greek Americans can be reduced to two main questions. Is there more or less variability within Greek Americans than between Greek Americans and other Americans? Is there more or less variability between Greek Americans and Greeks than between Greek Americans and other Americans? To pose such questions is a necessary first step toward an elaboration of Greek-American studies.

Similarities versus Differences

The prevailing interpretation of Greek Americans is to understand them in terms of cohesiveness and similarities. From this standpoint one views the ascent of many of the immigrants into the middle class and the relatively high economic and educational standing of Greek Americans of the second and third generations. Such a perspective also emphasizes the importance of Greek Orthodoxy in shaping the patterns of Greek ethnic identification in this country. While one might recognize ethnic differences between, say, a Greek American raised in Lowell, Massachusetts, and one in Orange County, California, the more salient observation might be how interchangeable the two would probably be in their social background and outlook. The old country localisms of the immigrants, moreover, tend to change into a common Greek-American identity among the offspring. Paradoxically enough, American-born Greeks have become more like each other in their common middle-class standing, social values, and communal participation than are the Greeks of Greece where class, regional, and political lines are more sharply drawn. The "melting pot" metaphor has been a better describer of the homogenization of American-born Greeks with regard to each other than it is of their absorption into the general American population.

Any appraisal of Greek-American similarities must take into account certain specific demographic and economic factors. Those immigrants who prospered in America were the most likely to remain in this country and establish families here. Not all who returned permanently to Greece did poorly in America, of course, but the proportion of returnees who were economic failures was certainly greater than those who put down roots in the United States. Even among those who did not do well but settled in the United States, a large number remained bachelors, thereby reducing the potential number of blue-collar parents. Overall, then, the Greek immigrants advancing into the middle class were the most likely to have families and pass on values to their children supporting both the American Dream and mainline Greek-American institutions. The fundamental question today is to what degree the experiences of the children of the new immigrants will replicate those of the children of the earlier immigrants.

To describe the Greek-American experience only in terms of similarities, however, would be seriously misleading. One must also be cognizant of the differences and conflicts within Greek America. A sizeable number of the immigrants, probably a majority, never escaped from the working class. Too much attention on middle-class Greek-American organizations obscures the fact that large numbers of Greek Americans are not part of them. There is some indication, moreover, that those at the very top of the success ladder and those locked in blue-collar employment are least likely to participate actively in Greek-American social activities. An anticlerical element, at odds with the mainstream where the denominationalism of Greek Orthodoxy holds sway, represents another differentiating feature in the Greek experience in America.

Throughout Greek-American history one could always find petty personalities in positions of leadership, now and again a descent into vitriolic clashes over organizational resources, language use, and political matters. Such divisions today, however, are more likely to be compounded by class differences than in times past. In the initial era of mass migration around World War I, all Greeks were in the same position of starting at the bottom. Today there is a juxtaposition between, on the one hand, a middle-class grouping of older immigrants and their American-born offspring, and, on the other, a large number of new immigrants who are still on the underside of the American social structure.

One other difference between the situation of the old and the new Greeks must be mentioned. The early immigrants confronted an antiforeign sentiment from among the people and institutions of American society. The contemporary public mood has much greater acceptance of immigrants and some might even say that there is a certain cachet to being a Greek American. The early arrivals had to stand together simply because all Greeks were looked upon with much the same hostility. In the more tolerant present, it may be that the imperatives for Greek Americans to feel bonded with each other are neither as operative nor as necessary as before.

Two general truths emerge from a dispassionate look at the Greek-American experience. One is that differentiation and dissension within the Greek-American community have been and are increasingly more pronounced than outsiders see or leaders of the Greek-American "establishment" will acknowledge. The other is that Greeks have successfully entered American society while maintaining strong communal ties more than faultfinders and leftist critics will admit. Both truths tend to operate in such a way that Greek Americans will always find what happens somewhat surprising.

Hellenic Diaspora or American Ethnics

The intellectual quandary of Greek-American studies is its relation to modern Greek studies.[6] Two versions of the Greek experience in America compete. One is that Greek Americans are part of a homeland extension, an *homogenia*, an Hellenic diaspora. The other is that Greek Americans are entrants and then participants in American history. Which of these—to be sure overstated—versions are we to accept? There is no simple answer, for each contains part of the truth.

Some of the issues in sorting out the differences between the Hellenic diaspora and American ethnic perspectives could be illuminated by looking at Greek immigrants in other countries. The modern branches

---

[6]In an important sense, one of the accomplishments of scholars of modern Greece has been to assert the legitimacy of their subject matter by differentiating it from classical Greek and Byzantine studies. In a parallel fashion, it can be argued, Greek-American studies will remain undeveloped unless they are separated from modern Greek studies.

of migration from Greece are particularly tangled, but even a cursory glance can help place the Greek experience in America within a broader framework.[7] Close to a hundred thousand Cypriot Greeks reside in England along with a smaller number of immigrants from mainland Greece.[8] Several hundred thousand Greeks have labored in the Federal Republic of Germany as *Gastarbeiter* or "guest workers" since the early 1960s.[9] A Greek community of indeterminate size has existed in what is today the Soviet Union since Tsarist times.[10] Smaller numbers of Greeks are found in the Near East, Africa, Eastern Europe, and Latin America. But the most salient comparisons of the Greek-American experience are to be made with the Greeks of Canada and Australia, the two other predominantly Anglo-Saxon continental countries that have received large numbers of Greek immigrants. There are over 300,000 Greek Australians and around 140,000 Greek Canadians, which represents 2.1 and .6 percent of the total populations of their respective countries— compared to about .5 percent of Greek descent in the United States. Some research has been done on Greek Canadians and Greek Australians, although it has not yet been placed within a comparative framework.[11]

The paradigm of the diaspora is that one's cultural roots and politi-

[7] A compendium of overseas Greek communities and migration statistics is *Greeks Abroad* [*Apodimoi Hellines*] (Athens: National Center of Social Research, 1972). The ten thousand or so Greeks residing in Istanbul, Turkey, today are, properly speaking, not an immigrant group at all, but the remnant of a three-millenia-old Hellenic presence in Asia Minor and on the Bosporus. It is probable that by the end of this century Greek life in Turkey will be virtually extinct.

[8] See A.D. Christodoulidis, *Report on the Problems of the Greek Colony in Great Britain* [*Ekthesis epi tou Provlimatos tis en M. Bretanni Hellinikis Parikias*] (Nicosia, Cyrpus: mimeographed, 1967). In 1978, Robin Oakely was completing a major research study on Cypriot migration and settlement in England.

[9] The results of attitudinal surveys of Greek workers in Germany and other Northern European countries are given in Elie Dimitras, *Enquêtes sur les Emigrants Greece*, I and II; and Elie Dimitras and Evan C. Vlachos, *Sociological Surveys on Greek Immigrants*, III (Athens: National Center of Social Research, 1971).

[10] Large numbers of Greeks settled along the northern coast of the Black Sea and in the nearby Caucasus during the 18th and 19th centuries. In 1944, Stalin, in one of his most ruthless actions, deported in mass the Greeks to central Asia, along with other minorities. Alexsandr M. Nekrich, *The Punished Peoples* (New York: W.W. Norton, 1978), p. 104. A quite different group of Greeks in the Soviet Union are the hundred thousand guerrillas and their families who sought haven there following the communist defeat in the Greek civil war in 1949. As late as 1960, there were some 300,000 reported Greeks in the USSR, of whom about 40 percent regarded Greek as their mother tongue. S.V. Vtechin, *A Concise Encyclopaedia of Russia* (New York: E.P. Dutton, 1964), p. 210.

[11] On the Greeks in Canada, see George D. Vlassis, *The Greeks in Canada* (Ottawa: privately printed, 1953); Judith A. Nagata, "Adaptation and Integration of Greek Working Class Immigrants in the City of Toronto, Canada," *International Migration Review*, 4 (fall, 1969), pp. 44–69; Peter Stathopoulos, *The Greek Community of Montreal* (Athens: National Center of Social Research, 1971); G. James Patterson, *The Greeks of Vancouver: A Study in the Preservation of Ethnicty* (Ottawa: National Museum of Canada, 1976); and Efrosini Gavaki, *The Integration of Greeks in Canada* (San Francisco: R and E Research Associates, 1977). On the Greeks in Australia, see the appendix to this volume.

cal senstivities must be nourished by a responsiveness to contemporary Greek realities—even if at a distance. The underlying presumption is that, whether residing or even born in the United States, Greeks in America share a destiny somehow connected with other people who call themselves Hellenes. The fact that most of the early immigrants continued to maintain strong emotional and personal ties to Greece—and that a sizeable fraction actually returned permanently to the old country—speaks clearly to the diaspora persuasion. Among the new immigrants, as well, there was a strong undercurrent to come to America on a trial basis. If things turned out well, they were prepared to remain; if not, they would pack up and return to Greece. Even among the American-born generations there are some who put their "Greekness" at the very center of their social identity. The diaspora perspective also raises the problems of crisscrossing, perhaps conflicting, loyalties toward Greece and the United States, problems normally hushed in the Greek-American community. Among its more analytical proponents, the diaspora view implies that the Greek immigrant phenomenon is better grasped as a profound outcome of the political economy of modern Greece than as a minor theme in the American historical experience.[12]

A quite different view is that Greek Americans must be placed in the broad context of the ethnic experience in the United States. I believe that this interpretation of the Greek experience in America is more valid than the other. Whatever the fullness of their traditional heritage and allegiances to the old country, the Greek immigrants who came here inevitably reordered their lives; initially, to the imperatives of the economic and social structure of the United States and, later, to some degree of conformance with American cultural norms. Among those born in this country, it seems clear that one's identity is not that of a transplanted Greek, but rather the sensibility of an American ethnic. The ethnic perspective, however, is not without its own controversy. It had long been assumed that immigrant nationalities would pass through successive generations in progressively diluted form until a point was reached where they would disappear as recognizable entities. This position has been strongly challenged in a renewed appreciation in American social studies of the endurance, even if modified or reconstituted, of distinctive ethnic subcultures.[13]

A useful distinction has been made between acculturation and as-

---

[12]The Hellenic diaspora viewpoint is not a homogeneous one, however. Compare, for example, the neo-Marxian interpretation of Mouzelis, *Modern Greece* with the demographic cum ecological perspective in McNeil, *The Metamorphosis of Greece.*

[13]Notable in this regard are Nathan Glazer and Daniel Patrick Moynihan, *Beyond the Melting Pot* (Cambridge: The M.I.T. and Harvard University Press, 1963); Milton M. Gordon, *Assimilation in American Life* (New York: Oxford University Press, 1964); Michael Novak, *The Rise of the Unmeltable Ethnics* (New York: Macmillan Co., 1971); and Andrew M. Greeley, *Ethnicity in the United States* (New York: John Wiley and Sons, 1974).

similation. Acculturation refers to the acquisition by the immigrants and their descendants of the cultural behavior—language, norms, customs—of the new society. Assimilation implies the entrance of the ethnics into the very fabric—the social cliques, business life, civic associations, and, eventually, the families—of the society.[14] Usually acculturation proceeds faster than assimilation. The pattern for Greek Americans, however, is different. Acculturation has probably lagged behind assimilation. This is the only way to understand continuing Greek Orthodox affiliation and the baroque structure of organized Greek America in the face of such assimilative measures as economic ascendancy, political representation, and even intermarriage. It has also been assumed that twentieth-century ethnic persistencies were mainly to be found in working-class neighborhoods.[15] Such a viewpoint does inform our understanding of the early and new Greektowns, but it has little applicability to upwardly mobile and geographically dispersed ethnics, such as American-born Greeks, where ethnic identification is more a matter of cultural choice than a constraint of the social structure.[16]

[14]The most influential statement of this distinction has been made by Milton M. Gordon who differentiates between "cultural assimilation" and "structural assimilation." See his Assimilation in American Life, pp. 60–83. Gordon has restated his concepts in his Human Nature, Class and Ethnicity (New York: Oxford University Press, 1978), pp. 166–208.

[15]See, for example, Stanley Lieberson, Ethnic Patterns in American Cities (New York: Free Press, 1963); Herbert J. Gans, The Urban Villagers (New York: Free Press, 1962); and William L. Yancey, Eugene F. Ericksen, and Richard N. Juliana, "Emergent Ethnicity," American Sociological Review, 41, no. 3 (June, 1976), 391–403.

[16]One of the problems in sorting out the different conclusions of the social researchers can be attributed to their near universal assumption that ethnic ties largely coincide with primary group relations. To put it simply, primary relations are informal, intimate, and bring into play the whole personality, while secondary relations are formal or casual, and deal, often bureaucratically, with a segment of the personality. The postulate that ethnicity corresponds with primary relations and that nonethnic activities fall more into the realm of secondary groups needs to be clarified. A study of American Catholics addressed one side of the issue and concluded that there was little empirical evidence that primary relations followed ethnic lines. Richard D. Alba, "Social Assimilation Among American Catholic National-Origin Groups," American Sociological Review, 41, no. 6 (December, 1976), pp. 1030–46. Among immigrant Greek Americans, it is virtually a certainty that closest personal ties are with fellow Greeks, nonrelatives as well as relations. For many of the American-born Greeks, however, primary relations are not usually confined to other Greek Americans, but can also occur with co-workers, neighbors, and relatives through out-marriage.

What has not often been appreciated, however, is that ethnic processes can also have powerful expression in secondary groups. On the Greek-American scene, one finds ethnic activities that many times are segmental in content: church attendance, voluntary association membership, eating in Greek-cuisine restaurants, and episodic participation in social, cultural, and political gatherings. Indeed, American-born Greeks can have strong primary ties with non-Greeks while simultaneously being actively involved in the organized Greek-American community. Secondary groups, that is, can be as much a definer of ethnic affirmation as primary groups. The differential weight given to ethnically bounded groups—heavily toward the primary side among the immigrants, more toward the secondary in the case of the American generations—is not, of course, clearcut. It does, nevertheless, introduce one important distinction between the Greek ethnic identity of the immigrants and that of their American-born progeny.

It is more productive to consider variables of descent, culture, and self-identification. By looking at the changing interaction of these factors from the initial arrival of the immigrants to the present, one can ascertain not so much the degree of continuity of the immigrant heritage, but, also account for the appearance of new forms of ethnic consciousness that may alternately wane and wax in relation to the common American culture—an ongoing process of "ethnogenesis."[17]

An ethnogenetic approach must take into consideration how the various generations are differentially socialized into an ethnic identity. Whereas the "Greekness" of the immigrant generation is a given, and whereas it is mainly an outcome of childhood experiences for the second generation, such variables do not operate into the third and later generations. Starting with the grandchildren of the immigrants the concept of ethnogenesis becomes applicable. For those two or more generations removed from the immigrants, maintaining a sense of Greek ethnicity is not an issue of ingrained sentiment, but one of conscious selection in an endless number of gradations in the choice of identity. Precisely because third-generation Greek Americans have the weakest commitments to the ancestral culture, their Greek ethnicity—if it is to exist at all—depends directly on their involvement with formal Greek-American organizations. One becomes an identifying Greek American, that is, to the extent that one's experience actively links with the collective experience of other Greek Americans.[18] For the grandchildren of the immigrants, and, even more so, the great-grandchildren, Greek ethnicity is not so much a matter of cultural transmission, but one of voluntary participation in Greek-American institutional life.

The brand of emergent Hellenism in America, therefore, should not be confused with that of the homeland. Such confusion is what underlies the periodic debates in the Greek parliament on the "dehellenization" of Greek Americans of the second and third generations. Rather than viewing Greek-American ethnicity as an increasingly pale reflection of an old country culture, we would be better advised to consider and respect it in its own right. Some of the educated Greek visitors to America disparage the Greekness of the American born. What such critics miss is that their rejection of the Greek-American subculture speaks more to the values of sophisticated circles in contemporary

---

[17]Greeley, *Ethnicity in the United States*, pp. 290–317. An ethnogenetic understanding of Greek-American identity was anticipated in Evan C. Vlachos, *The Assimilation of Greeks in the United States* (Athens: National Center of Social Research, 1968), pp. 165–84. See also John P. Anton, "The Greek Heritage and the American Republic" (paper presented at the Bicentennial Symposium on the Greek Experience in America, University of Chicago, 1976).

[18]An exception to this rule would be found among Greek-American families that alternate between residences in Greece and the United States, a life style that is evident among some of the newer immigrants.

Greece than it does to the ways an immigrant rural nationality has evolved toward a middle-class ethnic identity in a new country. Of Philistinism there is, of course, plenty in Greek-American suburbia, though one would be hard put to show there is any less in Athens or Thessalonica. Those who loftily dismiss the Greek retentions of the American born—a Greek Orthodoxy within the framework of American religious pluralism, attachments to old country foods and dances, ungrammatical Greek, the whole system of kinship life—should see that these tokens of the immigrant past are clung to because they remind the American born of parental and grandparental homes where Greek customs were kept.

Still we are left with the question to what extent the culture of the Greek immigrants has left a significant imprint on the lives of their children and grandchildren. This cannot be answered with finality, as the story of the Greek Americans in the suburbs is still unfinished. Yet a serious answer would recognize the presence of deep continuities. American-born Greeks have clearly carried forth the communal institutions founded by their forebears. There are times when one could swear that every Greek in town knows every other one, or at least everyone else's Aunt Helen or Cousin George. True, not many Greek Americans of the second generation speak Greek among themselves, and many of the third generation do not understand it very well. But in their deepest inclinations of conduct, religious approach, social bias, feeling for family, and affection for the old country, there are heavy signs of immigrant shaping.

Between the Scylla of assimilation and the Charybdis of ethnic chauvinism, the straits are narrow. So far Greek Americans have navigated well. May they stay on course.

A useful comparison can be made between Greek Americans and the Greek Australians.[1] A generation ago Greek Australians were an almost invisible ethnic group. Today some 300,000 Greeks constitute one of the country's major new nationality groups. Indeed, excepting those of English-speaking stock, Greeks make up the second largest ethnic group (after Italians) in Australia. Although their absolute number is less, there are proportionately four times as many Greek Australians as there are Greek Americans. The Greek presence in Australia is even more visible than numbers alone would suggest because nearly all are concentrated in a handful of urban areas. About 130,000 Greeks reside in Melbourne—which has a veritable Greek downtown on Lonsdale Street—and around 90,000 in Sydney. Seven out of ten Greek Australians live in these two cities, compared with four out of ten in the total Australian population.

Greek
Australians

The formal organization of the Greek-Australian community includes close to one hundred Greek Orthodox churches, several hundred voluntary associations, several well-edited Greek-language daily newspapers, a network of afternoon Greek schools for the children of the immigrants, and extensive modern Greek studies programs at the universities of Sydney and Melbourne. The Australian Greek Welfare Society has evolved into a professionally staffed agency, supported by government grants, serving a wide range of social needs for the Greek population of Melbourne. In the Hellenic manner, Greek Australians have also been wrenched by bitter factional fights within their own community.[2]

The first Greeks came to Australia during the Victoria gold rush of the 1850s, but only a few more arrived during the decades immediately following. Starting in the 1890s and continuing through the 1930s, larger numbers came over, though never approaching the magnitude of

---

[1]All interested in Greek Australians must make reference to Charles Price, ed., *Greeks in Australia* (Canberra: Australia National University Press, 1975). See especially the masterful social history of Mick P. Tsounis, "Greek Communities in Australia," *Ibid.*, pp. 18–71. On the Greeks in New Zealand, see J. Baddeley, "The Church and the Coffeehouse: Alternative Strategies of Urban Adaptation Among Greek Migrants to Auckland," *Urban Anthropology*, 6, no. 3 (fall, 1977), pp. 217–36.

[2]On Greek-Australian political struggles, see Mick P. Tsounis, "The Greek Left in Australia," *Australia Left Review*, No. 29 (March, 1971), pp. 53–60; and Christina Holbraad, "Ethnic Culture and Political Participation: A Study of Greeks in Australia 1926–1970" (unpublished doctoral thesis, Australia National University, 1978).

the Greek migration to the United States. By the eve of World War II the Greek population in Australia was estimated at slightly over ten thousand persons. The early Greek Australians entered the economy as manual laborers, either in the sugar cane and cotton fields or in smelters, railroad gangs, and lumber mills. Although the object of anti-Greek hostility and some violence, many Greek Australians were able to move on to their own small businesses—usually dairy bars, fish and chip stores, cafés, groceries—and a few did quite well in real estate. As in the United States, the entrepreneurial success of the Greek immigrants was attributed to the high premium they placed on individual effort, personal initiative, and plain hard work.

One contrast with America, however, was that the place of origin of Greek Australians was much more narrow. Three small islands—Kythera, Ithaca, and Kastellorizo—accounted for most of the Greek arrivals from the turn of the century until 1940. In time, the Kytherians concentrated in Sydney, the Ithacans in Melbourne, and the Kastellorizans in Perth. Greek regional ties carried over to the new country were very pronounced in prewar Australia—even more so than in the United States—and still remain strong among the original islanders and their descendants.

As in the United States, the initial Greek immigrants to Australia were almost exclusively male. It was only once the men settled down and knew their permanent home was to be in Australia that they sent for their wives or arranged for brides. The Greek-Australian family of the first half of this century was characterized by cohesiveness, a strong patriarchy, and wives who did not work outside the home. Most of the children of the Greeks who came before World War II were later to engage in white-collar pursuits, many becoming professionals. As the Greek immigrants ascended into the middle class, they formed ethnic communities. Those in the major cities were able to support Greek Orthodox churches. Many prewar Greek Australians were shopkeepers in small country towns, however, where there was no opportunity for a true Greek community to be established. In the late 1930s, the Australian Hellenic Educational Progressive Association or Ahepa—the acronymn was the same as the American organization that inspired it—began to initiate members and form lodges. Like its counterpart in the United States, the Ahepa of Australia served as a social vehicle for middle-class immigrants still closed off from the conventional status system of the larger society. The picture of Greek Australia at the time of World War II was one of marked embourgeoisement, social conservatism, and generally strong ethnic consciousness. In broad economic and social ways, though on a much smaller scale, the Greeks in prewar Australia replicated much of the experience of their contemporaries and coethnics in the United States.

All this was to change in the early 1950s. Over the next two decades close to 170,000 Greeks settled in Australia. The newcomers completely swamped the prewar Greeks and their offspring, thereby permanently recasting the Greek-Australian community. Unlike their counterparts in the United States, where the demographic balance lies with the more established older Greeks and the middle-class second generation, the numerical preponderance in Australia is clearly with the more proletarian new arrivals. The impetus for the postwar migration included restricted opportunities in Greece, a booming Australian economy, and the new policy of the Australian government to subsidize the relocation costs of many of the immigrants. The newcomers typically came from mainland agricultural regions or depressed urban areas and—though a surprising number did become proprietors—mostly found employment as blue-collar workers in the factories of Australia. Unlike the prewar immigrants, many of the new Greeks arrived as married couples, and it was not uncommon for both spouses to find gainful employment. This dual employment sometimes caused friction and strain within traditional Greek families confronting life in Australia. There also seemed to be an undercurrent among many of the new arrivals to come to Australia on a trial basis. Although repatriation has been a major feature of the Greek immigrants to the United States, impermanency in the new country appears to be even more characteristic of Greek immigrants in Australia.

A Greek Orthodox Archdiocese, headquartered in Sydney, was formed in 1959 and sought to introduce the "American System" of centralized church administration under a single Archbishop. This would replace the preexisting form of lay control and local ownership of church property. A vociferous battle broke out between the Archdiocese, on the one side, and the supporters of community autonomy, on the other. By the late 1970s, the Archdiocese had, with some compromise, generally prevailed. Over eighty churches—most of them newly built—were under Archdiocesan jurisdiction, while a dozen or so churches remained outside its control. In certain respects the fight within Australian Greek Orthodoxy paralleled the situation in America when Archbishop Athenagoras initiated his centralization policies during the 1930s. One important difference, however, was that where the American opponents of the Archdiocese were most likely to represent the ultraconservative camp, the Australian Archdiocese found its opposition coming mainly from the left. A more long-term and significant difference must also be pointed out. While Athenagoras was expanding Archdiocesan control, he was also taking steps—such as establishing a seminary—to professionalize the clergy and to insure that native-born priests would be able to supplement those from the old country. In Australia this has not occurred. Unless such policies are implemented, the hold of Greek Orthodoxy on Australian-born Greeks will likely be tenuous in the generations to come.

Because most of the Greek immigrants work in factories, they are part of the Australian trade union movement and are likely to vote for the Australian Labor Party. An empirical study of Greek labor union members has concluded, however, that they reflect little class consciousness in the conventional socialist sense.[3] Rather, fraternalism among working-class Greeks rarely extends to notions of working-class solidarity across ethnic lines. They view their unions as a concrete mechanism to articulate the grievances of Greek workers against management and not as a means to restructure Australian society through collective action with other Australian workers. On those occasions when the Greek-Australian community does mobilize its political resources, it is likely to take the form of realistic, short-term goals such as day-care centers, welfare relief, student aid, and translation services.

There is, nevertheless, a strong socialist and even Marxist component among many Greek-Australian intellectuals and university students as well as among working-class members. But much of this energy is directed toward Greek-Australian communal politics or issues in Greece rather than toward the political economy of Australia. Moreover, the Greek-Australian left replicates, almost unfailingly, the fissures of the Greek left back in the homeland. Despite these contradictions, the Greek-Australian left, organizationally and ideologically, promises to remain a major influence within the immigrant community for many years to come.

Within Greek Australia, the relations between the classes is one more of social distance than of any real hostility. Occasionally some second-generation Greek Australians complain about the newcomers taking control of the community and spoiling the good name of the Greeks in Australia. Yet the new Greeks seem to enjoy a generally good image as hard workers and law abiders in the wider Australian society. It is also evident that, as soon as the new immigrants attain a modicum of capital, they quickly move away from the inner-city-Greek-ghetto-working-class neighborhoods such as Richmond, Pren, and Brunswick in Melbourne, to better and more dispersed housing in the outer suburbs.

The long-term development of Greek Australia cannot be known exactly. Greek Australians are certainly much more "Greek" than are Greek Americans, though much of this can be laid to the recency of their arrival in the new country. Greek language maintenance is fervently supported by both family pressures and communal schools. One can hear people in Melbourne and Sydney say that Greek Australia can become an autonomous center of Hellenic culture rivaling that of the old country itself. But a look at the demographics already indicates some constriction in the Greek-Australian population. The mass migration of

---

[3] Petro Georgiou, "Migrants, Unionism and Society," *Australia and New Zealand Journal of Sociology*, 9, no. 1 (February, 1973), pp. 32–51.

the 1960s has crested, owing to improved conditions in Greece and fewer job openings in Australia. There are probably as many people going back to Greece now as there are coming in. Even more to the point, recent data show that over half of second-generation Greek Australians are marrying someone of non-Greek background.[4]

The Greek American who visits Greek Australia will encounter much that is reminiscent of Greek-American life in the large cities of a generation ago. Yet the Greek experience in Australia will probably not follow the same path as that in America. Different conditions have shaped the two. In Greek Australia the immigrant working class constitutes the bulk of the community and socialist organizations compete with the Archdiocese for dominance. In Greek America it is the middle class that sets the tone and communal life is essentially church centered.

A concluding observation, then, must be made concerning the atypical Greek community of Perth in Western Australia. Because it has few labor intensive factories, Perth has received few recent immigrants. Instead the Greek community there has come to consist mainly of second- and third-generation Greek Australians. The social ambiance of the Perth community is one of middle-class standing, political and social conservatism, and an ethnicity defined by Greek Orthodoxy rather than the Greek language. This description, while contrasting with the rest of Greek Australia, closely fits that of Greek-American suburbia.

---

[4]Price, *Greeks in Australia*, p. 15.

Selected Bibliography

Abbott, Grace. "A Study of the Greeks in Chicago." *American Journal of Sociology* 15, no. 3 (1909), 379–93.

Adamic, Louis, "Americans from Greece." In *Nation of Nations*, ed. Louis Adamic. New York: Harper & Row, 1945.

Anton, John P. "The Greek Heritage and the American Republic." Paper presented at the Bicentennial Symposium on the Greek Experience in America. University of Chicago, 1976.

Baddeley, J. "The Church and the Coffeehouse: Alternative Strategies of Urban Adaptation Among Greek Migrants to Auckland." *Urban Anthropology* 6, no. 3 (1977), 217–36.

Bardis, Panos D. *The Future of the Greek Language in the United States.* San Francisco: R and E Research Associates, 1976.

Burgess, Thomas. *Greeks in America.* Boston: Sherman, French & Co., 1913.

Chimbos, Peter D. "Ethnicity and Occupational Mobility: A Comparative Study of Greek and Slovak Immigrants in 'Ontario City.'" *International Journal of Comparative Sociology* 15, nos. 1–2 (1974), 57–67.

Chock, Phyllis Pease. "Greek-American Ethnicity." Unpublished doctoral thesis, University of Chicago, 1969.

Choukas, Michael. "Greek Americans." In *Our Racial and National Minorities*, eds. Francis J. Brown and Joseph S. Roucek. Englewood Cliffs, N.J.: Prentice-Hall, 1937.

Christodoulidis, A.D. *"Report on the Problems of the Greek Colony in Great Britain (Ekthesis epi tou Problimatos tis en M. Bretannia Hellinikis Parakias)."* Mimeographed. Nicosia, Cyprus, 1967.

Constantelos, Demetrios J., ed. *Encyclicals and Documents of the Greek Orthodox Archdiocese of North and South America: The First Fifty Years, 1922–1972.* Thessalonica, Greece: Patriarchical Institute for Patristic Studies, 1976.

————"The Greek Orthodox Church in the United States." Unpublished paper, Stockton State College, New Jersey, 1976.

Costantakos, Chrysie Mamalakis. "The American-Greek Subculture: Processes of Continuity." Unpublished doctoral thesis, Columbia University, 1971.

Counelis, James Steve. "A New Church: The Americanization of the Greek Orthodox Church." Paper presented at the Bicentennial Symposium on the Greek Experience in America, University of Chicago, 1976.

Cutsumbis, Michael N. *A Bibliographic Guide to Materials on Greeks in the United States, 1890–1968.* New York: Center for Migration Studies, 1970.

Dimitras, Elie. *Enquêtes Sociologiques sur les Emigrants Grecs*, I and II. Athens: National Center of Social Research, 1971.

Dimitras, Elie and Evan C. Vlachos. *Sociological Surveys on Greek Emigrants*, III. Athens: National Center of Social Research, 1971.

Doulis, Thomas. *A Surge to the Sea: The Greeks in Oregon*. Portland, Oregon: privately printed, 1977.

Doumouras, Alexander. "Greek Orthodox Communities in America Before World War I." *St. Vladimir's Seminary Quarterly* 11, no. 4 (1967), 172–92.

Dunkas, Nicholas and Arthur G. Nikelly. "The Persephone Syndrome." *Social Psychiatry* 7 (1972), 211–16.

————"Group Psychotherapy with Greek Immigrants." *International Journal of Group Psychotherapy* 25, no. 4 (1975), 402–9.

Fairchild, Henry Pratt. *Greek Immigration to the United States*. New Haven: Yale University Press, 1911.

Georgiou, Petro. "Migrants, Unionism and Society." *Australian and New Zealand Journal of Sociology* 9, no. 1 (1973), 32–51.

Gizelis, Gregory. *Narrative Rhetorical Devices of Persuasion: Folklore Communication in a Greek-American Community*. Athens: National Center of Social Research, 1974.

The Greek Texans. The Texians and the Texans Series. San Antonio: University of Texas at San Antonio, Institute of Texan Cultures, 1974.

Greeks Abroad [Apodimoi Hellines]. Athens: National Center of Social Research, 1972.

Hanac Staff. *The Needs of the Growing Greek-American Community in the City of New York*. New York: Hellenic American Neighborhood Action Committee, 1973.

Hecker, Melvin and Heike Fenton, compilers and eds. *The Greeks in America 1528–1977*. Dobbs Ferry, N.Y.: Oceana Publications, Inc., 1978.

Hicks, Sallie M. "Ethnic Impact on United States Foreign Policy: Greek Americans and the Cyprus Crisis." Unpublished doctoral thesis, American University, 1979.

Humphrey, Craig R. and Helen Brock Louis. "Assimilation and Voting Behavior: A Study of Greek Americans." *International Migration Review* 7, no. 1 (1973), 34–45.

Karanikas, Alexander. *Hellenes and Hellions: Modern Greek Characters in American Literature 1825–1975*. Urbana: University of Illinois Press, 1980.

Kiriazis, James W. "A Study of Change in Two Rhodian Immigrant Communities." Unpublished doctoral thesis, University of Pittsburgh, 1967.

Kopan, Andrew T. "Education and Greek Immigrants in Chicago, 1892–1973: A Study in Ethnic Survival." Unpublished doctoral thesis, University of Chicago, 1974.

Kourides, Peter T. *The Evolution of the Greek Orthodox Church in America and Its Present Problems*. New York: Cosmos Greek-American Printing Co., 1959.

Kourvetaris, George A. *First and Second Generation Greeks in Chicago*. Athens: National Center of Social Research, 1971.

————"The Greek American Family." In *Ethnic Families in America*, eds. Charles H. Mindel and Robert W. Habenstein, New York: Elsevier, 1976.

————"Greek-American Professionals: 1820s–1970s," *Balkan Studies* 18, no. 2 (1977), 285–323.

Lauquier, Helen G. "Cultural Change Among Three Generations of Greeks." *American Catholic Sociological Review* 3 (1961), 223–32.

Leber, George J. *The History of the Order of Ahepa*. Washington, D.C.: Order of Ahepa, 1972.

Malafouris, Bobby (Charalambos). *Greeks in America 1528–1948 (Hellines tis Amerikis 1528–1948)*. New York: privately printed, 1948.

Nagata, Judith A. "Adaptation and Integration of Greek Working Class Immigrants in the City of Toronto, Canada: A Situational Aproach." *International Migration Review* 4 (1969), 44–69.

Panagopoulos, E.P. *New Smyrna: An Eighteenth Century Greek Odyssey*. Gainesville: University Presses of Florida, 1966.

Papacosma, S. Victor. "The Greek Press in America." *Journal of the Hellenic Diaspora* 5, no. 4 (1979), 227–48.

Papaioannou, George. *From Mars Hill to Manhattan: The Greek Orthodox in America under Athenagoras I*. Minneapolis: Light and Life Publishing Co., 1976.

Papanikolas, Helen Zeese. *Toil and Rage in a New Land: The Greek Immigrants in Utah*. Salt Lake City: Utah Historical Society, 1974.

Patterson, James. "The Unassimilated Greeks of Denver." *Anthropological Quarterly* 43, no. 4, 243–53.

Petropoulos, Nicholas P. "Social Mobility, Status Inconsistency, Ethnic Marginality, and the Attitudes of Greek-Americans Toward Jews and Blacks." Unpublished doctoral thesis, University of Kentucky, 1973.

Politis, M.J. "Greek Americans." In *One America*, eds. Francis J. Brown and Joseph S. Roucek. Rev. ed. Englewood Cliffs, N.J.: Prentice-Hall, 1945.

Raizis, M. Byron. "Suspended Souls: The Immigrant Experience in Greek-American Literature." Paper presented at the Bicentennial Symposium on the Greek Experience in America, University of Chicago, 1976.

Rozakos, Nikos I. *Modern Greek Renaissance in Boston (Neoelliniki Anagenisi sti Bostoni)*. San Francisco: Wire Press, 1975.

Safilios-Rothschild, Constantina, Chrysie Constantakos, and Basil B. Kardaras. "The Greek-American Woman." Paper presented at the Bicentennial Symposium on the Greek Experience in America, University of Chicago, 1976.

Saloutos, Theodore. *They Remember America: The Story of the Repatriated Greek-Americans*. Berkeley: University of California Press, 1956.

———*The Greeks in the United States*. Cambridge: Harvard University Press, 1964.

———"The Greek Orthodox Church in the United States and Assimilation." *International Migration Review* 7, no. 4 (1973), 395–408.

———"Causes and Patterns of Greek Emigration to the United States." *Perspectives in American History* 7 (1973), 381–437.

———"The Greeks in America: The New and the Old." Paper presented at the Bicentennial Symposium on the Greek Experience in America, University of Chicago, 1976.

Scourby, Alice. "Third Generation Greek Americans: A Study of Religious Attitudes." Unpublished doctoral thesis, New School for Social Research, 1967.

Seaman, David P. *Modern Greek and American English in Contact*. The Hague: Mouton, 1972.

Selz, Thalia Cheronis. "Greek-Americans in the Visual Arts." Unpublished paper, 1976.

Stephanides, Marios. *The Greeks in Detroit: Authoritarianism—A Critical Analysis of Greek Culture, Personality, Attitudes and Behavior*. San Francisco: R and E Research Associates, 1975.

Stycos, Joseph M. "The Spartan Greeks of Bridgetown." *Common Ground* 8 (spring, summer, winter, 1948), 24–34, 72–86, 61–70.

Talagan, Dean P. "Faith, Hard Work, and Family: The Story of the Wyoming Hellenes." In *Peopling the High Plains*, ed. Gordon O. Hendrickson. Cheyenne: Wyoming State Archives and Historical Department, 1977.

Tavuchis, Nicholas. *Family and Mobility Among Greek Americans*. Athens: National Center of Social Research, 1972.

Theodoratus, Robert James. "The Influence of the Homeland on the Social Organization of a Greek Community in America." Unpublished doctoral thesis, University of Washington, 1962.

Topping, Eva Catafygiotu. "John Zachos: American Educator." *Greek Orthodox Theological Review* 21, no. 4 (1976), 351–66.

Treudley, Mary. "Formal Organization and the Americanization Process with Special Reference to the Greeks of Boston." *American Sociological Review* 14 (February, 1949), 44–52.

Tsounis, Mick P. "Greek Communities in Australia." In *Greeks in Australia*, ed. Charles Price. Canberra: Australia National University Press, 1975.

Vlachos, Evan C. *The Assimilation of Greeks in the United States*. Athens: National Center of Social Research, 1968.

———"Historical Trends in Greek Migration to the United States." Paper presented at the Bicentennial Symposium on the Greek Experience in America, University of Chicago, 1976.

Vlassis, George C. *The Greeks in Canada*. Ottawa: privately printed, 1953.

Xenides, J.P. *The Greeks in America*. New York: George H. Doran Co., 1922.

Yeracaris, Constantine. "A Study of the Voluntary Associations of the Greek Immigrant of Chicago from 1890 to 1948." Unpublished master's thesis, University of Chicago, 1950.

Ziogas, Elias K. *The Greeks of America: A Great but Unsung Epic (E Hellines tis Amerikis: Ena Megalo all' Atragoudisto Epos)*. Athens: Iolkos, 1977.

Zotos, Stephanos. *Hellenic Presence in America*. Wheaton, Ill.: Pilgrimage, 1976.

Index